DOG PSYCHOLOGY
The Basis of Dog Training

Dogs are happiest when used for the jobs for which men developed them by generations of selection. Happy, too, were these men (including the author at left) who used the Redbone Coonhounds the night before in treeing these raccoons.

DOG PSYCHOLOGY
The Basis of Dog Training

By

LEON F. WHITNEY, D.V.M.

1977—Seventh Printing

HOWELL BOOK HOUSE INC.
730 Fifth Avenue
New York, N.Y. 10019

Other Books by the Same Author:

The Basis of Breeding
How to Breed Dogs
Bloodhounds & How to Train Them
Dollars in Dogs
The Truth about Dogs
The Distemper Complex
The Complete Book of Dog Care
Your Puppy
This is the Cocker Spaniel
Natural Method of Dog Training
Wonders of the Dog World
The Coon Hunter's Handbook
First Aid for Pets
The Farm Veterinarian

Copyright© 1971, 1964 by Leon F. Whitney, D.V.M.
Library of Congress Catalog Card No. 73-161395
ISBN 0-87605-520-X   Printed in U.S.A.

To Julian Muller

Great Editor and Great Friend,
this book is affectionately dedicated.

FOREWORD

THIS IS NOT a book for psychologists, but rather my attempt to explain to dog owners what psychologists have learned and how to apply these findings in training dogs. If I have recorded any observations which will be useful to scientists also, so much the better.

PREFACE

ONE OF MY FRIENDS, a man for whose opinion I had and still have the greatest respect, was the first to suggest that I write this book. His name, Robert M. Yerkes, is well known to all professional psychologists, if not to dog owners. I know it will not detract in the least from the conclusions of others who work with dogs if I explain why Dr. Yerkes urged me to begin my book. It was his opinion that almost all of the psychological observations thus far published, where they related to dogs, were made within the artificial confines of laboratories. "You have had a unique opportunity," he told me, "of observing dogs under more natural conditions." He urged me to set down any of my observations which were not commonplace.

He enjoyed reading *Bloodhounds and How to Train Them,* and wrote me this was the first book on dog training which "showed that the author had any grasp of modern psychology."

It is difficult to distinguish the commonplace from the "special" because what may be commonplace to an experienced dog man may be excitingly new to a research scientist seeking something to measure. I hope that some of my notes may be of use to all of those who are in any way interested in dogs.

So, I thank Dr. Yerkes and others who have given me assistance in getting this book before dog owners. These include the host of psychologists on whose published work I have drawn, Mrs. Dorothy Livingston who helped me research this material, Mrs. Daniel Berna, who typed and edited, all of my friends who own and train dogs who cooperated in testing the methods herein described, and my assistant, William Evers who has worked with me these many years.

My especial thanks goes to the group of psychologists at Bar Harbor, Maine, Drs. J. L. Fuller, J. P. Scott, and Miss Edna DeBois and associates, for their excellent basic research and reports they have published. They deserve the gratitude of every person seriously interested in dogs.

Orange, Connecticut

Leon F. Whitney, D.V.M.

CONTENTS

CONTENTS

PHOTO ON THE COVER:
Newfoundland, Champion Little Bear Gemini
and friend.—*Photo by Vadim Alexis Chern.*

PART I

A timber wolf (Canis lupus).—Photo, courtesy of *The Illustrated Encyclopedia of the Animal Kingdom,* The Danbury Press.

The sled dog is a close relative of the wolf. In fact, some are pure wolf. This magnificent team of Greenland Eskimo dogs clearly shows the wolf base of the breed.—Photo, courtesy of Wm. L. Baldwin.

Cairn Terriers and Great Dane of the Cairndania Kennels. Every dog, from the tiniest Chihuahua to the largest St. Bernard, is a wolf in all its basic traits and its behavior.—Photo, Tauskey.

Chapter I

INTRODUCTION

Back in 1925, when I first started writing about heredity for dog breeders, almost no one had any conception of what genetics and genes and chromosomes were. Now, a generation later, we frequently see these words in print. Every high school student has an idea of what they mean; some a very clear idea. Many of the ideas about animal breeding which prevailed in 1925 seem silly to us now: birth marking, prenatal influence, the inheritance of acquired characters, and so on. It was commonly believed that blood was the medium of heredity. Educated persons, of course, no longer take stock in such discredited notions.

The public knowledge about psychology is today just about where genetic knowledge was in 1925. In the dog field, persons are still sticking puppies' noses in their stools to housebreak them, obedience class trainers are using the force system almost exclusively; and dogs are unconsciously encouraged in puppyhood to become shy (the buyer believing all the dog's life that "somebody abused this poor thing"). A pet dog bites a man, and the owner tells his friends that he is sure someone "kicked him once and he never has forgotten." And so it goes. But I doubt it will take another generation of dog breeders to become enlightened on modern psychology for the simple reason that they are eager to learn how to train dogs easily and achieve results in the shortest possible time.

When I think back to the dogs which were owned by my parents' friends, it is hard to recall a single one which was not trained in some way. One had a wonderful repertoire of tricks which delighted everyone. Another was trained to fetch articles for his owner. When asked, the dog would go upstairs and bring down his master's slippers. What always fascinated me was the accuracy with which he would bring his master's or mistress's slippers when given the sign or command. The owner wouldn't tell how he communicated to the dog which pair was wanted, but he would ask us which pair we wanted to see the dog bring, and one at a time, the right pair was carried down.

There were three blind men in my section of Brooklyn who had Fox Terriers which led them about; little dogs to which long canes were attached. These were trained, as I recall, even better than the large "seeing eye" dogs are trained today. Keeping dogs was lots more fun then because dog owners got their satisfaction mostly from training. Today it is my impression that the only satisfaction most dog owners derive is, first, in watching their pets eat and, second, in just having something "alive" around. Many dog owners would be just as happy with a tank of tropical fishes.

So, in addition to trying to help dog owners to better understand their dogs, one important purpose of this book is to bring greater happiness, too, into the drab lives of thousands of dogs who would so greatly enjoy the whole training process. Dogs can be a great deal of fun to have around. Try training yours and see how right this is.

It has often been said that to train a dog, the trainer must know more than the dog. There is *no* dog owner who doesn't know more than the dog! The truth is that in order to train a dog, one must know *how* to do it. In order to know how to best go about it, the trainer should know: (1) the nature of the animal he is training, (2) a little about the mechanical functioning of the brain, (3) a little about the means we have of reaching the dog or, to put it another way, the avenues by which the dog receives impressions, (4) the reflexes, normal and conditioned, and the needs and drives of the dog, (5) how the dog learns, (6) what incentives make him work, and (7) how to encourage and discourage individual actions.

That is what this book is about. I have been surprised and amazed at the time which can be saved by understanding the underlying principles which motivate a dog to action. Moreover, I have found training by modern methods not only far more rewarding, but certainly more appealing and interesting.

In addition to the training of dogs for kennel behavior and as home companions, I have trained a great many hounds—mostly coonhounds and Bloodhounds. Years ago it took me several hunting seasons to "break" a coonhound to become a "perfect" dog. Today I can do a better job in a few weeks of good weather. Bloodhounds once required about a year's training to develop them into really dependable trailers. Today I can do it better in six weeks and with a fraction of the expenditure of energy.

In this book, so far as possible, we shall use the scientific method. And this is the naturalistic method.

Scientific method questions the supernatural. There are innumerable matters which science hasn't yet got around to investigating thoroughly, but that gives us no right to call them supernatural. Perhaps there are supernatural phenomena, but in this book we can get along better if we forget them and deal with the natural. We want to be able to predict; science enables us to do this. Then, too, there are those who want us to believe that some of the as yet unexplained behavior is "metaphysical." We shall proceed on the basis that supernaturalism is nonsense, so amply demonstrated by Professor Alfred J. Ayer in his book, *Language, Truth and Logic*.

We are reared from childhood to use expressions which indicate that other animals possess the same mental characteristics that human beings have. We apply adjectives which belong properly only to human beings: *loquacious* parrot, *gentle* dove, *cruel* wolf. And, vice versa, we have been taught to apply adjectives properly belonging to other animals to our own kind of animal. It may be difficult for you to change your ways of thinking and to refuse to apply such language to your dog or dogs; but we must get to know the wonderful dog for what he is and not attempt to make him human. He is interesting enough as he is, and he needs only to be studied, not remodeled. Just because we see our dogs behaving in many ways like ourselves, does not mean that they are like us in all respects.

Man and dog live in different space-time worlds, and it is our duty to try to understand the difference so that instead of trying to bring the dog into our world where the dog can't enter because he lacks imagination, we can put ourselves in his world by using our unique powers. When we do this we are able to better understand the dog which is the object of our training.

Chapter II

OUR DOGS' IMMEDIATE ANCESTOR

IF ONE WANTS to know how best to manage any domesticated animal, he first must inquire what the animal is and, how it lives under the conditions with which it was evolved to cope. If I own a cat and have no books to read nor neighbors and friends to enlighten me, and I want to know how to feed that cat, I study its natural diet. Is it the flesh of horses? Of birds? Of rodents? I find the natural diet is mostly rodents. I can't spend time trapping mice and shooting squirrels to feed a cat, so I try to furnish him with the food elements in a different form—the most convenient form for me.

If I own a rabbit I do not try to make it live on cat food. No, I watch it eat its natural food and supply that kind of food to it. And in the same way, I try to provide living conditions as near to the natural as possible. I try to understand its natural behavior. I don't provide a scratching post for a rabbit; I don't provide a nest where the cat can pull out its wool to line it for a litter of young kittens.

Dog owners have in so many cases taken no trouble to investigate the dog's natural environment, what its forebears were, and how they lived, that it may come as something of a shock to learn that the dog itself is a wolf. What manner of animal is the dog? What manner of animal is the wolf?

To most thoroughly ground ourselves in the underlying foundations for dog training—to understand the dog's behavior— we might properly go back to the amoeba and study evolution. Since most educated persons have an idea of the theory of Darwin and the importance of adaptation to the environment, let us dispense with amoebae and consider this more recent ancestor of our dogs, *Canis lupus,* the timber wolf.

Psychologists talk about *adaptive* reactions. What they mean is this: That nearly every action of the individual has some survival

8

value. Everything the wolf does, he does to help him perpetuate the species. The wolf's environment has been the selector. The wolves which didn't fit, whose actions were bizarre, not helpful to perpetuation of his or her germplasm died and the species was well rid of that wolf.

Please note carefully in this chapter how *adaptive* the wolves' actions are, how each action helps the species to survive and how entirely dog-like every action is. If we understand the wolf we understand the dog.

We are fortunate in having excellent source material in the form of books and articles that deal with wolves factually, without humanizing them, or defending them, or condemning them. They were written by men who know wolves. After having read all of this source material, one is bound to conclude that these men knew *dogs*—dogs in their natural state.

First we must remember that just as man has, by selection—based on mutations—made the wolf into our many breeds of dogs, so adaptation to natural environment has changed wolves into many kinds. We might call them breeds of wolves. Timber wolves differ from brush wolves much less than dog breeds differ. All are fertile when crossed. There are differences in their inherited behavior patterns, in voice, as well as in appearance.

Timber wolf *puppies* (some call them *cubs*) when reared on domestic bitches often become trustworthy human companions. Wild wolves do not attack men. All the stories of such attacks you have read were products of imagination. The story of Little Red Riding Hood has done the wolf great injustice. In Algoma, Canada, for years the Wolf Club has had a standing offer of $100. to anyone who can prove he was bitten by a wolf. No one has claimed it.

The United States Bureau of Biological Survey says that its files contain no record of wolves killing anyone in North America. Dr. Wilfred T. Grenfell says in his book, *Labrador,* "The Labrador wolf has never been known to kill a man." Members of the Algoma Wolf Club say, "a wolf wouldn't even attack a baby; he'd be too afraid of being hit by its rattle."

Mr. Abe Martin of Algoma has summed it all up by saying that, "anybody who claims he was et by a wolf is a liar."

Some students have had unusual opportunities to observe them but a definition of wolves with which many agree is: "A howl in the night, a track in the snow." And this definition, as short as it is, is indeed eloquent.

Observations of domesticated wolves, of those in sled teams (many sled teams are composed entirely of Arctic Wolves) and those in zoos lead to the same conclusion so ably voiced by one of the wolves' most avid students, Ernest Thompson Seton:

"First, and in all ways, he is simply a big wild dog, living on flesh that he gets by open chase, recording his call on tree or corner stone, unsuspicious and friendly, wagging his tail for pleasure, or baying at the moon, more prone to attack the running than the facing foe—for all his instincts are for pursuit—unafraid of man, yet restrained by some unknown force from attacking him, very ready to become his freind, his follower, his helper and his slave.

"All this we see in the Arctic Wolf, and it used to be in the Timber Wolf until constant warfare changed him. A truer concept will be conjured up if we call them "Arctic Dog" and "Timber Dog"; for that is all they are—big Dogs, very doggy Dogs—only a little wild."

What is known about the wolf, our dog's ancestor, who yet lives as practically the basic breed of dog? It will be obvious to the reader that the following are not the observations of the author who makes no claim to being a student of the natural history of this wild dog. This is the gist only of what naturalists have written. In the appendix the reader will find these source books, all of which make for fascinating reading.

Adaptability. First, the wolf is an extraordinarily adaptable creature. This is one of the reasons for his survival. He is not only able to live in a variety of climes, but on an unusual variety of foods.

Then there are great differences among wolves, even among the pups in a litter. Those who have adopted wolf pups tell us there may be one or two in a litter which grow up to be docile and dependable while others with the same handling will become unreliable. The big timber wolves are easily tamed.

Eskimo and Indian children have been known to discover wolf dens and to play with the pups whose mother showed no fear, even permitted the children to play dolls with them and to paint the pups different colors.

The pups which are most vicious when captured have become increasingly so as they matured. Some are more forward than the rest and some so gentle and lacking in evidences of fear that they seem to want to become family pets. Some remain as friendly as a gentle old Shepherd dog.

The younger the pups are when captured, the greater percentage of them turn out to be reliable. Those raised on bottles are best. One naturalist who adopted a wolf pup and kept it at a park says, "The day I left the park I paid a last visit to the most freindly 'dog' I have ever known."

The wolf is uncommonly powerful physically and he uses this power to good advantage. When trained to draw loads the muscles become strong out of all proportion to his size. Six sled dogs, part or all wolf, can draw a load equal to what two horses handle. Wolves caught in traps which were attached to 100 lb. logs—drags, the trapper calls them—have been known to drag these logs for miles. One was found ninety miles away, the wolf still alive in the trap.

Relation to Man. The wolf's relation to man is one of avoidance unless circumstances have taught the animal not to fear. The Ojibway Indian name for our wolf is *Mahengun* which means a hungry sneak, eternally on the hunt for food.

It is probable that the tales of wolves attacking human beings come from the action of rabid wolves. In Europe wolf attacks were dreaded because so many bitten persons developed rabies.

Many are the factual stories of wolves coming close to men, especially at night but not molesting them. Men have fallen asleep drunk in the snow and next morning found rings of tracks around the place where they slept. One explorer was frozen to death and his body found two years later completely untouched.

For all this, people seem eager to believe the stories of wolf attacks. And so unquestioningly! There was the hunter pursued by twenty wolves, who took aim at the leader of the pack and shot it, whereupon the other wolves pounced on it and consumed it. This encouraged the hunter who snowshoed ahead but the wolves followed him, caught up and he again shot the leader. This process was repeated until he had shot the last wolf and so saved his life. Persons hearing of this exploit seldom question it. Yet, if they thought a little they would ask, "How much did the last wolf weigh?"

In the buffalo days wolves became tame. They learned quickly that they had no need to risk their lives killing calves so they would follow the hunters waiting for them to shoot and skin a buffalo and often sat no more than fifty yards away. The sound of a rifle was a call to dinner. All that the hunters wanted was the hide, the tongue, the tenderloin; all the rest was wolf food.

Reading about their actions one might think those wolves were a different species from others which are almost never seen unless a pack of wolf hounds drives one out into the open. But they are one and the same. The difference indicates a high order of animal intelligence and wonderful adaptability.

Endurance. The wolf has a prodigious amount of physical endurance and with it the stick-to-it-iveness to run its quarry to exhaustion. Sometimes a wolf will kill a sleeping deer but usually the kill comes at the end of a long pursuit. The fleeting exhausted prey feels less pain. The pursuit gait is estimated at between ten and twelve miles per hour; the running speed at twenty-eight to thirty. Wolves pursued by autos or airplanes have run as fast as forty miles per hour. One such wolf ran as fast as he could for forty-five miles, when he stopped exhausted.

Chases after prey often continue for 100 miles. Even in deep snow where the wolf cannot run on the surface, one may run 100 miles when pursued by a man on snowshoes. The wolf is no quitter. One was "walked down" by a group of men who took up a chase in relay fashion, using lanterns to follow the tracks at night. Even though the wolf was wounded by a rifle shot, he kept on and on for fourteen days when he was finally killed by a pursuer. Contrast this with the pluck and endurance of a moose which was "walked down" by a Vermonter in seven days with time out for sleep.

If a wolf makes a kill, he eats, then sleeps many hours. If he does not, he may hunt all night, return to his den, and sleep nearby for three or four hours and be up again rested.

An interesting fact concerned with hunting is the way wolves are reported to pursue an animal regardless of where it goes, until they exhaust it. Caribou pursued by wolves have been seen to run through caribou herds, the pursuers much closer to other specimens than to the one they trailed, yet they never turned aside, but kept on after the tiring animal. Some even went through several herds of its fellows but could not shake off the wolves.

Natural Environment. A single wolf's home range comprises an area anywhere from twelve miles to ninety and sometimes more depending upon the food available. Summer range is usually less than winter when search for food demands more travel and exploration.

If an Indian were taken off his hunting grounds he was frequently hopelessly lost but he often denied it. "Indian no lost; wigwam lost" was his reply. So says a man who lived for years among the Indians of Michigan. It may well be the same with the wolf. He has his hunting—or home—grounds and trails. The area is larger or smaller depending on the food supply. His runway through it is generally in the form of an irregular circle of from twenty to 100 miles in length. The overall diameter is usually under twenty-five miles.

In travelling the runways the gait is more often than not counter clockwise, and a steady jog-trot, with frequent stops to smell signposts which the wolf freshens with his urine. From his game trail, he makes frequent side excursions. By travelling in a circle his nose tells him of the presence of food or animals he can convert into food. He can receive odors from long distances especially when they emanate from herds of animals.

Observers tell us that the trails followed regularly often tend to lead through areas of the softest soil, as for instance through sand banks, in brooks and rivers where there are sand bars, as if the wolves wanted as much foot comfort as possible. When it snows, several observers state that wolves step in the tracks of other wolves. Their hind feet seek the holes from which the front feet are withdrawn so the gait in snow differs from that on hard ground. Sometimes one cannot determine how many wolves there are in a pack when they have been breaking new snow because of their propensity of stepping in each other's tracks.

When a family is at home with young, the parents hunt quite close: but when the family has been raised, the adults may make long circuits and spend days doing so. One excellent observation shows that two wolves methodically covered a seventy mile runway and passed a certain observation point every nine days. Another group covered a 100 mile runway every nine or ten days.

Travelling to a place they intend to reach, the family tends to travel fairly well bunched, but in snow they travel single file often, as previously noted, stepping in the foot prints of the wolf ahead.

Wolves travel many miles for food. In Alaska, Murie tells of a caribou herd which was calving; wolves from twenty miles away made the trip nightly.

Camouflage. If the word "intelligence" is taken to mean "the animal's ability to cope with its environment," the wolf is indeed intelligent because he has shown his ability to cope with such a wide variety of conditions and his adaptability makes an excellent intelligence all the more necessary.

Curran considers the wolf, "the most intelligent animal there is in the forest, and all his keen brain is used in camouflage to avoid man. He can conceal himself in long grass, behind a small shrub, and with a couple of twigs to help, can drape himself into a stump or fallen tree. His coloring helps him. A fox knows nothing of camouflage, of fading into the ground or a brush heap as does a wolf."

Another observer tells us: "A wolf on the run seems just an optical illusion that can conceal itself behind a couple of twigs or in some uncanny way disappear into the ground. A past master of camouflage."

Communication. Descriptions are given by various observers of the different ways in which wolves use their voices. First, the howl is the quality of voice which everyone associates with the wolf. One man describes it as "a prolonged, deep wailing howl, and perhaps the most dismal sound ever heard by human ear." One can question this statement by asking whether the dismalness may not be the result of previous conditioning of the hearer to "wolf tales."

To me there is something musical about it. So it was to an early colonial minister who left his impression of the wolf's howl as follows: "The wolves—give us as much music as six different cornets, the like of which I have never heard in my life." This sound is one indicating lonesomeness and there is enough variation in the voices of different wolves who may join in a chorus to produce a blending pastel effect. No hint of harshness accompanies the howl.

A good description of the wolf's howl—it is not a bark—is given by Pierre Berton in his book, *The Mysterious North.* "It is an eerie sound, plaintive, mournful, mysterious. - - - If the North has a theme song, it is this haunting cry, which seems to echo all the loneliness and the wonder of the land at the top of the continent."

In the full of the moon, or when a wind is blowing, wolves seem to like nothing better than to stand on a rocky prominence and howl. It is a long drawn out sound which undulates. This is taken up by all of the wolves within hearing and the chorus is even swelled by dogs in the vicinity. It is not possible to distinguish the wolf's voice from that of the dog's of the same size, say some students; others are sure there is a difference. Of course there is. Our modern dogs are of such different sizes and with differently developed throats.

The howling of a wolf pack is described as thrilling. "If any man can hear a wolf pack and not get chills he is made of corrugated rubber," one observed, after a pack howled not far from him. This man was studying wolves. He noted the wolves walked on the day-old snowshoe tracks, and would hide behind spruce saplings as long as they dared. They rested often and did not gather in a pack until a deer was sighted. He asks, "was their dreadful howling designed to frighten their prey and thus sap its strength and resistance?"

So much for the howl.

Second, the wolf at times emits a sharp staccato bark.

Third, a short, deep guttural howl, musical and with an eerie quality, apparently used as the call to pack and hunt game too large for one wolf to manage.

Fourth, the trail bark. This is not a steady, bow, bow, bow, bow, nor a drawl, but a short series of sharp, deep barks, followed by a silent pursuit and then another short series.

Fifth, the deep voice at the time of killing, almost a snarl which is muffled by the hair of the prey while the wolf sinks his fangs through the skin and twists his head back and forth to sink them deeper.

Sixth is the tone used while feasting when more than one wolf is present. This is a variety of sounds, the pitch and intensity varying according to the amount of food in their mouths, with their mouths closed, the sound coming through their nostrils or producing a humming sound. One man watching a pack consuming a buffalo carcass says the feast "is one of those sharp toned entertainments, which could only be compared to an old fashioned tea party composed of snappish octogenarians, paralytic and generally debilitated characters of both sexes, with a fair sprinkling of shrivelled virginity and a few used up celibates of the masculine gender. Each is guzzling to his heart's content and growling and finding fault with his neighbor." Let's call it the voice of greed.

Seventh, is the solicitous, plaintive whine used about the den. and especially near the pups. It is used by the mother and by other members of the family.

Eighth, a warning whine is emitted by females to warn the young. At the sound they scatter. Females also are known to have barked to warn pups to keep away from something the mother considers harmful or suspicious.

Ninth is that used by the female calling to her mate, more or less of a bark.

Tenth, wolves have been known to whine slightly from pain; young wolves when hurt in a fight may squeal as they run from the victor.

Last, wolves call one another in a tone they use when not hunting. A call which has been successfully imitated by hunters who have lured them downwind close enough to be shot. It may be that only the females use it because reports of such successful imitation indicate that it has been only males which answered.

Here then we have the language of the wolf. The natural, instinctive language which all wolves use and to which all wolves respond with but little education.

In general, is this not the language of our modern dogs?

In addition to vocal sounds wolves communicate with one another in sundry other ways: Scent and expressions or attitudes which can be studied. Some authors talk about ways mysterious to us. Seton calls one "a wolf wireless." So far as I can determine, no one has studied the sound range of a wolf's hearing which is doubtless far keener than ours, since our dogs possess that capacity. If so, wolves may emit sounds man cannot hear and does not therefore, comprehend.

Hunting. Most of their hunting is done at night; they rest during the day. When wolves hunt in packs they emit "hunting cries"—which probably attracts other nearby wolves who want to share in the feast. This cry is emitted on the trail of the prey before the wolves have seen the animal they are pursuing. When they catch sight of prey, they change their tone to a louder and different tone. There are many accounts by men who have watched and heard the pursuit and seen the pursued overtaken and killed. If it is a deer, she is pulled down quickly and seldom lives more than two minutes. And once this gruesome affair is concluded, half a dozen wolves will eat everything but the skin and hair within half an hour or less. What do they do then? Some walk a short distance, curl up in the snow and sleep for no one knows how long. The rest walk off in different directions, no two together and they too curl up and sleep.

Of the family members it is usually the males that do the hunting.

Murie describes the way a hunt began. He says it starts with considerable ceremony. He saw them "wagging their tails and frisking together. They all howled. A female joined the pack. She was greeted with energetic tail wagging and general good feeling. Then the vigorous actions came to an end, and five muzzles pointed skyward. Their howling floated softly across the tundra. Then abruptly the assemblage broke up. The mother returned to the den to assume her vigil and four wolves trotted eastward into the dusk."

On another evening a much more elaborate routine was followed with less apparent purpose, but eventually the pack started out.

Just how wolves communicate to organize killing or hunting parties no one knows. The best account of such a pack organization is related by Andrew Bahr, a Laplander who managed the drive of 3000 reindeer from Alaska to the MacKenzie River delta to be food for Eskimos. The trek took years and nearly everyone interested in the Arctic has read of it. Among their worst enemies were wolves. Following are excerpts from *The Beaver* (Sept. 1934) Winnipeg, as recorded by the Editor.

"Far away over the infinite distance of level snows came the faint wail of a wolf. There was challenge and unyielding patience and sinister warning in those long drawn signals. There was an almost imperceptible stirring of the deer. Even the animals which had not heard that cry before knew the menace of the tone. From a great way to the south came faint calls and answers like cocks crowing in distant farmyards.

"The first day there were no sounds and there were no tracks. At night the same eerie cries—came to the watchers of the deer. The direction of the cries changed from the south to the west. The wolves were still maneuvering at a distance.

"The leader saw a speck far off, it disappeared, appeared again. The men hid behind a snow barrier, each armed with a club, and on snowshoes ready to attack the wolves when they came.

"With what patience they came! What instinctive caution! Over the level snow the dark patch moved, halted, moved again. - - - - With tireless persistence they came on." The wolves would halt and seem to gather in close conference, and then a plan, an agreement, would seem to be made. The anxious men watched these strange consultations as the wolves advanced.

"At their last meeting the pack divided; part of them came on. The new division waited to select a new leader. Under his direction they moved off to the south as if utterly indifferent to the work of the others. But the men knew that this second pack had been given the task of making a great detour. Later they would appear on the opposite side of the reindeer herd."

The account goes on to tell how the men ran down the wolves and killed many, turned and went through the herd and killed some of those which were bringing up the rear but not before several calves had been killed.

Wolves are principally night prowlers. Hunters expect they will return home from their marauding so they start out just before daylight to hunt wolves.

At night wolves are much bolder than during the day. Whereas in daylight they might never be seen near a camp, after nightfall a pack may sit close to the camp and howl for hours.

Killing. In attacking a victim like a large bovine—a moose or caribou—the pair or more of wolves seem to try first to "hamstring" it. In the event you are not familiar with the hamstring, it is what in human beings is the Achilles tendon which reaches from the heel up the calf. In four legged animals it runs upward from the hock. Once this tendon is severed the creature is helpless in that leg. It cannot kick with it and so while standing on the other leg is vulnerable. With both severed, down it goes. Don't believe the stories of wolves turning a "thundering bird" of deer against a cliff; they are well content to capture only one laggard. They do not hamstring deer because no deer has been found with a severed Achilles tendon. The wolves catch the deer by the belly, the thigh or sometimes the throat.

But in killing larger animals, one, usually the female, keeps the animal's attention by jumping about or attacking the head. This permits the male, behind, to get in his deadly work. Stockmen used to call the wolf in front the "loafer wolf."

In a big wild sheep herd the wolves kill mainly the weaker individuals.

Wolves feed exclusively on caribou calves, not on adults unless there are no calves. Calves drop behind and, it is the weaker ones that are killed. So wolves have a salutary effect on the herds.

Feeding Habits. A large wolf eats a huge meal and digests it quickly. He can swallow huge lumps of flesh merely by puncturing it with his teeth but making no pretense at true mastication. He fills rapidly, then goes off and sleeps or drags meat to his den and sleeps, this, depending on whether there are pups at home.

Sometimes a whole pack will so engorge themselves that they are hardly able to walk and can be killed on the spot by hunters. This method of hunting, we are told, was a favorite used by Indians who would kill and cut up a buffalo for the food.

Careful observations show the wolf to be carnivorous but that he eats a large amount of vegetable matter by consuming the material in the stomachs of his prey. Even a growing wolf puppy, when eating a ground squirrel, takes pains to eat the stomach contents. Very little remains of even a large animal such as a reindeer or caribou when a pack of wolves has finished with it. Even the intestines are eaten.

Dan McDonald, in relating an experience in wolf capacity for food tells of finding three wolves which were still feasting on a large buck fawn where he surprised them. "All that was left was part of the front legs, neck and head." They had eaten the deer "entrails and all." They must have eaten twenty pounds each, thus accounting for their distended stomachs.

Probably wild wolves eat more than this after a long fast and a vigorous pursuit. The stomach has great elasticity and stretches into the shape of a watermelon. One litter of ten male wolf puppies raised by a naturalist weighed an average of ninety pounds when full grown. The investigator fasted them two days and fed them all they would eat of horse meat, beef and fat and then killed them and weighed the stomach contents. They averaged to eat eighteen pounds each.

We have seen how the wolf catches the kind of food which requires pursuit to bring it down. Let no one conclude that this is the only food of wolves.

Wolves are especially fond of lemmings, small mouse-like creatures. There are lemming years in the North and during these years the wolves prefer these little rodents to any other food and are often found with their stomachs bulging with them.

Sage bush buds, clams, rabbits, turkey, berries, snails in the shell, are all relished. So are foxes. And in captivity wolves are often fed on commercial dog food.

A wolf can be taught to eat any food, but if he has been raised on meat, he may be some time adjusting to other varieties of food. One pet wolf ate a boiled corn meal mixture.

There is some evidence that wolves may slaughter herds in advance of the whelping season. In one herd of caribou twelve head were killed one night, only the tongues of the animals being eaten. This slaughter may go on from February until the end of March for the purpose of providing meat for the pups when the caribou have moved on. Wolves will kill sheep and carry them to a den before the female whelps. One cache of five sheep was thus found buried in the snow.

Does this mean a reasoned providence on the part of the wolves or is it instinctive, like the squirrels burying nuts? Some instances of apparent foresight are related, such as one of a herd of eleven horses which had become snowbound in a yard. The wolves had not killed them all nor harmed any yet alive but had apparently killed and eaten them one at a time and dragged their meat to the den, 200 yards away.

Reproduction. Much of the most interesting phases of the lives of wolves is concerned with the reproduction of its species. That, of course, is its chief concern; all of its characteristics and attributes are developed as adjuncts to insure survival, not only its own but the next generation as well. That's why the wolf exists. And all of the phases of its mating and home life are most interesting.

The selection of a mate is a matter of propinquity unless there are several males in an area and then furious fights ensue between them. Observers have made many records of hearing these savage battles and of following bloodstains in the snow. Sometimes it has seemed to these men that the wolves must have lost sufficient blood to have died of hemorrhage but no dead one has been reported so far is I can discover.

Once the pair has decided on being mated, they run off together and from then on remain mated, both being monogamous.

The female does not come into heat until she is, according to the popular opinion, two years old. Actually, she first comes in heat at twenty-two months of age.

According to Seton wolves mate from the end of January until the first week in March; "the colder the country is, the later." Today we would say, on the basis of information chiefly amassed since Seton's death, that the farther north, the later, because it is the lengthening day which causes the change in the female, not the cold. Yet this does not alter the sense of the observation; he stated a fact but ascribed it to the wrong cause, yet a perfectly logical one. The opinion did not conform with nature when tested.

Wolves are great diggers. Sometimes they tunnel ten or twelve feet in a season. The hole may go straight into a side hill or down into the ground.

Wolves hollow a saucer shaped place in which to whelp. One of these measured six inches deep. Even the ground in a cave is scratched into a saucer shape. The dens are not necessarily caves into which wolves crawl; any sheltered spot will do. Perhaps it will be under some gnarled roots of a tree, in a depression dug out of the ground when there is no protection as in a prairie, or if there are rocks, among them. Apparently wolves prefer a natural cave when they can find it and make their bed not far inside; usually not nearly as far in as they might go. Many dens have been found in hollow logs. Nearby to the den, there are sometimes found eight inches deep saucer shaped depressions which wolves have dug to sleep in. Sometimes a wolf family will renovate a fox den, enlarging the burrows. One of these was found with eight entrances in an area twenty feet long.

No one reports having seen a wolf carry anything to line a nest, nor do they shed like rabbits and many other species, to afford a lining for the nest.

The gestation period from the first observed mating is usually sixty-three days, sometimes as long as sixty-six. No one knows whether these matings were in the middle or at the end of the acceptance period of the heat.

The cubs or pups number five to fourteen with the average between seven and eight. They open their eyes on the ninth or tenth day unless prematurely born when they may open them later.

The mother in the wild probably seldom lies on a pup but of this no one can be sure. In captivity the females will eat any that die. They are often nervous and acute for any minor disturbances when they may start carrying a pup about, either to a new nest or back to the old one. But when hunters have entered a cave, the female often crawled to the back and made no effort to prevent her babies being taken. Many records of this attest to the fact that the mother is so overpowered by fear that it is far greater than her maternal instinct.

There are records of "she-wolves" having adopted the orphan young of others.

Wolf dens or nests are always completely free from feces and are dry because the mother laps the cubs to cause them to urinate and defecate. No one seems to know how long this process continues, but probably, in this case, we can judge from our own observations on our dogs; until the pups are well out of the nest— five to six weeks old.

Care of the Young. Generally the female whelps in her den.

However, in the case of wolves there is not always warning or pre-monition to insure that she stay at home. Several instances are re-ported to indicate that mother wolf was too far from home when parturition began and thus had to find a substitute place to whelp. After a time the young are carried to their proper den. She-wolves, as they are called by trappers, have been seen carrying quite young pups, by holding them in the center, head and tail projecting from the sides of the mother's mouth. Some have been seen carrying young by the loose skin above the neck and shoulders.

The father wolf practically disappears during the nest period of the young but soon joins the family again. In the case of coyotes, foxes and some other carnivores, the male stays away from the mother during parturition and until the young are several days old.

If a mother wolf is killed, and the pups are old enough to get along without milk, the father takes over their care, even moving them to a new den if the old one is disturbed.

The male, according to Browning, takes over the work usually ascribed to the mother: He eats food and brings it home in his stomach. At the den he disgorges it. (We may question this state-ment because recent work indicates that the disgorging of food by bitches is under hormone control and is tied up with reproduc-tion and lactation.)

That this is done by the female wolf no one can doubt. In Colorado "as much as 150 lbs. of disgorged beef was noted at the entrance of a wolf den." This produced an abundance of flies and evil odors. The observer who records this finding says that some families of wolves move four times during the period of raising the pups—for sanitary reasons.

One male wolf was known to carry food home a distance of twelve miles for the female to eat and feed the pups.

Not only the parents bring home food. Apparently all the mem-bers of the pack carry it to mother and pups. Some is brought directly to the den and some cached anywhere from 100 yards to half a mile away. Probably the hunters eat until satiated and carry what is left home because seldom do the hunters eat from the caches near the den.

Family Life. Wolf pups leave the den at three months of age, sometimes even younger. With the parents, they follow the runways stopping for a day or more at protected places while at night the parents lead them to a kill for food. Those who have watched the youngsters have remarked at the freedom of their play at such times. The parents' absence does not make them hide and remain quiet. But the discovery that a man is in the vicinity will produce panic and they will dive for a hiding place.

Wolf pups remain with the parents through the first winter and at least until March. It is possible that they disperse with the coming of a new litter to the den. Some may remain for several years.

Wolf hunters and trappers who have caught pups tell stories about finding the parents nearby. Seton observed the devotion of a male to a female. The male often acts as a sentinel, usually on a prominence and he acts as a decoy, trying to draw the attention of the person who goes too near the den.

The attitude of the male toward the litter is evidenced not only by this watchfulness and decoying but of his providing food while apparently not entering the den. Yet if a cub is taken out and left he will guard it.

The young cry when hungry and are answered by their mother. They stay in the nest even though able to crawl away. In the day time only, the young, when about a month old may crawl out of the den. They soon learn where the solid food comes from and when hungry jump at the mother's mouth until she vomits.

There is disagreement among observers as to the length of time the mother wolf suckles her pups. One man says for five or six months, another for six weeks and still another for eight weeks. By the time they are three months old, the mother may take them for short walks or hunts.

One of the favorite ways of trapping females and males is to kill a cub and stake it out fifty yards or so from the den. The trapper is as likely to catch the male as the female. There is one record of a pregnant female caught in a trap where she had her litter. Apparently in an attempt to help her, the male was caught in another trap in the same set. The whole family was dispatched by the trapper. Seton, who relates it, remarks: "What a commentary is invited by all this! Our only chance of trapping and destroying these wonderful creatures is by playing on their noblest emotions—love of their young and devotion to each other."

Trappers use the family loyalty characteristic effectively. They find that if they can trap one member, kill it and remove the carcass, the others will come to investigate, apparently to determine what happened to their member. The entire family has been taken in this way in traps set close to the spot where the first was trapped.

Family members will often attempt to free another from a trap. Their affection is touching. They will stay around, scratching at the confining chain, will howl and keep long vigils until frightened away by the trapper whom they never attack.

The mother stays in or close to the den until the pups are three weeks old. When the pups are two weeks old, the father and other family members may venture in. When the pups are old enough to toddle about, all of the family members are attentive to them. Even other males will permit the pups to crawl over them. There are reports of a litter having been raised in one den and the parents taking the pups to a larger den occupied by another litter.

In one den in Alaska there were seven adults and five pups that lived together and worked together as a family unit. This family consisted of the adult pair and their pups and the other five adults (1 female, 4 males) could very likely have been pups from the previous year which had not yet established families of their own. And this brings to mind the question of wolf packs. What are they?

Wolf Packs. Observers tell us the wolf pack is a family which lives together, or sometimes, a group of families. As many as thirty-two wolves have been counted in a pack, but most packs consist of five to seven adults. It is a mark of sociability. "No other carnivore," remarks Seton, "exhibits it in so high a degree."

The notion of the wolf pack has brought forth many stories of what someone told someone else about seeing two males battling for the foremanship. So far as I can discover, no one has yet reported such a fight from first hand observation. After all, why should such fights ensue when the pack is just a family? This is quite different from fighting between males when one of his family attempt to invade the territory occupied by another family.

About the lone wolf, students say they are simply outcasts. Some are old ones, unable to kill any longer because of teeth worn

down to the gums. Some are wolves which have lost their mates.
It is possible that among such wolves even the females do not mate
again. So as progenitors, they are a closed issue.

Education. Wolf education begins at an early age. A growl
from the mother means instant response. Punishment is extremely
severe, and especially so when the smallness of the pups is considered. If the pups try to nurse when she doesn't approve there is a
warning growl, then a snap which causes a terrific scream of terror
(and serves as a warning to the others.) The scream is akin to that
emitted by many species. It seems to cause pain—actually—in the
others and in one way they learn without having to feel physical
pain. This is a most important point to remember. Sometimes the
mother shakes the pup, sometimes throws it sideways hard. She tells
it, *NO!*

The next education they receive is learning as they play together. Later when they are old enough to learn by example (if
they do learn this way) the mother takes them hunting. The
mother is able to inspire her pups to fear a trap by her actions
when near one. Whether she emits an odor, we do not know.

When the pups are old enough to run, the mother and probably
the father, too, chase down a deer and the family eats it. After
many such experiences each cub learns which are the most de-
lectable parts. This training does not start until the pups have
their adult teeth. Some ascribe their learning to imitating the
parents. But is it imitation? The pups like to chase anything which
moves. Who knows how many hares they may have pursued, or the
young of larger animals, perhaps calves? If the parents are present
and help to kill the calf, the young wolf may not know that it was
not his own hold on the calf which killed it, whereupon he develops
confidence and courage, as his conquests with larger animals, in
company with his parents, become frequent. This is a most important point. If his first attempts consisted in an attack on a bull
which turned and all but gored him to death, would he try again?
Possibly, and then another lesson might finish him. But he learns
and develops prowess by assisting as an apprentice and may never
know that it was not his strength which threw the prey. There are
stories of lone wolf attacks, but attacks on large animals are almost
always by packs of wolves.

A year old cub has become proficient at finding his own food, but he is two years old, and some students say three, before he has lost his puppy look and become adult in appearance.

In Water. Puppies have been seen to wade brooks and rivers. Older wolves swim across deep rivers and lakes. In pursuit of a deer, one was found swimming a mile from shore. Deer can swim faster than wolves and frequently take to water. Upon emerging from the water the deer has a greater lead than when it entered. The wolves will plod on fearlessly.

But when ice starts to form on lakes, most wolves will hesitate to plunge in. Like any other creature soaked in ice water, they will eventually slow down and drown. It is likely that those wolves which have been hesitant to enter water after game have at some previous time had some frightening experience with water. Perhaps ice broke, or perhaps they have been slowed down so much that upon emerging from the water they were too stiff and weak to run farther. For whatever reasons there are, wolves which end a chase when their prey takes to water have been seen many times. Or if a lake is small, they may run around the shore to the farther side and take it up again.

Memory. Few animals have better memories for minute details than wolves. Trappers know well how necessary it is to disturb nothing which the wolf will have seen previously. Even sticks thrown onto or moved in a runway is a subject for a wolf's suspicion, and he will shy from the spot.

Fear. A wolf pleading for mercy will usually roll on its back when it realizes it is no match for the wolf or wolves which are its adversaries.

If a stranger wants to join a pack he is often run off by mild attacks and nipping at his rear as he runs. Or if he persists in staying, he may be killed.

Alertness. While a wolf is abroad mostly at night he does travel in the daytime, keeping eyes and ears working so he can locate an enemy and avoid it. In areas where wolves are man-shy anytime a man sees a wolf first, lupus is falling down on the supreme wolf rule, which is Safety First. Alertness and celerity are the first two virtues of the wolf mind.

An able observer and hunter who knows where to look, saw

sixteen wolves in sixteen years, besides those he saw on organized hunts with hounds. He says, "The man who sees a wolf is one of the elect, and it is quite true that you can walk a wolf-infested woods all your life and never get a glimpse of one."

Reaction to Hunger. Hungry wolves, instead of being ferocious are very abject and unresisting. It is very unlikely that a wolf will attack even when cornered.

Because wolves have so few enemies and are not often frightened, one naturalist walked right into the midst of a family before being noticed. There were pups to protect, too. All ran from him. He says: "The strongest impression remaining with me after watching the wolves on numerous occasions was their friendliness. The adults were friendly toward each other and were amiable toward the pups at least as late as October." Of three captive wolves which this student knew, he says that he was impressed with their innate good feeling toward each other.

Facial Expressions. The wolf's facial expressions can indicate the gamut of emotions. They have been said to smile, to express pride, to curl the lips in a snarl, baring the front teeth. Some have a squint-eyed appearance, and in many the eyes are yellow, giving a somewhat wild expression.

Identification. Young and Goldman tell us the wolf has a special scent gland, bluish in color and located in the upper side near the base of the tail. Dogs all possess anal glands but they are located below and to either side of the anus.

When wolves meet "the tail is thrown almost at right angles to the backbone, held stiffly a moment, when the animal's friend or foe takes a sniff."

Wolf urine is individualistic, each being indentifiable by it. Urine from a strange wolf when placed where the wolves of a given territory can smell it, causes great excitement. This elicited excitement is well known to trappers who use urine to lure wolves which may throw caution to the wind.

When male wolves smell urine from a strange outsider the hair along the nape stands up to give the appearance of a mane. The same thing happens in females, but to a lesser degree.

The biologist has a theory: Ontogeny recapitulates phylogeny. Long words. Here is approximately what they mean: Each individual in reaching its present form, passes through the stages which his kind passed through during the long process of evolution. Of course the classical example is the human being. It starts as a single cell. The cell becomes two, the two four, the four eight, and so on, until it becomes a hollow ball-shaped mass. From that stage it goes on, growing more and more complicated until finally it has legs, gill slits, a tail. The tail shrinks, the legs elongate, the front ones become arms. The gill slits disappear and finally it becomes a human baby. When the baby is a few hours old it has such strong hands and arm muscles that it can hold its weight if it grasps your fingers and you raise it.

Phylogeny is the history of the race in terms of millions of years of evolution; onotgeny is the history of the individual as it goes through approximately the same stages in nine months or so. It is a lowly single celled animal, a water-living creature, an ape-like animal and finally a man. Even in its childhood it recapitulates the later history through which the race passed.

But while this theory has much evidence to substantiate it, only recently have psychologists come to recognize that what applies to the physical history of man and the lower animals, applies also to their behavior. The dog is no exception; its behavior during its natural development exemplifies that of the history of its forebears. We have now a fair idea of the behavior of the wolf, our dogs' immediate ancestor, or we might say, of wild dogs untouched by selection and civilization. We who have lived with and observed dogs and are able to consider them objectively must realize that every characteristic of our domesticated dogs is, in some degree, but a modification of characteristics inherent in the undomesticated dog, the wolf.

With this basis established, let us proceed to the further consideration of how dogs got to be as we know them today.

Chapter III

HOW THE WOLF BECAME THE DOG

T HERE WERE WOLVES, very much like the wolves which exist today back in the Pleistocene Epoch the Ice Age. Very likely there was great variation among them then as there is now. Wolves - even timber wolves - are by no means uniform. Some weigh upward of 150 pounds, muscle-hard and not fat like our giant dogs of such great weights. Some weigh under fifty pounds. Some have been killed which were forty inches tall—taller than our tallest dog today. Others are quite short-legged in comparison. There are those that have short stiff tails and others with longer bent tails.

Wolves range the same color scale as the German Shepherd: From black to pale yellow. Some have been reported spotted with white. Some are red and occasionally albinos appear.

At least nine sub-species of wolves have been distinguished, each differing from the others in some distinct manner. While they tend to breed within their own sub-species, they are fertile when they mate with any wolf.

All of the wolves are fertile when they are crossed with dogs and the off-spring are not sterile hybrids but just as fertile as either parent.

Many wolves have been domesticated and proved as safe to have around, as loyal, and as useful as any dog. Big wolves, taken as young pups and raised with Eskimos or with white men in the Arctic behave so much like dogs in dog teams that the drivers call them dogs, seeing no difference in their behavior from that of the others in the teams.

All those differences among the wolves! The Indians making friends of the wolves, painting the faces of the pups! Does it require much imagination to see an Indian child carrying a particularly amicable puppy home and adopting it? Was the first such adoption a freak with a coat spotted with white? The picture of the dogs (or were they wolves?) found buried in the sand in an Arizona cave of the Basket Maker Indians, and having lain there for 3,000 years are illustrations of what might well have happened to alter the wolf enough so that we today call our changed wolves, dogs.

The dog is a wolf which represents a series of captured mutations or sudden changes in the germ plasm each of which bred true. Mutations are occurring today as they have throughout the long history of wolves. They are occurring among dogs, so that anyone who wishes can produce a new breed.

During my own dog breeding experiences, I have found several interesting mutations. One was an ideal screw-tail (ideal for a Boston Terrier) which appeared on a pup which was a cross of Bloodhound and Irish Setter. Another was a short legged Cocker Spaniel, so short legged that he could have passed for a long haired Dachshund. I could have developed a new breed from either.

The wolf survived because he possessed the quality of adaptability inherent in the species. He proved he could live from the Arctic cold to the heat of tropical Mexico. And this is one of the most worthwhile traits of the dog not lost by domestication. The wolf changed when his environment changed so he could live in it. Man changed the wolf to be the dog to suit his needs or whims. How much has he changed it *basically?* Almost not at all. For every dog, from the tiniest Chihuahua to the largest St. Bernard, is a wolf in all his basic traits, in his anatomy and his physiology, but most of all in his behavior which is the subject of this book. Surely no one doubts the essential adaptability of the dog. A Beagle, for instance, lives in a Park Avenue apartment and is fed from a can, while its littermate sleeps in an unheated barrel with some straw for a mattress up in Northern Vermont where the temperature reaches thirty below. The Vermont brother comes out in the morning, stretches, eats a meal of dried dog food from a pan, laps some snow to quench his thirst, barks at the moon and when the dog across the river howls, he howls too. He loves to accompany his owner to the woods where he promptly leaves him, and finding the trail of a snowshoe rabbit, trails it, baying merrily for several hours until it is shot; when he finds another and trails that, continuing with the process for perhaps eight hours. The Beagle is adaptable. But no more adaptable than wolves kept in zoos and their litter-mates which avoided capture. One lives by his wits and strength, and the other as the guest of the zoo-keeper.

With the foregoing in mind it will be easier to understand *why* the dog possesses certain capacities and to see that, in some degree, all of his behavior patterns were in the wolf, the reservoir from which he came. Or to put it genetically, the genes of the dog came from the genes of the wolf. And most likely, if we were to scramble all of the genes of the different breeds of dogs we would come up with a product very much like the wolf.

The dog has been man's companion since long before the beginnings of recorded history; the crudest cave sketches show us that. Several thousand years ago there had been sufficient mutations for early man to have differentiated dogs into more than one kind. At least 5000 years ago there were shepherd dogs, sight hounds, guard dogs like Mastiffs, and trailing dogs.

As time passed, certain wolf (or were they always dog?) traits were intensified by the selection of mutations until dogs were made increasingly more useful to man. This usefulness was principally with their modes of behavior. Every trait of the dog's ancestor has been found useful in some way. His propensity to dig has been the basis for the terrier breeds (terrier comes from terra firma) dogs which dig, or as the fanciers say, "go to earth." The wolf's sense of curiosity and the pause before attack has been the basis for the bird dog breeds. His barking on the trail has been the basis for the hound breeds; fetching home food, the basis for the retrieving breeds; his sticking with one quarry until it has been caught even though it runs through a whole herd of others of its species, the basis for the Bloodhound's and other hound breeds' stick-to-it-iveness. Its natural friendliness and loyalty with others of its family has been the basis of the friendliness and loyalty of the dogs kept for companions and pets. And so it goes. The adaptability is surely the basis for the infinite variety of environments in which dogs live happily today.

There must have been mutations among wolves which would have proved a hindrance to survival yet many of these are the very basis of the differences in breeds which man has produced. One must conclude that many if not most of the dog breeds if put back into the wild, even if they were suckled by wolves, would scarcely be able to survive. Can anyone imagine a Bulldog with its short legs, short coat, inability to stand a chase because of the difficulty it has breathing, surviving in a natural environment and perpetuating its kind? Or could a lumbering St. Bernard catch food and survive? Or a dainty Chihuahua? or a Bloodhound? Imagine one of the new-fangled wooly Cocker Spaniels existing for long? Its coat would collect filth, flies would lay eggs in it, maggots develop and poison the dog, even if the unfortunate animal didn't find itself hung up on brambles and unable to free itself!

Our breeds of dogs have not evolved to be better physically nor more generally intelligent than the wild dog we call the wolf. But for specialized tasks they are far superior.

It's probably the fault of the great majority of dog owners that our dogs are only more competent in their specialized areas and not in general intelligence. We are at fault in insisting that all of our dogs be conformists in behavior. If one shows that he is more intelligent than the rest, he is usually eliminated as being too much trouble. Generally he shows his intelligence by learning quickly how to escape from confinement. He is called an escape artist and is no longer desired.

On a Greyhound track, with a low fence, an intelligent hound quit chasing the rabbit, jumped the rail, ran across the track, jumped the other rail and was there to catch Rusty when he came bobbing along. Rusty was destroyed, the hound suffered a broken leg. The leg was set as good as new but the dog of course was useless for his job; he was too intelligent, nor was he used at stud for fear some of his pups might also be too intelligent.

One of my own Redbone Coonhounds first learned to get his nose under the door, raise it and let himself out into the run at night. The door was fixed so he could no longer get his nose under it. But the chain which was attached to it, via pulleys, ran across the top of his kennel six feet six inches above the floor. He learned that he could jump up, catch his front legs over it and hold on until his kennel mate went out. Once she was half out, he would let go and get his head under the door before she was all the way out and thus follow her, the door dropping behind him. This was a nuisance because they could not get back in and they barked during the night. So his owner disposed of him. He should have been used to breed a more intelligent strain of dogs.

The only dogs I know about which were bred for general intelligence were the English Lurchers and they were invariably crosses.

They were bred to be thieves, to steal anything the owner wanted to send them to steal, whether it was hares on estates or clothes hanging on lines. They quickly learned to hide in the landscape wolf-fashion, to be alert, to respond to signals of hand or sounds. When the British conscripted dogs for war work, Lurchers stood far in the lead in general intelligence and in quick response to training. What a pity it seems impractical to select for general intelligence instead of for conformity and specialization.

PART II

Salt in solution is odorless to man, yet dogs can smell it down to a teaspoonful in 13 gallons of water. This is artist's sketch of the Bloodhound, Nick Carter, the greatest trailing dog that ever lived. Nick trailed for V. G. Mullikin (see facing page 265), and was responsible for over 600 convictions. His successful run of a trail over 105 hours old stands as a record.

Chapter IV

THE DOG'S NERVOUS MECHANISM

BEFORE ONE CAN MOST effectively and efficiently learn to train, one should know how a dog learns and how to make him respond. Basic to all this is your realization that a *dog's behavior is never uncaused.* There is a reason or a cause for everything he does, be it to open an eye when he appears to be asleep, to twitch an ear, sit down or stand up, to bark, to eat, to save a human life. This fact is basic in understanding something about behavior.

The exterior of any dog is interesting. We see his eyes, ears, skin, hair, tail and so forth, but the interior of the dog is the real dog. The skin is only one of his organs. Of his whole physiological mechanism, that which controls his body is most interesting of all to us because it controls what he does with his body.

Knowing a few rudiments about the nervous system of all dogs, the mechanics, if you will, by which dogs are able to do the things they do, and the logical inferences from this knowledge, makes training ever so much more interesting. Of course one can train a dog and know nothing about it, just as one can operate an automobile without the slightest knowledge of what goes on under the hood. The top drivers who can get the most out of an automobile are the mechanics who know more than others about the intricate mechanism. How much more they enjoy and appreciate the automobile!

How much more they know what to expect of the car! They know why the car can't climb trees, or fly. If all of us who train dogs knew how the dog's nervous system operated, and just what it could do, what not to expect of the dog, we should be better trainers, and like the mechanic, get more satisfaction in our work.

The Natural Dog. In his natural environment there are three drives which are uppermost in the life of every dog: He must eat, he must save himself from enemies and he must reproduce. All these he does because of his complicated nervous system.

A system of behavior organs holds all three drives together. That part of the nervous system which controls digestion, the beating of the heart, elimination, does not concern us as much as those sense organs and nerves which watch over or guard the dog; the part which controls his behavior.

We now have a mind picture of the natural dog because we know something about the wolf. Just what are his capacities? In the natural wild dog are all of the behavior patterns we know in domestic dogs at least in some degree. As we have seen, he uses his nose to trail, to smell danger and food. He momentarily pauses before he charges (a pattern which, by selection, has been lengthened in the pointing breeds.) He swims, he retrieves, he barks and guards his food, he fights, he digs holes. He is full of natural instincts which govern his behavior—behavior patterns which he was never shown —never needed to have shown him.

But our natural dog also has many faculties which have to be educated. He hears, but he has to learn to localize the direction from which sounds come. His senses too have to be taught what he may not do. He may eat a frog with impunity, but he soon learns that a toad which looks so much like the frog had better not be chewed on. He even learns that hopping insects are good food, while flying insects are to be avoided; so many of them sting.

Once he is launched in the world, grown to maturity, the natural dog is quite well educated for living in his natural environment.

Even the unnatural breeds, as we have seen, still possess in some degree all of the native behavior patterns and instincts of their ancestors. Why? Because the nervous mechanisms are the same, with some few changes. Changes so inconspicuous they are, that no neurologist can look at two dog brains, one from a shepherd, another from a retriever and show us where in the nervous system the mechanics for this difference lie.

Therefore we are going to examine in a gross way, the nervous system of a dog, knowing that what applies to one breed applies to all, and the wild ancestors and related species as well.

When a dog is lying on the floor, apparently unconscious of external happenings, and when he suddenly springs from his comfortable nap and rushes to a window and barks, what happens in his body?

He has been apparently asleep, but the dog has a capacity of sleeping "with one eye open." This is not literally true. It means that he is more aware of noises and jarrings than is his human companion. A noise to which he is not accustomed has startled him. From the nerves of his ear an electrical impulse has run to a certain spot in his brain. The stimulation of the nerve tissue of the brain affects another set of nerve tissue, which controls the movement of a certain muscle or the movement of many muscles. In response to the stimulation there is a jerking of co-ordinated muscles and the dog is seen to spring up and move in the direction of the sound. He has to learn every one of these actions.

His barking results from further nervous stimulation and so, by a system of electrical transmission over nerves, the dog is motivated. In back of the head lies the organ which controls the entire behavior of the dog. It is the clearing house for all exchanges which come to it from the special senses of sight, hearing, taste, smell, feeling. Remove all of these outside paths by which the brain is affected and the dog could not learn.

Head Shape. The head houses the brain, hence many persons mistakenly believe that the narrow headed breeds have smaller brains than do those dogs with wide, high, apple heads.

The extremely narrow, long head of the Collie appears as we see it, because the muscle is thin over the skull and the bones which project along the side of the skull are close to the head.

The admirable high dome of the Newfoundland is mostly hair and a high occipital ridge, and deep muscle tissue over the head and alongside and large sinuses in the skull. The brain case, in comparison with the size of the dog, is no larger than is that of the Collie. Views of the tops of dogs' heads are just as illuminating. We must conclude that the shape of the head is not the real reason for the difference between the breeds, or their intelligence; a fact which puzzles many people.

The older types had been selected primarily for their ability along the lines for which they were intended. The modern dogs are often selected only for show and seldom used for any other purpose than picture dogs. Naturally therefore, one would expect the result to be apparent. The correlation is between the amount of selection and not between the shape of the heads.

Indeed what little correlation there is between the physical appearance and the behavior patterns is not to any degree between the skeleton and the behavior patterns, but rather between the appearance of the fleshy parts and the behavior patterns. I was amazed one day when the Curator of the Peabody Museum at Yale University and I could not tell which of the two skulls belonged to which dog. Without looking at the identification numbers on the skulls—one of an Irish Wolfhound and the other a Bloodhound—we were stumped to say which belonged to which dog because of their great similarity. And yet the behavior patterns of the breeds were about as different as one could find.

The brain is very well protected. It is contained within the skull, and around the skull there is considerable padding so that the brain is isolated from the jars, and yet it is in a place where it most efficiently controls the body.

When we think of the dog's abilities, we naturally compare them with our own—a perfectly natural act, so long as we do not expect as much from the dog as we do from a fellow human being. The brain case in the skull is much smaller in the dog. So is the weight of the brain. If you compare a dog skull with that of a horse, you will see an even greater difference.

The comparison of brain size with the size of the whole body gives a greater contrast still. Man has by far the largest brain. The dog's brain is much larger than the horse's in proportion to body size.

Anatomy of the Nervous System. The general appearance of the dog's brain and spinal cord is familiar to many readers. It weighs from one ounce to five ounces depending on the size of the dog. From and to the brain and cord the nerves run, making a system of living "wires" over which electrical impulses travel.

The Cerebrum. The brain fills the cranium, the cord fills the spine. The larger part of the brain is the forepart and called the cerebrum. It has a cleft running from front to back which divides it into right and left *cerebral hemispheres.* In these deeply grooved hemispheres, the processes of memory and association take place. The rest of the brain and cord are concerned with automatic unconscious actions.

Remove the cerebrum of a dog and what can he do? Breathe, walk aimlessly about, sleep, eat, but he is not able to hunt for food, and never shows any sign of hunger or that he enjoys food. So perfectly helpless is he that if the keeper fails to put food in his mouth, he won't eat. He can't recognize food as food. Hurt such a dog and he will snap at you. Dogs without the cerebral hemispheres perform all of the unconscious acts. Such dogs have all of the senses of normal dogs. They can smell, see, hear, feel, taste, balance and use the other senses about which we hear less, such as the sense of well-being.

Studies report the surgical removal of whole sections of the brain in efforts to learn precisely which parts of the organ control what sections of the body or are concerned with reacting to stimuli such as smell, sight, hearing. This is one way in which scientists have learned a great deal about dogs' brains.

If a cerebral hemisphere is looked at in cross section we see two kinds of tissue. Close to the surface is a layer of grey matter. Below, we see a large area of white matter, white because it is composed of an immense number of individual, tiny nerve fibers.

A nerve is actually a cell, but unlike any other kind of cell in the body. There are in general two kinds of nerve cells. One is called *afferent,* the other *efferent,* depending upon where the main part of the nerve cell is located. The efferent nerves lie in the grey matter of the brain or in the ganglia (see below, of the *autonomic system*). Each has a body and nucleus (neuron) but besides the body it also has extensions like tentacles which reach out in many directions (dendrites) and one long extension (axion) which has grown out, in many places, great distances. Some go all the way from the brain or cord to a toe on a rear foot—a distance of perhaps five feet in a large dog. Each is about as thick as a human hair. We know from research that the impulse that travels over these wires of cell protoplasm goes at the rate of about 400 feet per second. At least, the results of the current, as measured by the body's reaction indicate such a speed. If a dog burns his paw the sensation of pain in the foot must travel to the brain and a reaction travel back, 10 feet in all. This requires about a fortieth of a second, a fact to remember in dog training.

Not all of the impulses go all the way to the brain. The fibers from any one muscle going to the spinal cord can affect all of the muscles. If part contracts due to stimulation of a fiber, then that fiber through a reflex via the cord, without the brain, causes contraction of the whole muscle.

It is interesting to know what *ganglia* are because these are of great concern in the nervous mechanism of the dog. A ganglion is a group of nerve cells usually located outside of the brain and spinal cord. Many nerves do not go all the way to their destinations but rather end at a ganglion. Here the impulse may be transmitted to one or to several other nerves.

Behind and below the cerebrum in the dog lies the *cerebellum*, while below and behind that the *medulla oblongata* lies, and from it the spinal cord, almost round in cross section in the dog, proceeds along the length of the spine.

Below and in front of the cerebrum lie in long bulbar lobes which are concerned with the sense of smell. Sight impulses come from the eyes over two optic nerves which join under the brain and then separate sending fibers to the parts of the brain concerned with vision. They also interact with other complicated nerves.

The several sections of the brain each have an important connection with the outside world: the forebrain with smelling; the midbrain with hearing; the hind brain with seeing; the spinal cord with feeling and tasting. Yet all these parts of the brain are linked with their nerve fibers so there is instantaneous communication between all parts. The reports come in and the forebrain sends out orders. The grey matter on the roof of the forebrain — the *cerebral cortex* — is the most important correlating center of the nervous system. It is not developed in the dog as greatly as in the human being but to the dog as well as to the man it is of the utmost importance.

When the cortexes were removed, dogs became easily fatigued, body temperature fluctuated, digestion difficulties developed and a certain amount of sleepiness was shown. But, and most important, the main personality traits remained unaltered to any extent. Greedy dogs continued being greedy; apathetic dogs, apathetic; slow dogs, slow. So the researchers have concluded that the traits considered have their origin in the sub-cortical part of the dogs' brains.

Just behind the junction of the optic nerves, lies the *pituitary* gland. This is a master gland over most of the other glands.

All of the soft pink tissue of the central nervous system consists of nerves. The fibers from the cell bodies run to other nerve cells making a tremendously intricate system. Using a microscope one can see the tiny fibril ends of the nerve tentacles clasping the fibers of others.

In each nerve bundle one finds nerve fibers which carry impulses in both directions. The *sensory* nerve impulses go over the afferent fibers while the *motor* or movement impulses travel over the efferent fibers. An impression comes from a muscle nerve. It travels over a fiber to the brain as a sensory impulse. The brain's action comes back over a motor fiber which causes a movement in the muscle.

If you think you have seen a nerve with your naked eye, what you probably saw was a large bundle of fibers bound together by a tough coat for protection. These fibers branch out from the cord and brain. The cranial nerves, of which eight emerge from each side of the head, also run about the body.

Dogs seem well balanced and are equally dexterous with either side of the body; ambidexterous, they are neither left nor right handed. Some reader may express a doubt that dogs are ambidexterous because he has observed some dog of his own running around his pen, always in the same direction. This action can probably be explained by the fact that he started in that direction. In that respect he may be right handed, but had he started his running in the other direction, he might now be considered left handed. What started him running one way in the first place would be the deciding factor. Certainly dogs shake hands naturally with either paw at the start, and only through the formation of a habit do they come to always give the right paw when requested to shake hands.

Psychologists generally separate the functions of the brain in man into two general classes, namely those of thinking and of willing. Or the realm of the reasoning and the realm of the affectivity. The distinctions between these realms is loosely drawn. The seat of thought is in the upper brain or the cerebral cortex which, as we have seen is the great development of the forebrain, especially characteristic of man. The dog, too, has some development of that section but nothing like as much as man; the dog lives to a great extent, if not altogether, in the realm of affectivity.

The nerve systems are divided into the autonomic which supplies fibers to the muscles and digestive organs (the system used by the dog with no cerebrum) and the craniospinal system, which sends fibers to the muscles of locomotion and movement. Part of the cells of this system are also located in the cerebellum and cord.

In dog training we must keep both systems in mind - autonomic and craniospinal.

Nerves are working all the time. Even when a dog is resting his muscles are in *tone* and that because nervous energy is going to them ceaselessly. If a nerve going to a muscle is cut in an accident, the muscle gradually becomes soft and flabby.

We are particularly interested in the dog's senses. The sense organs are generally divided into external and internal. The former keep track of the external condition of the body, the latter with the internal - hunger, intestinal pain, balance, discomfort from gas distention, pressures of other kinds. The external senses are sight, touch, hearing, taste, smell.

If a stimulus is steady, the reaction to it becomes less and less pronounced. It is the new stimulus, a change in conditions, which gets action. A dog lies on a porch looking at a stream of automobiles passing. He grows used to them until a truck suddenly passes with a horse on it. His interest is keen again. It is illustrated by ourselves who can get so used to any odor as not to smell it clearly and then not at all. But let any new odor stimulate our olfactory tract and we smell it and react to it.

This explains why dogs are so keen to see movement and learn to recognize kinds of movement at long distances. Psychologists tell us dogs do not see details at great distances which are clear to human beings but I know that they can distinguish the walk of one person from among many at 100 yards.

Likewise they distinguish the body odor of one person from many for distances up to a quarter of a mile, or one animal from another for long distances.

Reactions to sounds are also good examples. Your dog may hear the purr of automobile engines along the street in front of your house all day long, but he becomes excited at the sound of your own car's engine.

When we study what is known about what a dog can see, smell, taste, hear and feel, we get a better idea of what to expect of him and how he differs from us. We shall find that he excels us in several respects, in keenness of some of the senses, while he is simply not in the same class with a human being in other uses of his brain. And this is most important in dog training because it shows us what to expect and what not to expect. We strip the dog of all the build-up which persons' imaginations have elevated him to, perhaps. But we get a true view of the material we have to handle and can therefore do it better.

A Dog is not Human. And right here let me disillusion some; I hope not you, but the thousands of human beings who on the basis of what they have read, have come to ascribe to dogs so many, if not most of the attributes of man. Hopes, fears, aspirations, ability to imitate, to recall ideas, are not within the ability of any dog. All the instances of dogs' thinking in familiar dog stories and movies, all the tales wherein dogs are made to have human intelligence, and the delightful anecdotes wherein dogs reason, and reasoning, save lives, are figments of the author's imagination. If you want to believe them because it is comforting or because you saw them in print, do so, but I warn you, if you do, you cannot be as proficient a dog trainer as you will be if you have an open mind.

It is highly probable that a dog cannot call up past images; the past does not exist for him, nor the future, because he lacks imagination. He lacks a framework of time. He can vegetate comfortably and happily for long periods if well fed. He holds an image but a short time because it is crowded out of his consciousness by many new sense-impressions. Our beloved dogs may recognize us when they see us, and after a long absence, more quickly when they smell us, but while we are away they are not remembering us and reflecting about us as we are them during that same interval. How, without the power of imagery, could they?

Our dogs have no language. A man or woman thinks in words and images. Dogs do not think as a human being does and when they seem to, some other explanation must be wrought to explain their actions. We must be open-minded. There is no psychologist living who would not welcome a demonstration of thinking by a dog. Even a dog who responds to 400 words, when tested, could not seem to use them to evolve new ideas.

The apparent knowingness of some dogs is actually often the reflection of their master's conscious or unconscious teaching. The real test of a dog's intelligence is in the things it can find out by itself with no help from a human trainer. What problems can a dog solve? What simple, less than childish problems? Dogs learn by trial and error; let's face it. But more about this later. Here we simply want to observe that dogs are quite generally different from human beings. And now let us see specifically how they differ in regard to the several senses. To understand canine behavior we must learn how a dog interprets, and acts on, the messages it receives from the sensory nerves. Contrasting this behavior with our own then helps us better to manage our dogs.

Few of us, in our moments of mature consideration would say that a dog is intellectual or rational. He behaves in such a manner that to us he as a personality, and we know almost as many differences in personality in our dogs as we do in the people about us. In fact, there are no two just alike, so far as we can remember. We would hardly find such personalities in so many frogs or worms, so we must conclude that the dog has an individuality, even if reasoning and thinking are not part of it, save for certain very rudimentary acts which some have thought at times they have seen dogs perform that border on thought. However, by and large it is by their acts that we know them. By their reactions to different situations; by their faithfulness; their usefulness. We can hardly deny that a dog has a personality; we would quickly observe that a worm had none.

The dog's nervous system is a collection of analyzers. The eye discerns oscillations of light by the effect on the retina. The ear detects the oscillations of air, wave lengths and amplitudes. And so what the nervous system does is to break up, decompose chemicals, vibrations and so forth into many component parts. And in many ways the dog is far more competent than we. He can detect, as we saw in the wolf, the odor left by one animal from the others in a herd and he relentlessly pursues this one, perhaps through a herd of the same species. The Bloodhound follows the trail of one man among many which walked in the same path.

First a conditioned reflex is formed as a general form and then specialization takes place: discrimination.

So the analyzing constantly goes on; formation of new connections between the lower and higher parts of the brain and then more delicate analyses. Everything that happens to a dog comes down to these two kinds of activity: (1) formation of new connections, and (2) analysis. His education, the habits he develops, his orientation with other dogs and his surroundings represent one or both of these functions of the brain.

The whole process is a matter of "ever-increasing concentration of excitement, and then probably in gradually beating a path between the points of the central nervous system which are to be connected."

When a dog associates he thinks in a small degree. He forms connections and then begins intellectual activity. In the human being, thinking is nothing else but associations and finally chains of associations and as associations grow in number, thinking becomes more profound.

Chapter V

THE DOG'S SENSES

W E SAW THAT THE dog's behavior is never uncaused. The causes are impressions made on the brain by happenings (stimuli). There are many organs whose tasks are to receive external stimuli and transmit them to the brain for appropriate action. Formerly the only recognized senses were: Sight, touch, taste, smell, hearing. But now many more are recognized such as balance, well-being, hunger.

And since dogs have been a favorite of psychologists the world over, as an animal to study, and because these investigators have left us records of their findings, much information is available.

Hearing. A dog is born into the world deaf. His ears are closed until about the tenth day of his life, and then what he hears is of small consequence to him as compared with the impression what he hears makes on his mind as he becomes mature. His mother's barking, his mother's growling, or that of other dogs, are not instinctively reacted to. He has to learn that a growl is generally followed by a pain inflicted with teeth. He gradually learns that what we call barking means that he must be alert.

He cannot even tell from what direction a sound comes until he has grown fairly mature. I have never seen scientific references to this fact but I have observed it over and over in my training. You can too. Take a young dog into the country where there are many places to hide. Then when he has dashed off to play, just hide, and sneak around to a different direction from where he last saw you. Then watch him, and when he has turned away from you, whistle. He will as likely dash away from you as toward you. Then in a few lessons he will learn to run toward a sound. This is not instinctive, but a learned ability.

Few persons have thought of the great importance to a young puppy his mother's hearing is. I have tried to raise puppies on a deaf bitch. If she raises any it will be good luck. She will lie all over them and because she cannot hear their cries she will not know when she has stepped on one or laid on one. A deaf bitch is often almost worthless as a mother.

Balance and hearing use much the same mechanism for accomplishing their purposes. This is, the semi-circular canals set at angles to one another.

Hearing is accomplished by pressures. Everyone knows what a dog's ear flap looks like, and the hole which it surrounds, which leads into the head. All the delicate mechanism of hearing is embedded in the heavy bone at the base of the skull. Technically the outer ear which we see is the *auricle*. In natural dogs with erect ears, these cone-shaped organs can be moved to better collect the sound waves and conduct them down into the cavity where these vibrate against the ear drum. This is a membrane (the *tympanic*) which lies across the end of the auditory opening and is very thin and delicate. It has no vibrations of its own and is able to pick up vibrations of a variety of lengths and intensities.

Many students consider the mechanism of hearing far more wonderful than that of sight, as marvelous as sight is. Behind the ear drum there is a small cave (*tympanic cavity*), a tube (the *Eustachian*), drains it from its lowest part down to the throat of the dog and allows air to enter to insure equal pressure on both sides of the ear drum. Within the tiny cave there is a most ingenious arrangement of delicate bones - the mallet (*malleus*), the anvil (*incus*) and the stirrup (*stapes*). The mallet is attached to the ear drum while its body attaches to the body of the anvil. This bone in turn attaches by its other end to the stirrup, the flattened area of which fills the end of a crooked tube called the *cochlea*.

While these three small bones undoubtedly make hearing more acute, a dog can hear fairly well without them, as was shown by a student who surgically removed them from a dog who was still able to hear after the operation.

Intense sound can destroy the end organ of hearing, the sensory part of the cochlear duct, called the *Organ of Corti*. Changes which are permanent can be produced by certain sound frequencies of considerable duration. This is nowhere nearly as severe as a loud blast which may deafen by rupturing the ear drum and is of an entirely different nature.

In the matter of hearing, dogs and human beings live in the same world, but at times quite different ones. By that I mean that the dog can hear everything we can hear, but a lot more, too. He can hear fainter sounds coming from a somewhat greater distance. But he really puts us to shame when it comes to hearing notes of a higher pitch - higher on the musical scale.

Everyone today reads about kilocycles, megacycles, cycles, as they apply to radio and television but how few know what the terms mean? High school physics students are taught these interesting facts and dog owners will better appreciate their dogs if they know what a cycle is. An electro-magnetic wave - a sort of vibration - is given off by a transmitter of some sort - a noise-making device. Anything which makes a sound sends off waves which must reach an ear to be heard, or an instrument to be detected. The waves carry some distance and die down, just as a pebble dropped in a pond causes a series of concentric waves which die out in a few moments.

The frequency of the vibrations - cycles - can easily be measured by a meter made for that purpose. Middle C on the piano sends off 256 cycles per second. The cycles are fewer as the scale descends, more frequent as the notes on the scale are higher. Of course the cycles do not need to be musical notes. A buzz made by an electrical vibrator is what is generally used as a test. I have sat in a study, next to a chimpanzee, each of us wearing a pair of head phones. When a buzzer sounded my job was to tell if I heard it, the Chimp's job was to pull a lever and receive a piece of banana (or an electric shock if he pulled the lever when he didn't hear it). To me the signals became fainter and fainter until they were inaudible, but my neighbor kept right on hearing sounds and getting pieces of banana.

In the same way dogs can hear cycles far up the scale. A man's hearing capacity begins at about twenty and stops at about 20,000 cycles per second. Dogs' start at about twenty but go up above

30,000 and some experimenters claim as high as from to 35,000 to 70,000. (Cats hear up to 50,000.)

Besides the cycles we must consider pitch. This is the quality of sound that depends on the rapidity of the vibrations. We hear best at about 2,000 vibrations per second, a dog hears best at about 4,000. Dogs respond to sounds to which we are deaf. The so-called silent or Galton whistle is heard loudly by a dog, while we hear only a hiss of air. And incidentally, many Galton whistles are worthless. To be useful, all should be calibrated and set.

Loud noises elicit a much greater response than the same note when weak. True, dogs may be trained to respond to weak signals but when their attention is on something else, it requires a sound of great intensity to elicit a response. Every kennel owner knows how useless quiet tones are to stop barking. A loud sharp *"Quiet!"* will, in trained dogs, produce a rapid effect. Sled dogs, trained to understand the snap, crack of the whip, will react quickly to a loud crack. One famous driver tells us how, in transporting a pack of these northern dogs, a free-for-all fight started which could have ended disastrously with many dogs and men badly gashed before they could be separated and chained to individual kennels. One loud crack of his whip, and every pair stopped fighting! But these dogs had first been trained to understand the pain that a lash can inflict.

The closer one is to sound, the louder it is, so the ear closer to the sound hears it loudest. When he has learned, the dog can localize sound coming from behind him. A human being is not as accurate. A dog with one ear covered or blocked with wax cannot localize. Dogs do not localize noises above them as well as those on their own plane. (Cats can do much better in distinguishing sounds above.)

When trained, dogs can localize the point from which the sound originates with amazing accuracy. They excel human subjects in this ability. If you imagine the circumference of the circle surrounding the dog to be divided into the usual 360 degrees, dogs could locate sounds as closely as 5°. Imagine yourself standing in a room and holding a rifle. A buzzer sounds. You shoot in the direction the buzzer is sounding. You would not be as accurate as would a well-trained dog, who would go to where he had heard the buzzer to obtain food.

The dog localizes sound in one or two ways, since sound waves travel at only 1000 feet a second, the time difference between the sound reaching the two ears is probably most important. It has been quite well substantiated that it is the difference in the time the sound strikes the two ears. This difference is only three ten-thousandths of a second, and still perceptible.

Many theories have been put forward to explain how a dog knows to such a fine degree where sounds come from. Some think, on the basis of many observations that he does it simply by facing toward the sound. One dog, when the distance was five and one-half yards could localize sounds that were only five inches apart.

Many studies of dogs' hearing ability have been made, some by most ingenious methods. The dog must be conditioned to respond to a sound, either by reaching for food, nodding his head, lifting a paw, or some other indication.

Cats were found to be able to discriminate between tones only one tone apart. Can the dog do the same? Better! A dog can discriminate one-third of a tone. How could this be determined? Two dogs were conditioned to salivate; and at the sound of a buzzer to act positively; at the sound of a weaker buzzer they acted negatively. The frequencies were brought nearer and nearer together until they were finally one-third of a tone apart. Other studies on tone differentiation have been made by using paw withdrawal. A comparison of the two shows the methods to be equally effective in conducting a study.

The question of where on the scale of tone - cycles per second - dogs hear best, was found to be about 4000. For man, the maximum level of sensitivity for pitch is 200 to 5000, for tones 27,000 cps. To hear tones toward both upper and lower limits there must be a great increase in their intensity. The tones of the upper piano octaves are heard best by human beings; tones not even on the piano keyboard are clearest to dogs.

This has a practical application in calling dogs. Fog horn whistles are the kind to avoid, while those which sound shrill to us can be heard farthest by the dog. The tones of Galton whistles do not carry as far with the same force blowing as do the tones which sound clear but shrill to us.

A loud sound is felt as well as heard. Man and dog are about equal in this ability. The lower the kcps the higher is the threshold of feeling. Those who have heard it know how the great deep blast of the ocean liner seems to be felt in one's very spine. The high note of the bird's song produces no feeling except aesthetic. The shrill, unfelt note produces an unpleasant sensation in one's ear.

Dogs can learn to respond to tones quite accurately, although much patience is required to teach them. If tone G is sounded, the dog may be taught to go to its food box for food, to stay away when A is sounded, to go again at B and in short to respond differently to odd and even tones. The student who first investigated the problem feels that the stimulus is a chemical one brought about by food at the sound of the G, etc.

One of the studies of dogs' abilities to hear pitch involved the use of pure oscillator tones under rigidly controlled conditions, demonstrated first that dogs could distinguish between tones of 19,000 and 20,000 cycles and then between tones of 29,000 and 30,000 cycles. They were less accurate where the tones varied by only twenty-five or fifty cycles. No dogs tested could discriminate between different *intensities* of a tone of 35,000 cycles. The author reports the differentiation of tones depends upon pitch and not intensity discrimination. The study indicates that, contrary to the previous ideas of some researcher that dogs fail to hear high tones because of low intensity, this is not true; he made them of high intensity and still his dogs could not respond to tones above 35,000 cycles.

Two students found dogs to be less sensitive to sounds than human beings, even though they could hear a greater range of sounds.

When a dog is eating, noise upsets his flow of saliva and of gastric juice. At 600 cycles and 30 db. of noise there was a significant reduction. At 100 db. tone and 2000 cycles, dogs showed a considerable decrease in gastric secretion. At 5000 cycles, two dogs showed a reduction in the amount of acid in the gastric juice.

Dogs studied in noisy environments were found to have increased pulse rates, faster respiration and tenser muscles. It would be interesting to study the dogs at a show when the benches were filled. Surely an enormous difference would be found among the various breeds as well as various dogs within breeds. Noise can require considerably more oxygen consumption by dogs and cause expenditure of fully 25 per cent more energy even when the dog himself is not exercising.

Taste. The senses of taste and smell function by the stimulation caused by dissolved chemicals. The receptor cells for taste are located in *taste buds* in the back of the tongue and in the soft palate. In man there are five kinds of tastes: *sweet, sour, bitter, salt* and *metallic,* and presumably dogs are also affected by these same sensations.

How then can a dog distinguish almost instantly between the flavors of two substances which are very similar in appearance: fish and beef, for example, provided both contain the same amount of salt? By odor, of course. The difference in odor diffuses up into the nose. What we call *flavors* are to dogs, most likely odors.

A dog can do with foods what we cannot, except in a very small degree. Give us soup and we taste a mixture with a characteristic taste and smell a characteristic odor. Let the dog smell or eat some and he can unscramble the separate ingredients. A dog gets variety even in a mixture, where we have to eat separate items, a fact difficult for many dog owners to understand. Instead of feeding their dogs a sensible wholesome meal of mixed ingredients once a day, they serve variety as they do to their families - cereal and milk for breakfast, dog biscuits for lunch, meat for supper, a snack of something else at bedtime.

How a dog's sense of taste via the taste buds alone compares with ours, we do not know for certain. The faculty of tasting is probably of least consequence to a dog of any of his senses. Less has been written about it, less investigative work has been done so far as I can determine.

There is a nervous connection between the taste sense and that of smell, as there is in many of the animals, but it seems to be dull in comparison with our own.

Because of the feeding methods of the dog's forebears, he gulps his food. There is little need for chewing except to render his food small enough to pass through his gullet - an extremely expandable organ. And in eating, the dog mostly tears flesh and organs, puncturing them with fang holes and using his back teeth to cut the flesh loose. With his powerful molars he breaks bones into pieces small enough to swallow.

He relies on his sense of smell, but very little on taste to accept or reject food. For this reason the dog is one of the easiest of all animals to poison. If the toxic substance has no odor, it may be gulped down regardless of how it tastes. Hundreds of dogs die annually from eating caustics thrown carelessly into garbage pails. If they tasted the food even a tiny crystal would cause rejections but it is swallowed before being tasted.

One of my tasks once was evaluation of 52 different materials which were added to dog food to enhance palatability. Standing before the dogs hour after hour and watching their acceptance of these foods one is struck by the fact that once it passes the front teeth, almost never is a food spat out. The acceptance is mostly a matter of olfaction - smelling - and on that the dog principally relies.

Foods which dogs refuse raw they often eat avidly when cooked.

Dogs normally hungry, often refuse to eat dog flesh, or food in which they can smell it. But this is not so with all dogs. Of a group studied, two consistently refused to eat it, eight ate the raw flesh on more than half the trials, five ate it all the time. No dog refused cooked dog flesh. The investigator who conducted the study learned that after the flesh was cooked all the dogs ate it well. One dog which had an aversion to dog flesh, when made so intensely hungry that he ate it, from that point on, relished it. We have observed that wolves ate foxes. Apparently the smell of the meat was repulsive, not the taste.

Nearly all dogs unless they are famished will refuse raw raccoon meat. Even raw fat from raccoons is refused. But cook the flesh and fat and dogs do not object.

Dogs will however, eat rodents raw. As we have seen, wolves feast on lemmings to the exclusion of other food. Most dogs eat squirrels raw, and some eat rabbits. Apparently, decomposition, like cooking, changes the odor of flesh foods. Dogs may not eat some animals when they are freshly killed, but after a few days of ripening they will eat them. This may partially explain why dogs bury food. Usually they cover it with a shallow cover of dirt.

There is no doubt that dogs enjoy the odor of ripened carrion. When a decomposed animal body has passed the stage where the dog will eat it, he will often roll in it, smearing his coat all over if he can. Most suburban dog owners are fully cognizant of this fact. But we are considering the sense of taste and the foregoing shows us that there is a point after death of an animal where the dog will eat the ripened flesh and that this condition soon passes and the dog thereafter refuses it.

Animals which dogs ordinarily refuse are eaten at this time. I have known several skunks to be eaten. Dogs dislike skunk spray only when it is strong and sprayed into their eyes and nose. A mild "skunk odor" is not objectionable as is shown by dogs eating skunks, scent glands and all. The taste of the glands does not preclude the consumption of the whole skunk.

How often do we hear that once some animal "gets the taste of blood" he will be a killer. This is probably untrue. Dogs which kill sheep may, the first time, have found a dead one and eaten it. But usually sheep killed by dogs are not eaten so it is not the taste of blood which drives them to kill. Dogs which have fought with other dogs and tasted their blood are not necessarily savage dog killers thereafter.

Hunger drives dogs to unusual behavior. Men with dog teams lost in the North, may kill a dog and feed him to the rest of the team to save the lives of the team.

It is certainly not the taste of blood which drove German Shepherd dogs to pull babies from their carriages, kill and partially eat them. These dogs have smelled the babies and other human beings but have never tasted of them nor any of their blood; jealousy may have been the motive for killing, but not for eating. The dogs have never been studied because they were all killed immediately.

One of the nastiest sights in a kennel is to see a dog eating his own or other dogs' feces. Here certainly taste enters the procedure and taste should tell the dog to reject it. Consuming feces seems to be dictated by hunger first, smell second and taste last. I have seen dogs on deficient ration smell of feces, pick some up and drop it as if it tasted bad, but later eat it. Apparently they do not like the taste.

Smell. Smell is a chemical sense. To compare our own feeble sense with that of a dog would be ludicrous. If you have seen a Bloodhound which followed a three day old trail of one person whose tracks have been covered sometimes by a hundred or more others walking in both directions, and see the hound unerringly lead right to the lost person, making right and left turns during the journey, you would realize that the dog lives in a different world from that of the human being. I have seen Bloodhounds perform remarkable feats with their noses.

How does the odor of something the dog smells arouse him to action?

The inside of the nose and the air passages back to the throat are lined with cells which are actually chemical receptors. The area of cells over which the air passes is enlarged by a marvelous arrangement of bony supports called the turbinate bones, scroll-like labyrinthic passages covered on both sides with these cells. The passage is not a straight tube as most persons imagine but by this spreading out of the tissue the air can come into contact with millions more cells than it would passing through a tube lined with them. The lower part of the passage is a fairly free passage, but while the bulk of the air and the chemicals it carries pass without much interruption directly to the lungs, some of it moves about in the turbinate bones in the upper part of the nasal area.

Smelling is achieved not only over the olfactory nerves but via the fifth cranial nerve two of whose branches have fibers in the mucous membrane of the nose. It is interesting that impressions of certain vapors are carried by one set of nerves and not on another. Anise, asafetida, benzol or zylol affect the olfactory nerves alone. Camphor, eucalyptus, pyridin, buteric acid, phenol, sheep dip, ether, chloroform impressions are all carried over both paths.

It has been calculated that the area in a dog's head over which air containing odors passes is about the size of the skin on his body, while our own for the same purpose is about as large as a postage stamp. No wonder the dog lives in a different world! And just as his scenting apparatus is much larger, so is his memory of smells. All of us can remember how, as adults, we have smelled an odor which perhaps had not been smelled in twenty or even forty years. Yet the odor at once called up some happy childhood scene. Or it could have called up some unpleasant experience in which case the memory could have been of a protective nature.

And this being so in the case of ourselves, how much more so in the case of dogs? When all other memories have faded the smell memory of a dog lasts. One dog I trained is an excellent illustration. We were together a great deal. When he was six months old I treated him several times a day during a seige of Carre's disease. I ran him good days, on trails from the time he was a year old, for several months. Then I sold him to a professional man trailer. Only six months later I visited the trainer. The hound was with two others in a yard. All barked at me - a stranger - and the hound in question as vociferously as the rest. I called to him. No recognition even when I used his name. I called him to *come* to see whether he, remembering my voice, would stop barking and recognize me. Nothing made him lose his aggressive action until I went deliberately to the fence and pressed myself against it. He stopped barking and sniffed. One sniff and his aggressive attitude changed instantly to recognition. He squealed like a puppy, relaxed, and rubbed himself against me through the wire, whined loudly.

Dogs recognize places they have been where they have had happy and also disagreeable experiences. If I walk into my personal kennel dressed in my business clothes my dogs politely greet me. If I come in dressed in brand new hunting clothes I receive the same greeting. But if I wear some old clothes with the odor of the outdoors, perhaps some animal smell or the smell of a training cord, the dogs' keen noses know it and their boisterous reception is almost deafening.

What is the mechanism for this recognition? We have seen that the nose is amply provided with receptor cells - chemical receptors, that is. But without water covering the cells there would be little smelling. Every healthy dog's nose waters profusely. Water floods the cells. The chemical odor - all odors are chemical in nature - first, instantly, dissolves in the water.

By expanding his nostrils and sniffing briskly the dog can fill the area in the turbinate bones readily. The more odor he pumps in

which is dissolved in the fluid, the stronger his impressions become. You may often hear a dog almost snorting as he trails or rises
on his hind legs to catch an air draft he wants more of.

It is the nerve-stimulation by the dissolved odors which produces the sensation of smell. What the dog does when he receives
these sensations depends upon what the odors are and on his inherited behavior patterns.

Some experiments have given us a vague idea of the difference
between a dog's and a man's olfactory capacity. We are told that
ordinary salt is odorless. Salt in solution is odorless to a man. Yet
dogs can smell it down to a teaspoonful in 13 gallons of water. A teaspoonful of acetic acid in 1300 gallons of water (1:1,000,000) is recognized by an ordinary dog. Sulphuric acid, he can smell at 1:10,-
000,000.   We are told by purebred Negroes that white people
have a peculiar odor. White people can detect a different odor of a
Negro person, but not if either has recently bathed and put on new
clothes. Yet I have never known it to fail that my Bloodhounds,
without seeing anyone, if a Negro comes within a hundred feet of the
kennels and the wind is right, will set up a roar, which they never do
in the case of a strange white person. Probably if my hounds were
kept by a colored person in a colored community and a white man's
odor came to them they would roar just as loudly.

We may have no idea of a dog's acuity, unless we are in the field
with him when he is trying desperately to detect a certain odor. Any
laboratory experiment yet devised is not nearly as sensitive as,
for instance, the odor from a raccoon which comes down the breeze
to a coonhound. I have seen one of my dogs stand on his hind legs
and delicately sniff the air, then drop to all fours and disappear into
the night not to be heard from again until he was a half mile away
upwind, where he had found the coon's track.

Bird dogs do miraculous feats of smelling and birds have less
odor than mammals.

The Norwegian Elkhound ("Animal Dog" in Norway) is a dog
with only mediocre scenting ability. He is used as a game detector,
not to trail but to airscent. He is led to the general vicinity of elk
or bear, lets the hunters know when he smells the game's odor, and
then leads the hunters upwind close enough to shoot.

The difference between dogs of different breeds and even within the same breed are tremendous. German Shepherd dogs were found by the Berlin police department to be accurate of man trails up to twenty-seven minutes. A Bloodhound, Nick Carter, successfully ran a trail 105 hours old, and another Sappho, ran one over four days old; both made convictions. Hundreds of three day old trails have been run and Bloodhound detectives are seldom asked to use their dogs on less than twenty-four hour old trails. In the chapter on Conditioning Trail Hounds, we shall consider these interesting facts in detail.

Within the same breed, setters for instance, the difference in native ability is marked. Often in training a lot of young dogs of the same breed one will so out-perform the rest by scenting far off birds that the hunter thereafter spends his time principally on that dog. The best illustration of this difference I ever saw was the performance of a Redbone Coonhound. He and two other truly expert hounds were hunting in a swamp. Raider, the dog in question, sounded off. Although the other two could smell the track faintly in the wet spots, as soon as the trail led out of the swamp onto dry land frozen two inches deep, they could not recognize it. Raider followed the trail a mile, to a mile-long strip of woods in which a pack of Bluetick hounds were hunting. He carried it right through the woods and not one dog could detect it. The Bluetick hounds' owners laughed and it took real faith in Raider to believe he was not following a phantom. By the time the track had crossed frozen wheat fields and gone on over three miles, Raider's companions began to be able to smell it a little. At the end of four miles they treed the coon. And we hunters walked beside Raider for at least two and a half miles watching a magnificent performance.

Was that coon odor in the nature of a 1:10,000,000 dilution? No, far, far more dilute than that. In fact, so dilute we have no way, chemical or otherwise, of measuring it.

From earliest infancy the sense of smell is probably the most important of the senses to the dog. As a tiny puppy, he is guided toward his mother's breasts by smell, and as he grows older the odor of food which his master offers him is his guide to whether or not it is the food for him. He may even become very finicky about what he eats and what he doesn't and, it is thought that his sense of smell controls this fully as much as does his sense of taste, and probably more. When a dog likes liver and when liver is sprayed on another food which may be only cereal, the dog will generally eat it because of the smell of his favorite meat.

By sight alone a dog cannot recognize unfamiliar food as food; he must smell it and even then he may not always recognize it. Raise a puppy on milk and he will recognize milk as a food as far away as he can see it. But then show him meat and he will not recognize it as food. The pup must smell and taste of the meat first before it becomes a stimulant. This applies to mature dogs as well. I have taken a stale steak which a butcher has trimmed from the end of a ripened quarter of beef, thrown it to dogs which had been raised exclusively on meal-type dog food, and found the steak in the run hours later. If dogs have been fed beef fat mixed with their meal-type food they will accept meat more readily.

Every dog uses his olfactory ability for many purposes. And it is very unfortunate that our own sense of smell is of such a low order, because were it even half as good as a dog's we could then understand how important it is to a dog. As it is, we can't appreciate the dog's smelling ability. We can't experience it as he does. We have to be content with smelling mixtures of odors as one odor whereas the dog can analyze odors. As a good illustration of this, I think one of the most marvelous experiences which ever happened to me with dogs happened in the summer of 1934 when I was attempting to find a lost baby with my Bloodhounds.

During the hunt, the dogs put their noses into the air and started up the wind. We handlers ran as fast as we could, holding onto their leashes. Without putting their noses to the ground they ran a distance of three eighths of a mile. There was a crowd of at least two hundred persons standing between us and the house to which the dogs went, but they had smelled the little girl's odor coming from the house. That meant that all the odors from all the people must have mingled on the breeze and been wafted to the dogs and yet the dogs were able to analyze them, so to speak, and distinguish one from all the rest. They then went out of the house and trailed correctly to where we found the baby.

I have seen these dogs run one trail accurately through a maze of literally thousands of foot tracks, without making an error, and sometimes the trail which they were following would be the oldest one of all, often over two days old. This is a refinement of the wolf's staying on one trail regardless of where it goes or how many other trails it crosses.

Every dog possesses this ability of unscrambling odors to some extent. The habit of urinating on the same post day after day by all the neighborhood dogs has some basis in survival, and in the facts that the dogs are able to analyze the urine and to thus know which dogs are "in town," just as wolves do.

Why do dogs congregate in such large numbers around a house where a bitch is in season? May it not well be that they smell the foot tracks of many dogs and see dogs pass their homes all leading in the same direction and they feel the urge to join the procession? We shall consider this more fully in Chapter XI on the subject of drives.

Dog food manufacturers can tell many interesting facts about what foods dogs like but every one who has studied the question will have to admit that what smells good to a human being - substances which one would be sure would tempt a dog - may actually repel him. The only way to test such apparently alluring aromas is to try them on the dog.

Another obvious illustration of the vast difference in olfactory ability in dog and man is the fact that most human beings smell pretty much the same to each other, but to a dog every one is different. I used to entertain the children's friends at their parties by giving a demonstration with a Bloodhound. The children would be placed about the room in a ring. I would take the handkerchief of one, go outside, bring in the hound and simply flash the handkerchief across close to his nose, and releasing the dog, say, "find him." The dog would walk into the room and without walking about smelling all the children, would walk straight to the handkerchief's owner and wait for his reward. It would seem that was recognizing the child by the color of its clothing instead of his or her odor.

Hunters have often tried to rate the wild night animals in American outdoors on the basis of their appeal to hounds to trail them. The consensus of one large northern group was as follows: Deer, porcupine, mink, fox, rabbit, raccoons, skunk. They were not attempting to say which left the strongest spoor, but which tempted an untrained hound most to follow the trail.

When a dog follows the trail of a person or wild animal, what is it that his nose smells? One study implies that it is crushed grass or vegetation. But this does not explain trails followed in snow or across ice, or on country roads. Apparently what is followed is the by-product of exercise. A coon hound can walk within a few feet of a sleeping raccoon, one in a semi-hibernated state and not know it is there. I have taken excellent coon hounds to den trees, looked in and seen coons asleep and gone away when the hound failed to recognize the coon was there. A few hours later when the coon had waked and come out, the odor was strong and the dog followed it.

It may be foot tracks which the dog follows but body odor enters the picture. I have trailed men with bloodhounds, had them break into farm houses, steal boots and leave their shoes and have the hound continue trailing them.

When the wind is blowing, the scent followed may be fifty or more yards away from the foot tracks. It is as if the dog follows along in an invisible tunnel of scent. In a valley near our home, if we had a man take a walk along the brow of the level land, and if it was after five o'clock in the evening, we would start the trail on the brow, but the hounds would invariably go down the hill to the brook in the valley fifty or more yards away and trail along the brook as if the trail was clean cut there. At the end of the trail when the scent "ran out," the dogs would circle back and then airscent and go up the hill out of the little valley to where the "fugitive" would be waiting, and get their reward. Generally the dogs' heads would be held high while "trailing" up the hill.

This should interest those who make rules for trailing contests: They should not require the dog to run along the path taken by the person making the track because only the dogs with the "poorer noses" need to stick to a trail that closely.

How does a hound know the direction taken by his quarry? Any dog which back-tracks is usually destroyed because he is useless as a hunter, and there is some evidence that the tendency is inherited. Through all his evolution, the wild dog must follow in the right direction or he starves. Nor must he leave a track being followed for a more attractive, perhaps fresher one.

Many opinions have been expressed to account for this astonishing ability. One which has captured the fancy of many is that the dog obtains a mental image of the shape of the foot and sees with his nose. Persons who have watched a Beagle, for example, approach a rabbit track at right angles and appear to spin ninety degrees with his nose almost in a foot track and start off in the right direction have some substantiation for their opinion. Some suggest that the heel of an animal's foot smells stronger than the toes.

But those of us who have used dogs on stale tracks or have run dogs on snow which has covered tracks, or have hunted hounds from automobiles, realize that a better explanation is needed. Watching fine coonhounds perform ahead of a car, fully illuminated by the headlights, is an education in dog olfaction.

The hounds may be loping along at twelve miles an hour; they run over a track which has crossed the road and immediately try to stop. I have many times seen one flop over on his side in his eagerness to turn back. The age of the track is what determines which direction the dog will take. The chances of his following in the right direction is, of course, 50-50. If he takes the wrong, he may run fifty yards backward if the trail is old, two or three yards if fresh. The experienced hunter right then gets a good idea of how far he may have to walk by how far the dog ran the track backwards (backtracked). If only a short distance the trail will probably be short, but if the dog ran back fifty yards the trail is old and the hunter knows the coon made the track perhaps an hour or two earlier so he is a long way off unless he has stopped to eat close by.

It would seem that the dog knows which way to follow by the way the trail odor diminishes or freshens.

Some trails are not trails at all. If a large number of animals use a single den, any gentle breeze will waft the odor for a half a mile. A dog starting on it will trail directly toward the den just as if an animal had made a trail to it. When I kept a lot of raccoons, it was necessary for me to learn which way the wind blew and hunt so that my hounds could not be on that "beam."

It would seem that a dog follows in a long narrow cone whose apex is the animal leaving the spoor. The closer he gets to the animal the narrower the cone becomes and the easier to follow.

There are conditions which make trailing more difficult than others, and vice versa. In our section conditions are worst when the Southwest wind is blowing and the weather is warm. Conditions are best when there is no wind, when it is night time, when there is a little fog a few feet deep and the temperature is cool. Dogs which failed to follow an hour old trail in the afternoon of a hot day could follow the same trail that night when conditions are as I have described them and follow it as if the trail were a white line.

A newly plowed field will almost always slow a trail whether it be a Beagle after a rabbit, a foxhound after a fox, a coonhound after a coon, or a Bloodhound after a man. If the quarry crosses a moist hog pen, its odor seems to be masked by the hog odor it has picked up. Even a man's trail is masked by this odor.

Sheep and cattle flocks and herds are no deterrent. I have watched hounds of all kinds pursue trails through flocks of sheep. Nor do cattle and horses deter. Water is no deterrent because body odor rises and lies on the top. Animals pursued out into a pond are easily followed. Running water will carry the spoor of an animal which crosses it, far down the stream leaving enough on both banks for a good hound to follow it upstream along the water's edge as if it were a fresh made trail. Convicts in prison camps where Bloodhounds are kept all know this fact and many a fugitive has been lost because the dogs followed his trail down the banks of a stream when he went up and climbed out on a vine or tree which hung over the stream and got out some distance from the stream's edge. Most clever dog handlers know it and act accordingly.

Touch. The senses of touch and taste are less important to a dog than any of his other senses. With sight and hearing developed about as well as a human being's and with the sense of smell developed probably as high as that of any animal, the dog could almost dispense with his sense of touch entirely.

Very young puppies depend largely upon their sense of touch for orienting themselves. At least until they are twenty-three days old, puppies, when separated from their litters, make turns rather than walking in a straight line, and when very young, make motions as if they were swimming rather than walking.

Soon after birth, puppies appear to feel the mother's teats and grasp them with their lips, finally wrapping the tongue about half of the teat and sucking. Puppies used to the feel of the mother's teat may be reluctant to suck from a nipple until they feel the warm milk from the holes in the end.

Temperature of milk must be quite close to blood temperature for puppies to suck it from a bottle. Even five degrees may mean the difference between acceptance and rejection. Many a well-meaning person attempting to raise orphan pups on a bottle fails to understand this fact. When the temperature in a bottle is just right, by the time the contents of the bottle are half gone, it has cooled off sufficiently to be unacceptable, leading the owner to think the puppy has had enough. This is a matter of temperature *felt* by the pup.

Dogs feel the heat and register it by panting which is the way they reduce body temperature, the evaporation of the water from the lungs and throat making marked reductions.

Vibrations felt through a dog's foot are about the same as those reported for man. That a dog actually feels the vibrations via the foot, and that they are not transmitted to the ear, was determined by tests with deaf dogs.

Dogs probably also feel vibrations through the skin as can be observed by the actions of deaf dogs to the step of a person in the room or even on a remote porch.

Then, probably for the reason that a dog has more salts in his blood, he feels electric shocks much more acutely than does a human being. In using electric currents in training, I find that a shock which is no more than slightly unpleasant to me will have a profound effect on a dog.

Do you think a dog is more or less susceptible to pain than a man is? One study indicates that so far as the skin of the back is concerned there is very little difference; both feel certain very slight pains - have about the same threshold - evidenced by muscle twitching.

Considerable research has been done to determine the dog's sensitivity to cold. Pictures of sledge dogs sleeping through blizzards are familiar to most persons. Forty degrees below zero with the wind blowing does not freeze them. Dogs which become acclimated to cold tend to grow thicker coats and are able to live in hutches with doors uncovered and, provided they have deep bedding under them, live at zero degrees in apparent comfort. And this applies to relatively short haired dogs. If they feel the cold one cannot tell it from their actions. I have never known a dog under such conditions to freeze.

In a study with a recording thermometer when dogs were kept in a 3x3x2 ft. hutch with deep bedding and a burlap hung over the door opening, the hutch containing two sixty pound hounds, the thermometer went to seventy degrees when the temperature outside dropped to ten degrees. When the dogs went out during the night the temperature dropped one time to forty-five degrees.

Compared with a naked human being, dogs are practically cold proof. They have their overcoats of hair and enough fat under the skin so they survive intense cold. This, however, is only when they have been acclimated. Dogs kept in heated apartments have been known to die of cold when they were lost. Studies show however, that dogs kept in out of doors kennels at night may spend some time in homes during the day without discomfort during the night.

The dog's skin is of such a nature that severe thrashing with a whip does not raise welts on it as occurs in the case of horses. But this does not mean that they do not feel pain as much.

To see dogs fighting one might judge that they felt but little pain. I have seen Bull Terriers and Pit Bulls fight so they tore ears off, broke legs and had blood flowing freely when neither adversary seemed to realize he was hurt. The explanation for this is probably that the anger felt has caused large amounts of adrenalin to be secreted, and this may partially anaesthetize the dogs.

But having been for so long a veterinarian and having watched the suffering of so many dogs with all sorts of ailments from abscessed teeth to broken bones and great gashes which had to be sutured, once such dogs have come out of their state of shock, I am sure they do feel pain, probably as acutely as we do.

Anyone who has watched that distant cousin of the dog, the raccoon, feeling its way around and has seen the delicate sense of touch in those delicate fingers realizes how callous, by comparison, is the foot of a dog. True, a dog will paw at some object trying to tip it over but his feet, as we have seen in the wolf, are made for digging as well as running and walking, and so could scarcely be sensitive.

Sight. The dog does not see as much as a human being, but some dogs can probably see farther and some dogs can doubtless see much better than other dogs, and have the aptitude of looking for moving objects better developed than many of the representatives of certain other breeds.

When I say a person sees more, I refer to the fact that a person can see colors while a dog can see only shades of grey, just as we see a photograph. But before we get into this subject, a few words about the construction of the eye and how a dog sees will not be amiss.

When the eyelids are open, the eye appears as the front part of a ball. The large transparent part is the *cornea,* the white which encircles it is the *sclera,* the tissue under the lids is the *conjunctiva.*

Behind the cornea we see a colored area, the *iris*, with a hole in the center, the pupil. The iris has muscles which run around it circularly and muscles which lie radially in it. When it is dark, the circular muscles relax and the radial muscles pull the iris back thus enlarging the pupil. When light is bright, the circular muscles tighten and the pupil becomes smaller, the eventual size depending upon the intensity of the light.

Behind the pupil lies a tough lens through which light rays pass and come to rest on the *retina* which covers most of the back of the inside of the eye ball.

Between the iris and the cornea there is a watery fluid, the *aqueous humour;* between the iris and the retina is a thick viscous fluid, the *vitreous humour.*

How do dogs get around in the dark? Many animals have in the retina of the eye a substance called visual or retinal purple. Dogs, and cats too, have little or none, and where we have a regeneration of visual purple which helps us greatly to see in dim light, there is none for our dogs. But dogs have a wonderful system which opens the pupil greatly to allow more light through the lens - and besides this, dogs use organs of touch. Even on "pitch black" rainy nights dogs get about well. So do many almost blind dogs. My favorite coonhound had so little sight left that he ran into men and automobiles in the first exuberance of starting hunting. As he sobered down, he got about rapidly without injury and even felt his way up and down rocky hillsides. When stimulated by the track of a coon he trailed rapidly, missed trees, and even managed to get over or under fallen logs and trees.

A dog has a wider scope of vision than we have. At least the dogs used in one study indicated as much. If a line equivalent to the horizon is considered as a base, the dog can see from fifty to seventy degrees above, twenty to sixty degrees below it, 100 to 125 degrees out to the side and thirty to forty-five degrees on the nasal side with either eye. Undoubtedly, these figures will vary greatly with breeds. Those with deepset or protruding eyes must have different values from the above. A human being has a field of vision of 180 degrees (half of a circle) or ninety degrees on each side of his nose.

Not only dogs, but cats and raccoons are color blind, if we are to judge from data collected by students. By their data the animals could not distinguish between brightness and actual color (chromatic) differences. One group of investigators end their study by concluding that dogs, cats, and raccoons are color blind or so nearly so that they are only slightly, if at all, dependent on color stimuli.

Dogs who go blind have come in for considerable study. Those totally blind show a natural decline in conditioned motor reflexes. Castrated blind dogs show even more rapid declines.

This may partially explain why old dogs which develop a tumor on or in one testicle become more and more phlegmatic. A tumor in one testicle usually causes a shrinking in the other. Removal of the cancerous testicle permits the shrunken one to gain normal size and the dog usually seems to shed several years of his age.

Every dog has to learn to use his eyes. If experiences of blind human beings who gained their sight when adult are any guide, then a dog is learning all the time. At first he has to learn how his mother looks, how his owner looks and he associates certain facts with the appearance. If a black dog bites him he may be afraid of all black dogs until he learns to distinguish among the black dogs he sees. If a person wearing a skirt steps on his toes he may fear any woman until he learns they do not all step on his toes. If he touches a red hot coal and is burned, he may shun all bright objects for some time.

Whether a dog *can* see as clearly as a human being is less important than whether he *does* see as clearly. Suppose there is a gate with a trick latch in the dog's run. The dog learns that all he has to do is reach for that latch, press down on it and he can escape. Now suppose you move the gate to the other side of his run. There it is plainly visible. Will he run to it and open it? No, he will keep trying to open a latch which is no longer there. If he used his sight, he would escape as readily in one place as in another. Perhaps if the incentive were great enough he might try.

For a doctor studying narcotic addiction I once addicted a pen of dogs to huge amounts of morphine. (These dogs were later used by the pharamacologist to discover how to denarcotize them without harm, painlessly.) To the dogs I represented something they must have found pleasant, for whenever they saw me, they drooled copiously. The pen in which they were kept was 120 feet from our driveway beside the house. People came and went and the dogs never drooled. But if I were in even a group of others, they picked me out unerringly and drooled. We watched them through glasses. Perhaps it was my style of walking they came to recognize, or my form. I feel sure I was as clear to them as any one of them was to me.

That there is considerable difference in visual acuity among the various breeds is quite certain. The sight hounds used principally on level land to pursue game by sight undoubtedly see moving jack rabbits, coyotes, deer and other game at great distances. Possibly this is because they try to see. In my kennel there are always dogs which will see a stranger 150 to 200 yards away and alert the other dogs by barking. To judge by their actions some of the dogs never learn to discern strangers so far away; they seem to look everywhere until the stranger approaches closely. To compare two breeds, the Redbone coonhounds seem to see much farther than the Beagles.

A moving object elicits responses which still objects fail to evoke. But the difference is rated by two students as very great. They say vision for still objects is decidedly inferior.

How far away dogs can recognize moving and stationary objects was investigated by a German whose data show one dog could recognize a moving object at about 1000 yards, two at almost 900 yards. A stationary object was recognized by one dog as far away as 600 yards.

Do dogs enjoy moving pictures? Some do, at least. Dog owners will tell you that dogs never respond to movies or television screens. But this is because they do not own the right kind of dogs. Others, because they do own the right kind, think that all dogs do. American type Fox Terriers were found to be much more attentive to movies than some other breeds in a careful study, whereas Springer Spaniels showed no interest.

What do dogs see when they observe something? Students now know that dogs can recognize patterns readily. It has been possible to photograph the images on the retina through the eyes of dogs. This image is so sharp and clear after it has come through the lens that it is most likely dogs see as sharply as we.

Balance. As we saw earlier, hearing and balance are both more or less dependent on the labyrinths of the ear. Dogs have been studied to learn about their sense of balance and what affects it. Dog owners have many bizarre notions about balance, some of which are negated by research.

For example, William James, an eminent psychologist, tells us that one of his correspondents wrote him: "If a dog grows up and his tail is cut off suddenly, he staggers so badly he cannot cross a foot log. Many believe this to be true. One hears it argued that shortening a Pointer's tail, as is done so often in the case of the German breeds, causes him to lose balance. The Germans cut the tails short to prevent the dogs from flailing them on brush and making them raw.

Some experimenters, to shed light on this question, taught two dogs to walk a two-inch runway, twelve feet long. Then they amputated the dogs' tails. Next day the dogs could run the line as well without their tails as they had done with them.

Dogs learn readily to get about when legs are amputated. The loss of a hind leg is less serious than loss of front because the hind are more concerned with pushing while the front bear more weight. Dogs which have lost both front legs learn to walk on the two hind legs in two or three months. But without labyrinths of the ears they never do learn to walk. This illustrates quite well that the sense of balance is a side to side matter and not front to back. Even blind dogs can learn to walk on hind legs if they lose their front.

Carsickness is a condition which is of concern to all dog owners. Some students, in undertaking the study of the effects of swinging dogs in suspended boxes at a rate of thirty cycles per minute learned that the normal movements of the stomach are inhibited and vomiting is produced - usually in five to fifteen minutes. In some cases the gastric tone recovers while the swinging goes on, but usually increased movements of the stomach develop along with a lower gastric tone.

The sense of balance is not alone a function of the ear mechanism, but has its seat in the brain. Dogs with brain inflammation or permanent injury from it may be left without the normal ability to balance. It is often quite amazing to see a dog with a temporary loss of balance on one side, learn to compensate and walk fairly steadily. When the brain inflammation heals, the dog goes the opposite way and then has to compensate back to normal.

It has been shown that even embryonic puppies possess a well developed sense of balance. X-rays indicate that when the mother is turned over, the embryos may turn the opposite way to be right side up.

Hunger. That hunger is one of the dog's senses may be news to some, but it quite definitely is. This sense is used more in dog training than any other.

Food consumption has come in for much study but most of it has been in the fields other than dogs. Poultry, rodents and other kinds of animals all point up some interesting principles which apply to dogs, as does the research with dogs themselves.

Hunger by itself is only part of the picture. Food consumption is another part. Some psychologists speak of "two-compartment" theory. Dogs by themselves under one set of circumstances will eat a given amount of food; another need or drive is added and they will eat more. These other drives may be the time, habit, competition, food quality, the locality where fed, fear, the presence of a different handler and so forth.

Time Sense. Dogs have a fairly accurate time sense. They can be trained to open trap doors, or go from place to place at given time intervals. The farm dogs which used to go from the barn for the cows or accompany the children to school or go for them were seldom late or early by more than a few minutes.

A dog trained to open a trap door every $1\frac{1}{2}$ minutes became very accurate. Behind the door was some meat. The dog became so keen and eager that measurements revealed that his breathing rate increased, indicating an antagonism between the desire for food and waiting for the time to expire from one feeding to the next.

Chapter VI

THE DOG'S MENTAL AND
EMOTIONAL STATUS

WHAT WE SHALL learn in this chapter may disillusion some persons but is should help us all to have a sounder basis for training. How? Well, for instance, if we know that a dog doesn't think to any considerable degree then we can't expect too much of him; if we know his memory for odors is excellent, we can use that fact in training.

EMOTIONS

It is natural that we should start with a consideration of emotions because dogs live in the realm of emotions much more than in the realm of intelligence.

And dogs resemble human beings more in their emotional behavior than they do in their intelligence. Many dog owners probably unconsciously harm their dogs by misjudging from their behavior, attributing to them emotions which they think they should have, when perhaps they don't. Such persons often harm themselves as well as their dogs by such misdirected sympathy.

Understanding dogs helps both dogs and owners. Sitting next to me in the movies one night was a woman exhibiting misdirected sympathy. The picture concerned a Byrd polar expedition and showed a short sequence of a Malamute curling up in the snow while a blizzard was slowly covering him. The woman said she was going to "write to Washington so as to see that such cruelty was stopped."

It is common to find a mature woman with plenty of prolactin in her system, using a dog as a substitute for a baby; playing dolls with it, if you will. There is nothing wrong with this and much that is exemplary. This very act may have been the cause of childless women finding themselves happily pregnant. A documented research study established the fact that adoption of a baby by a childless woman may set up a hormone action in her body which helps her become pregnant. And perhaps a dog may actually substitute for a baby.

Our emotions are expressed by such words as fear, anger, cowardice, timidity, aggressiveness, calmness, jealousy, selfishness, love, greed, shame, joy, exuberance, satisfaction, happiness, sadness and so forth. If dogs feel these emotions can we know it by any way other than by our observations of their actions?

And if dogs feel emotions, is there any degree of difference between them? Also, are the emotions dependent on glandular secretions as we know certain ones are in mankind? What is known, briefly, about such matters?

Most of the studies of dog psychology have dealt with emotions. These reactions to stimuli are not reasoned reactions. Emotions exhibit themselves in many ways such as timidity, boldness, aggressiveness, effect of stimuli on heart rate, rapidity of respiration. The degree of the dog's activity is one form of emotional reaction, the effect produced by noises is another; whether or not a dog "freezes" and how long it takes to return to normal. In one of my studies where we used a drug called Malucidin to produce resorptions of fetuses, I learned that a small desensitizing dose before the main dose was necessary to prevent a drastic fall in blood pressure. However, in dogs which became so seemingly afraid that they "froze," no desensitizing dose was necessary, probably because adrenalin was secreted due to fear and adrenalin prevented the blood pressure fall.

Fear. Fear paralyzes and extreme fear can result in a loss of almost all feeling in a dog. Terror in dogs is expressed by an emptying of anal glands, which act may be regarded as symptomatic of an acute state of fear. Various guesses have been made at the purpose of these glands with their acrid odoriferous material. To the dog its own odor is not obnoxious, but to another dog a strong dose of anal gland odor is so repulsive that, in a dog fight, the winning dog will often cease fighting and leave; in short, this is probably how a losing dog says "uncle" in a fight. I can think of no other purpose for them. One always smells the odor on a dog which has been a victim of an accident, and often on a dog after a convulsion, in which the dog generally experiences terror.

Fear is a strong emotion, stronger than others, as we saw, far stronger than hunger, but it is not one of those we can very often use in positive dog training because we do not want timid dogs. Fear of the consequences of certain actions can act as a deterrent and that we can use.

Sustained fear is accompanied by increased hydrocholoric acid secretion in the stomach. This has been measured by many students in several species. The dog is no exception. He probably digests his food more quickly as a result, but the human being may develop stomach ulcers.

A dog's anxiety can actually be measured by the encephlograph, which fact has helped students learn much about fear. Dogs are often afraid of new objects, new situations. One investigator studied 26 home reared dogs with various stationary objects and objects with moving parts, such as toy lizards, skulls, soap bubbles. He could tell what frightened the dogs by their avoidance responses such as turning away from, running from or crouching. The objects with moving parts were more frightening. But the dogs soon learned there was nothing to fear in these objects. Anything new may cause avoidance.

Some dogs will act this way toward strange animals. Some dogs with great natural courage may seem to display timidity when actually their actions are misinterpreted by the handler. Dogs who will not be bullied by other dogs may crouch as if they feared the new animal. I have seen this many times in hounds. One whole family of hounds behaved this way. All that it took to remove the attitude of fear was for the young dog to get close enough to the animal to be bitten, perhaps only on the lip, and the whole mien of the dog changed; it boldly and furiously attacked the animal and tried to kill it.

The Shepherd dog's bravery with the flock he guards is most interesting. Darwin ably tells about it in *The Voyage of the Beagle*.

"While staying at this estancia I was amused with what I saw and heard of the shepherd-dogs of the country. When riding, it is a common thing to meet a large flock of sheep guarded by one or two dogs, at the distance of some miles from any house or man. I often wondered how so firm a friendship had been established.

The method of education consists in separating the puppy, while very young, from the bitch, and in accustoming it to its future companions. A ewe is held three or four times a day for the little thing to suck, and the nest of wool is made for it in the sheep-pen; at no time is it allowed to be with other dogs, or with the children of the family. From this education it has no wish to leave the flock, and just as another dog will defend its master, so will these the sheep. It is amusing to see, when getting near a flock, how the dog immediately comes forward barking, and the sheep all close in his rear, as if round the oldest ram. These dogs are also easily taught to bring home the flock at a certain time in the evening. Their most troublesome fault, when young, is their desire of playing with the sheep; for in their sport they sometimes gallop their poor subjects most unmercifully.

"The shepherd dog comes to the house every day for some meat, and as soon as it is given him he skulks away as if ashamed of himself. On these occasions the house-dogs are very tyrannical, and the least of them will attack and pursue the sheep dog. The minute, however, the sheep dog has reached the flock, he turns around and begins to bark, and then all the house-dogs take to their heels. A whole pack of hungry wild dogs will scarcely ever venture to attack a flock guarded by even one of these faithful shepherds. The whole account appears to me a curious instance of the pliability of the affections in the dog; and yet, whether wild or however educated, he has a feeling of respect or fear for those that are fulfilling their instinct of herding together. For we can understand on no principle the wild dogs being driven away by the single one with its flock, except that they think, from some confused notion, that the dog with the sheep gains power, as if in company with its own kind.

"F. Cuvier has observed that all animals that are easily domesticated consider man as a member of their own society. In the above case the shepherd-dog ranks the sheep as its fellow-brethren, and thus gains courage; and the wild dogs, though knowing that the individual sheep are not dogs, but are good to eat, yet partly consent to this view when seeing them in a flock with a shepherd-dog at their head."

Patience. Patience is not alone a trained characteristic, it is quite definitely inherent in some dogs. A good example of patience is afforded in a Bloodhound and Bull Terrier cross named Bill. Bill had been used to treating dogs for me. He licked cankered ears, cuts which were inaccessible to the dog himself and Bill always forced the ailing dog to stand and be treated. He would take more bullying from other dogs than any dog I ever owned. On one occasion a large Black-and-Tan Hound was put into Bill's run. The hound tried to dominate him and seemed to be succeeding, but we who knew Bill wondered why he was so patient with the bully. For three days he took insults. The morning of the fourth we found the big hound a pathetic mangled semblance of the proud hound he had been. He was curled up in a corner, eyes closed. The run was red with blood. Bill however was wagging his tail and except for a cut in an ear looked as if he had spent a comfortable night.

Frustration. In a number of experiments the students relate the effects of frustration on dogs. The animals may be in a harness as subjects for experiments. If they become frustrated they may take it out on the harness, chewing and fighting it, or any other object at hand. This destructiveness therefore is a frustration reaction. The stimulus is present but the dog cannot react as he usually does. Try as he may, he is thwarted and frustrated.

Few dog owners realize how important frustration can be to them, especially those who own large undisciplined dogs. Put any dog in a situation where he wants something badly but is barred from obtaining it and he becomes either passive or frustrated. Many a hunter can tell you of his dog's actions when he had left him shut in the automobile and taken a companion dog hunting. He planned to return and change dogs but when he returned to make the swap, he found the inside of the car a wreck. I once had a new hound which appeared not to have taken our leaving him too hard. But he did; he ripped all the upholstery loose, tore the cloth lining off the car's ceiling and made it necessary for us to sit on metal springs to drive home.

A Boxer owned by one of my clients tore up the owner's apartment, chewed chairs, rugs, tore the bed clothes, pillows and mattresses apart, burned his mouth on electric light wires and thus blew the fuses. The total damage was in excess of $6,000.

These are not rare occurrences. Even the dog left home in his kennel when mates are taken out may become frustrated and when he does, he may seem to go beserk, chew wire mesh, dig, scale fences, actually harm himself physically and still not stop. Some owners express the opinion that these dogs are teaching the owners lessons. Lessons are to be drawn from the actions but the dog had no such purpose; he was simply frustrated.

Neuroses. Dogs, like human beings, have phobias. Some fear heights, some automobiles, some fear other animals. An experiment to learn whether phobias could be established was undertaken by using a dog which some one had previously thrown down a flight of stairs. This experience plus experimentally induced "weakened inhibitory processes" established an excessive fear of height. This was done by early castration and causing a long series of difficult discrimination experiments. The dog was ordinarily fed at the edge of the stairs but he soon developed an intense fear of this location.

Dogs do not become neurotic in natural environments. Behind every neurosis will be found some inability on the dog's part to solve a conflict which it feels it cannot escape. And dogs in kennels cannot escape so occasionally one becomes neurotic. Take the circler for example. He has great energy. He feels cramped in his quarters from which he cannot escape so he starts to run around. Soon he is running in as large a circle as he can within his small run. And before many weeks he has made a racetrack for himself. If this neurosis becomes established he will run in a small circle even when placed in an acre run.

In studying neurosis in dogs, one investigator found his experimental subjects broke down when the problem became too difficult. In this case they had to distinguish a circle from an elipse. When the ratio of their axes became as 8:9, the breakdown occurred, showing it by either becoming subdued or wildly excited.

Studies of neuroses in several species show that there is a threshold of neurosis and that the differences tend to be hereditary.

Dogs which show mental breakdowns or those which develop "abnormal" behavior patterns under environmental stress, do so to some extent because of hereditary factors.

When dogs of entirely different breeds, temperaments, and

behavior patterns are all raised together in as nearly a same environment as possible, they all turn out differently. The difference depends on their inherited behavior patterns. I pointed this out years ago and others have since. Many others will in the future. My observations covered such breeds as trailing hounds, raised with pointers. When birds or butterflies flew over, the hounds showed no interest while the pointers tried to catch them.

Dogs developing neuroses show it in the early stages. Any upsetting procedure may produce a neurosis-like behavior and the severity of the disturbance depends upon the type of dog. Complex reflexes are more susceptible to disturbance than are simple ones and the same applies to newly formed reflexes; they are liable to disturbance. Internal inhibition is less stable than the excitatory process.

The difference in dog types can be amply illustrated by the description one student gives us of the actions of one dog which, as he puts it, was faced with life's difficulties. This dog was of a highly excitable and aggressive nature. He became educated but it took him two years to learn to differentiate between 120 beats of a metronome per minute and 60 beats. And even then he was unstable unless he was sedated with bromides. During a summer vacation he was not worked, had poor care and by the fall had lost the metronome differentiation entirely. He was "morbidly sensitive" toward it. Each time the metronome was presented he would become violently excited and the excitation was followed by a general loss of what he had learned and the onset of experimental hypnosis.

That dogs will develop neuroses as the result of finding they cannot perform a certain task with the certainty they will feel pain if they do not, was established with both a German Shepherd and a Basset hound. A weight was affixed to a foreleg. When a buzzer sounded, the dog was supposed to lift the paw, weight and all; if he failed to, he received a shock. The weight was gradually increased up to the point where he couldn't lift it. The fear of the shock brought on neurosis in the German Shepherd gradually and suddenly in the Basset.

In human beings psychologists find that behind every neurosis lies an unsolved conflict, and as we have seen, the same is true of dogs. Our training should be as free from conflicts as possible. Switching a dog from one kind of behavior to another constitutes a conflict. Trying to make a dog behave in opposition to his native behavior patterns produces another kind of conflict. Square pegs do not fit into round holes in dog handling any more than they do in the case of human beings. Students can, for example, cause neuroses in dogs by confronting them with problems too difficult for them. I made a dog neurotic by preventing him from attacking others. He was three-quarters Bull Terrier. From puppyhood on he attacked, not just bullied, any dog put into the kennel run. I decided to break him of it. One morning I put dog after dog in the run and stood beside each, holding a strong slat in my hand. Each time the terrier attacked I slapped his side and drove him away. Finally he went to a corner, laid down and whined. He behaved as though I had trained him but actually I had simply caused a mild neurosis. He refused to eat all that day.

Those who like to compare dogs with ourselves will find much of interest in the observations of two scientists who tell us about fear, and how it is especially prominent in dogs, how some dogs are egocentric, some dominant, some submissive, envious, jealous. When dogs commit crimes they are aware of it. Hate, they tell us is usually the result of bodily punishment and will not replace love, once the latter is well established. Canine deceit, which shows by malingering simulates the behavior of human neurotics.

We could add a lot to this report. One of the most obvious characteristics is respect. The man who is firm, yet just, wins the dog's respect.

Do dogs ever develop obsessions? Yes, but infrequently. In one study a dog started to fall forward and look under a table toward the source of a noise. Later on, this reaction generalized to other stimuli, not a part of the study, and included visual stimuli. Sometimes these actions appeared when no stimuli were seen or heard. Such action represents an obsession as in mankind:

> Late last night upon the stair
> I saw a man who wasn't there
> He wasn't there again today
> Oh how I wish he'd go away.

There have been many reports in lay literature about dogs who saw ghosts but perhaps they heard some sound and their actions seemed to the observer to indicate these dogs saw, when all they did was cock an ear, the better to hear, and this gesture made it seem the dog was looking. It might also signify the dog had been obsessed.

Jealousy. Dogs often exhibit this reaction. One sees it displayed when a new dog is introduced into a home, when a child is adopted and sometimes when a new baby gets attention which has been lavished on the dog. Resentment shows in several ways: by open antagonism, by sulking, even by running away. Jealousy has been blamed by those attempting to explain the basic cause for dogs killing babies they were supposed to guard.

Hunters know the characteristic well. Their dogs often resent having other dogs do their work. Greyhounds chasing an artificial rabbit must be muzzled to prevent one dog from attacking another; many coonhounds will attack other dogs who bark tree with them. One of my Bloodhounds insisted on having her track to herself. She did not object to another dog trailing behind her, but let that dog come even with her and put its nose close to hers and she always reached sideways and snapped; she jealously protected what was hers.

Independence. Dog owners often say that their dogs are independent. What they should say is that the dogs are improperly conditioned. What I refer to as independence is a characteristic exhibited by certain dogs and certain breeds. The English Foxhound—one of the truly great breeds—is a pack hound par excellence. Turn half a dozen out together and they hunt as one dog. They "hark in" quickly to the bark of another and run together. For this they are trained, to be sure, but for this they have been bred by hundreds of generations of selection.

In contrast, we have the old American Black-and-Tan Foxhound. It exhibits independence in hunting. Turn a group of them out and soon each will be hunting its own fox. I have seen them entirely ignore a kennel mate who had started its fox. I have heard three of these hounds running different foxes on a mountainside at the same time. Occasionally one finds a hound which will not follow a trail which another dog is running.

INTELLIGENCE

Are dogs *intelligent?* "Intelligence is the ability to use one's past experiences effectively for the solving of present problems and the anticipation of new ones."

Some contradictory conclusions have been stated by various investigators as to the relative intelligence of domestic animals and wild animals partially domesticated. Several have found the dog definitely superior to the wild dog or wolf. Most of the ratings have placed ape, monkey and raccoon over the dog with the cat a step below the dog. Of course a great deal depends on the particular animals observed by the investigator, and even the time of the year. Some raccoons become phlegmatic in the winter months. Some dogs are far more responsive than others. Having kept a great many dogs of many breeds as well as raccoons from various parts of the United States, I would rate the coon definitely higher than the dog, speaking generally.

Intelligence or the use of the dog's ability to solve problems involves such topics as reasoning, thought patterns, abstract thinking, insight, foresight, decision, counting, imagination.

What a dog can find out of its own accord with no human help is the test of its intelligence. How can intelligence be tested? By arranging some problem for the dog to solve with no help from a human being. How quickly the farm dog learns by himself to catch woodchucks is one test. How quickly he can solve a puzzle box is another. Let us arrange one with a lever which our dog must trip to open a door to let him get inside and receive a reward he knows is in the box. Finally he masters it, never makes a mistake. Has he mastered the workings of the mechanism or merely learned to paw a certain place? We rotate our box a quarter turn. Does the dog stand back and study the change? No, he simply paws at the place the lever was, or at the door and then takes nearly as long to learn to paw the lever in its new location as he did in the old.

Real intelligence is the capacity or faculty for understanding, not for learning. So in this predicament the dog is not really intelligent. But set him at some natural job such as catching woodchucks and it becomes evident that some dogs master the knack far more quickly than others.

A good measure of canine intelligence is how few mistakes the dog makes in learning a new problem.

No one questions the relative intelligence of the higher apes compared with dogs. Can an ape recall events or plan for the future? If he can and does he shows no manifestations. Nor do dogs.

Apes can learn some words but they are always words for *how they feel*. So far as I can learn no ape ever learned any words for things—only the human being has such words.

We read about the language of wolves—the sounds they make. Apes make far more but still they cannot talk. Dogs have been trained to make about eight sounds for things they want but this is not naming things. They may want food. A certain cry may be uttered. This is not saying "food" but, "I'm hungry." Some of the dog's sounds resemble our words and funny stories have been composed based on that fact.

One dog was said to have made a noise which sounded like our word *rough,* or like some persons pronounce the word *roof.* Another could say *out* and did when he wanted out.

Abstract Thinking. A rare quality in man, probably the highest accomplishment of the human brain, abstract thinking has for its basis, knowledge and interests. In some small degree dogs may think, as their attachment for man awakens an interest in his doings. Dogs do not think by themselves according to two authors. It is idle to argue the point. The only way conclusions can be reached as to the mental life of animals is in the light of human intelligence. We study dogs only through isolated performances and these have no significance, they say, except as seen in relation to the totality of the mental life.

Thought Patterns. If we can draw a conclusion from a study involving children and monkeys—and I think we can on the basis of observations of farm dogs or dogs hunting—then a dog stores in his brain patterns of thought which represent the solution to problems. An individual accumulates a sort of file of thought patterns on which he can draw to solve puzzles or problems with which he is confronted. A dog kept in a kennel has nowhere nearly the chance to accumulate patterns which the farm dog has or the dog which has access to the outdoors. If dogs could speak they might have the kind of index to thought patterns which we possess, but they do not use words so do not reason to any extent.

Reasoning. A good illustration of lack of reasoning in a dog is his reaction to a cord about his neck. He can stand up and not choke but once he pulls down too hard and chokes he will not hold his head up and he will die.

Another illustration is the habit which so many have of urinating or defecating in their feeding or water dishes as soon as they have finished eating or drinking. Without inquiring into why they do it, isn't it obvious that the urine renders the water unfit to drink? Any dog should know that he will want to drink again and can't if he has spoiled the water.

Insight. Several thousands of persons watched a Border Collie, Roy, perform at a great American exposition. The American champion sheep dog was being put through his performance. On that day there was an exceedingly balky ram among the six sheep and he gave the dog trouble right to the end when the dog's job was to run the sheep up a gangplank into a trailer attached to his owner's car. Roy drove the five ewes in and in masterful fashion, but the ram refused to go and began to run around the car and trailer with Roy in pursuit. The crowd was enjoying the spectacle enormously but suddenly Roy dashed forward, caught the sheep by one ear and dragged him up the gangplank. His owner told me he had never seen Roy touch a sheep before. Was that insight, reason, frustration, or just what? Roy's patience was exhausted and he refused to allow a sheep to master him.

Foresight. When a dog buries a bone is he putting it away consciously to be prepared for tomorrow? Or is he performing an instinctive action? Probably the latter. And there are few other actions on the part of dogs which come even that close to demonstrating foresight.

Word Understanding. Dogs do not understand words. They do not have vocabularies which enable them to think. The same word spoken by different persons may not have the same significance. Take, as example, a dog trained to step from one chair to another at the word "spring," to jump to the floor and run to its mistress at the word, "off." If words coinciding with "spring" and "off" were spoken, the dog became confused. When the changes were at the beginning rather than some other part of the word, confusion was most frequent. When the mistress left the room and a stranger gave the commands, the dog was confused, and greater confusion existed when the words were spoken through a loud speaker.

If a dog is to understand words and not simply sounds, one author tells us, he must have mental sensitivity, will and attention, memory, ideation, association and intelligence. Does the dog give evidence of these processes? This author who wrote in 1931 assures us that he does. Contrary to other later students, this man is sure that in understanding of words, the dog is not dependent on cadence of the sound, on lip movements, nor on sensory cues other than actual word sounds. He assures us that dogs exhibit will in the same sense it is found in man; that is, in the ability to inhibit an action. Attention depends on intensity, novelty of stimuli; movement and change in the dog from day to day. The dog demonstrates memory. He has ideas which play an important role as is indicated by evidence of dreams and actions carried out at a long distance from the handler. The dog experiences conscious learning and conceptualization. All of the above was deduced by watching three dogs over a period of time.

If one discusses the actions of outstanding, apt, Border Collies and their handling of sheep, one would agree with all of the above. If one watched some of the less intelligent breeds, one might not. In their natural tasks in the open is where one observes the real workings of the brains of dogs and this cannot be said too often.

The famous German Shepherd dog, Fellow, had much written about him by newspaper writers and scientists. I was fortunate enough in 1928 to witness a demonstration by this remarkably trained dog and his master. He was almost five years old and according to his patient trainer "understood" some 400 words. He was a "one-man dog" which limited psychological test but with the cooperation of the owner, it was determined that "scores of associations between verbal stimuli and definite responses have been fixed" as a result of training by the owner. In a later report on their tests these same psychologists tell us that only word sounds were necessary and that no visual cues were needed.

Space Perception. Perception of space is a kind of unlearned behavior and it does not develop until relatively late in puppy-hood. Put a young pup on the table, and he flops off completely unable to accurately gauge the distance to the floor. But now take a litter mate who has never been given an opportunity of jumping, place him on the table at about the time puppy number one has demonstrated that he can gauge the distance to the floor. You will find that puppy number two can gauge it just about as well.

Or you can arrange a distance jump. There too the untrained pup shows that he can judge distance almost as accurately as the trained.

A dog can distinguish up and down, right and left, and forward and back, but how far in distance would he normally go from a small area which to him is home? Lions are said to move over an area two thousand miles long. But how far is an ordinary dog ever found naturally away from his home? I do not mean the hound which pursues game into unknown territory. One of my partly trained coonhounds followed a deer from North Branford to New London, Connecticut, in one night and needless to say did not find his way home.

A dog has his neighborhood, his home, and my impression is that, with the exception of the hunting dog, which is driven by a compulsion to go to some familiar hunting grounds especially if he has a companion, his neighborhood is only a quarter mile in each direction. This is the area he ordinarily inhabits. This is the territory in which he could be set down anywhere within it and able to return directly home. Exceptions of course, occur. There is a bitch in heat perhaps a mile away which a dog visits. There is a hunting companion or the companion in mischief. Two hounds which lived two miles apart would, on damp nights in fall or winter, manage to get together and go to their hunting grounds and after running a fox all night, go home to their own homes. Two Bluetick Hounds of mine would try to escape on such nights and "bark themselves out" about two miles from our home. They might be picked up five miles away if they found no game nearer or if the coon track they found led that far away.

A pair of Boxers from about four miles away on what was to them a lark, went down a country road and killed everything they could; all the ducks in a man's yard, many rabbits in a boy's rabbitry, after tearing the wires off the cages, two calves, and ended up killing six of my lambs and damaging the old ewes.

There are exceptions such as the sheep-killing farm dog who generally does his marauding several farms away—a distance of several miles, or the shepherd dog which went to school with the children. But the usual neighborhood is still a quarter mile in diameter, one-eighth of a mile in each direction.

Even uneducated persons get lost easily. The classic remark of the Indian who when lost said, "Indian no lost; wigwam lost," is not the figment of someone's imagination. The Indians' natural hunting ground was not over too great a territory and the un-educated dog's is quite small too. Indeed in the case of city dogs the neighborhood is but a few city blocks square.

Memory. How well a dog remembers what he sees has been demonstrated by the experimenter placing a piece of meat under one of three containers in full view of the dog which was leashed and about nine yards away. The dog was liberated, and, provided the delay was not over thirty minutes, he would remember under which container the meat had been placed. A wolf tried in the same experiment couldn't remember where the meat was if the delay was over five minutes.

Dogs, after some experimenting, learned to open a cage in one way for meat and in another way for bread, but only when they could see the food. The author of the study concludes that the dogs remembered very well how they had opened a wire door, but when the food was not visible, they had not remembered what they had obtained as a result of their actions.

A dog can hold an image only a few short hours. It gets crowded out. Not all people can recall them. We think by images. Dogs can't recall images.

A dog probably is unable to remember and reflect about his absent master. He looks for him at an accustomed time. He can remember and recognize him by his movement, however.

Many ingenious experiments have been performed in an endeavor to study the memories of dogs. Some observations of hunters should be well worthwhile to psychologists.

When dogs hunt in strange territory they range out much less than they do in country they know. After two or three visits to a new place they usually range as well as they ever will. It is quite amazing how well they remember that terrain. Even when taken back to it three years later they start out ranging widely as if they had hunted it within a matter of days.

Dogs remember smells far better than appearance.

Some of the studies to determine dogs' ability to remember are conducted by investigating how accurately they can alternate. Can they go through a door, walk across a room which has two doors on the opposite wall, go to one door, press a lever and obtain food, go out of the room and return later and go to the other door, press a lever and get food? In other words, can a dog remember to alternate and without errors and if so after how long intervals? Yes, he can, fairly well, but dogs do not do as well as raccoons. Some raccoons remember after twenty-four hours. Dogs were accurate after only a matter of minutes. In mazes dogs can solve only the most elementary patterns. One dog in a maze learned to make two right turns and then two left but that was the extent of his ability. Another dog developed an experimental neurosis.

Decision. To demonstrate the capacity of dogs to show both inhibition and excitation and to make decisions, several were trained to go in one direction when one signal was given; in the other at a different signal. This was not difficult. It shows that a hungry dog can decide which way to go by rejecting one direction and going in the opposite.

Counting. Dogs, as we have seen, do not count very well. But these studies concerned laboratory conditions. What can we learn about a bitch's concern for her puppies? Day after day she may live intimately with them but from a large litter she will generally not appear to notice the absence of several. She will be as well content with seven as with ten. Some bitches will not notice the removal of two out of seven, provided they do not see the puppies being removed or be able to hear their cries or smell them.

A Beagle bitch with two acted extremely uneasy when I took away one, and another Beagle with eight three weeks old, sniffed around and showed she knew something was wrong. A Redbone bitch with four pups was greatly upset when two of hers were removed and glad to have them returned. All of these pups were removed while the dams were outside and a slide closed so they could not know the removal was going on. But could we call this counting?

Hunters have several times told me their coonhounds could count. They treed coons and barked tree up pines or hemlocks where they could not see a coon and kept barking after a coon was shot out, stopping only when there were no more in the tree. I had this experience with one of my dogs in New Hampshire. He treed and we shot a coon. As soon as our hound was satisfied it was dead he went back and barked until we found another and shot that. Again he returned to the tree and barked. We shot another and then he was ready to hunt elsewhere: his interest in the tree was over. He had apparently known he had trailed three coons and had counted. Unfortunately the last coon was the old one, the real coon he had trailed. And all of my similar experiences in each case the dog stopped when we shot the old coon and we could still see more eyes of young coons still in the tree.

Imagination. In studying imagination in dogs an investigator tried a method of accustoming a dog to a certain food box in a room. When he was accustomed to the location, the dog was given new trials by using a second box in the room. When it was mealtime the dog went directly to the second box. This indicates that some imagination is evoked regarding the new location of food. If the act of going to the old food box is not reinforced by food in the box, the dog stops going to the old box much sooner than to the new. He goes about the room seeking food. This is a form of individual behavior and it develops to such an extent that automatized behavior always drops out.

The highest mental capacity of any dog has been expressed by one investigator as the fact that future activity can enter his consciousness, provided it is already familiar to him.

When memory begins to function the dog expects food, pain, or whatever excites him. His past is not reviewed in memory and cannot be pictured. Memory plays a greater part in behavior than perception. In present situations he can remember clearly his previous behavior. Experience is directed toward the future.

Imitation. To date psychologists have not been able to demonstrate that a dog possesses the ability to imitate. Laymen often contradict the scientists and offer instances of what they call true imitation. Too often their observations are faulty or their imaginations are working overtime. All psychologists are eager to find dogs with this capacity.

One scientist, using a method of free movement is sure he has demonstrated it. A brief starvation period increases the reactions and after feeding the imitation reactions disappear. He says the imitation is conditioned by the increase of excitation of the central nervous system. Imitation movements of one animal were conditioned by the movements of the other one and not by food.

On the other hand, in a laboratory test on thirty-one mongrels ten dogs were given an opportunity to watch others being taught a lesson. A bell rang, the dog lifted his paw. When the ten were trained the watchers required just as much training as the ten other dogs which had not had the opportunity to watch the first group being trained. "No evidence was obtained of either imitation or of social facilitation," from this study.

I felt sure I had seen a dog imitate once but further consideration convinced me there was another basis for it. One of my hounds which I had handled from puppyhood and trained carefully was seemingly very fond of me and looked to me constantly for encouragement. One night I happened to look up at a full moon and he did too; he looked until he seemed almost hypnotized by what he saw. But was this imitation? It might have been so construed if we did not know about contagious behavior.

Contagious Behavior. Behavior which seems like imitation is sometimes called *contagious behavior* or technically *allelomimetic;* a word made by combining two Greek words: allelo- mutual and mimetic- mimicking. Yet it is not truly mimicking, if by that we mean true imitation. What we are referring to here is behavior which is contagious and not always produced by the same stimulus. If one of a flock of pigeons sees a bath pan, flies to it and begins to splash, most if not all of the rest of the flock do likewise.

If one of a herd of deer is frightened and dashes away, the rest of the deer in the herd dash with it.

This kind of behavior represents a sort of group activity. A flock of homing pigeons flies in circles above the loft for many days until, with what appears to be one accord, the whole flock starts out and flies for two hours, going far away from home. Where it goes without a leader, why it goes there, one cannot say. The desire is contagious, sparked no doubt by a few of the more adventurous of the flock and the rest follow. This is different from spring and fall, north to south, migration of birds which is caused by a change in the physiology brought about by lengthening or shortening of the day.

Most of the instances reported to me of what dog owners took for imitation have been this type of behavior. You read about how the wolf family forms a pack and goes hunting—contagious behavior it is.

This behavior is one of the most important aspects of any dog's life, for it helps him learn many things. It exhibits itself early in life and from then on is basic in self preservation.

When I am starting three week old puppies to eating gruel, they may not have any interest in it whatever. Their natural mother, if they were wild would have vomited her partially digested meal for them. So to get them to eat I add an acid smell to the diet and a reflex sends them to trying it. Without the acid odor how better can I elicit the eating response? By starting one eating and affecting the others through their sense of hearing. This may be the result of early education; they have already associated the sound of sucking their mother's nipples and hark to a similar sound coming from the food pan.

Once they have learned that the pan means food, there may be two pans in their pen. If one puppy starts to eat and they see him the others flock to the pan and eat too. It has been repeatedly observed by psychologists and laymen alike that two puppies fed together grow faster than one. Is this based on greed?

A thin partition divides true imitation from this contagious behavior common to the higher and many lower species which one might well call follow-the-leader behavior. If you have ever driven sheep, or even watched the way they are driven in an abatoir you know well what I mean by follow-the-leader. It takes but one sheep to start in a given direction and another follows. The trained goat which leads the lambs up the long incline in the slaughter house is used because of this common characteristic.

Even stupid fishes follow-the-leader. All animals which herd, pack or school do it. If only two animals are maintained together, in the absence of knowledge of this instinct, the observer will likely mistake the action of the second animal in following the first, as true imitation.

Dogs exhibit the instinct occasionally, but seldom in the laboratory. And generally this is because in the laboratory, hunger is almost the exclusive drive used. Where the fear-of-being-left-behind is a drive, one sees some remarkable demonstrations where dogs learn quickly. In no situations which I have observed is there more eagerness on the part of the dog than when hunting in well fenced land.

We come to a fence where no hole in the mesh is larger than 6 x 6 inches. Our dogs cannot possibly get through. The bottom wire is on the ground. The only way to get past the fence is to climb it, jump it, or wait for a human companion to lift the bottom wire enough for the dog to squeeze under.

Let the man lift the wire for the dog once and the untrained dog next time stands at the fence and barks until his companion comes and lifts it again. If the man fails to return, then the dog is on his own and must find another way past this barrier.

Even in learning to crawl under a bottom wire which the man pulls up, one sees what looks like imitation, but isn't. The untrained dog does not realize why the wire is held up. Below it, there is usually no more than six inches to squeeze through. Even calling him, snapping the fingers of the free hand, fails to entice him under. Now let a trained dog slither under and the untrained dog nearly always follows. Is it imitation? Is is only follow-the-leader instinct?

The same applies to learning to jump low fences. The deserted dog tries vainly to get through the holes and cannot. Suddenly a fence-trained dog comes up behind him and jumps the fence. Immediately the smart deserted dog will generally try to jump the fence.

And what are we to say of the dog who is trying vainly to get through a fence? A dog comes toward him from the other side, jumps the fence, whereupon the untrained dog jumps it in the opposite direction from the trained dog's jump, the way he wants to go. I have seen these things happen many times and all can be demonstrated in hunting dogs. Certainly the dog which jumps a fence in the opposite direction from the trained dog's jump is not following-the-leader or he would turn around and follow him. But when he looked up and saw the way out of his difficulty he came pretty close to exhibiting imitation.

To my mind imitation is a development of the follow-the-leader instinct and indeed "thin partitions do their bounds divide."

From watching the actions of animals which exhibit allelome-metic behavior one must conclude that the only time they exhibit it is when a need is felt by all of the group, whether it be a flock, herd, or pack.

As I watch my pigeons quit their perch on the roof of the loft, fly down to the entrance and go in, allelomemetic behavior is not apparent. One goes but this departure from the rest is no signal for the others to follow. Obviously he feels a need, probably hunger or thirst, and goes to satisfy it. Occasionally two or three go at once but it is to be expected that of sixty birds, two or three would feel the same need at the same time.

A pack of dogs in a large run may be lying about in the sun. One feels a need, to satisfy thirst. He gets up, goes to the pail and drinks. No other dog moves. This kind of movement is distin-guished from the quick movement of needing to escape which communicates itself to the companions when they would then show their allelomemetic behavior.

Adaptability. As we observed in the case of wolves, one of their most outstanding characteristics is their adaptability.

As an example of how adaptable dogs can be, here is a descrip-tion of the behavior of the Soviet dogs, Belka and Strelka while they were orbiting the earth in the U.S.S.R.'s space ship. Tele-casts were transmitted of the ship's cabin so that the dogs and other species of animals aboard could be watched:

"At the moment of the start the dogs pricked up their ears

and looked in bewilderment at the floor of the cabin: What was that unusual noise? During the first seconds of the flight the dogs were worried and tried to rush about. As the ship's speed was accelerated, the dogs were gradually pressed to the floor by the increasing force of gravity. Strelka tried to resist by pressing firmly with her legs and anxiously looked around her. Then the animals stood stock-still. The ship had reached its orbit.

"After the great overload, a condition of weightlessness set in. The dogs found themselves in mid-air in the cabin, their heads limply lowered. At first glance the animals seemed lifeless.

"I will not conceal the fact that we were greatly worried during those minutes. Only the readings of the telemetric system reassured us: The pulse and respiration of our travelers gradually returned to normal. We realized that the animals were simply resting during the take-off and were becoming accustomed to the new and extremely unusual sensations.

"Gradually, they started to raise their heads and move their paws. Everything was unusual: It was not so simple to manage their own paws in such strange conditions. Belka even became angry and started to bark; but one gradually becomes accustomed to everything, and the animals became accustomed to the condition of weightlessness. They started to eat . . .

"There were times during the flight when they again became alarmed, but gradually they began to feel at home."

It is because the dog does not show rigid instinctive behavior that he may be trained. The dog who normally urinates on every tree on which he smells urine can be trained not to do so—because he is adaptable. Any hound whose instinct prods him to follow the spoor of any animal can be trained to let all alone except the tracks of one species—because of his adaptability.

Because the dog is so adaptable he is able to make adjustments to his environment. We have all seen or known of dogs taken to city apartments, which become happily adjusted. Several students set out to study the problem and found that dogs make these adjustments quite readily.

COMMUNICATION

How do dogs communicate? Most animals do so principally by sight and sound. But dogs have other ways. Placement of urine and the sense of smell are important. Here we find curiosity at the base and it is difficult indeed to dissuade a dog from expressing it for it is his way of knowing what other dogs are in the neighborhood and of notifying the other dogs of his own presence, just as his wolf ancestor did. "A dog's idea of heaven is a full bladder and a long row of trees" is not altogether true. To the adage there should be added, "on which other dogs have urinated." Man uses sight mostly but dogs use smell more than any other sense. Seeing another dog is not sufficient, the dog wants to smell him. Hearing another dog bark does not often attract the hearer to rush in the direction of the barker; hearing does not evoke curiosity as much as sight.

I have had an excellent opportunity to watch dogs using their sense of smell. Some of us who hunt raccoons will often hunt until we are tired, then get in our cars and let the hound trot along in front of the car on back-country roads. It is a simple matter to train a dog to do this (see Chapter XXI) and most interesting to observe the behavior. The dog is easily kept within the car's headlight because the dog jogs at between five and fifteen miles per hour. As he proceeds he passes thousands of trees lining the roadsides. He stops at every one on right or left side when there is urine on them. And it is amazing how he can smell trees on the opposite side of the road and how he will shuttle back and forth depending on the trees on which another or other dogs have deposited their distinctive urine.

This action is so ingrained and instinctive that it is extremely difficult to stop. The dog is under no compunction to urinate (micturate, some call it) because of a full bladder, but simply because of the urine odor of another dog—an unconditioned reflex. And, lest anyone holds the opinion that it is learned, let him take a dog raised in a pen along a lonesome road and note his behavior. The dog will not urinate as often as an experienced dog, but he will often enough.

Dogs communicate by sound by barking, and growling, baying, whining, screaming in terror. One dog's barking alerts his kennelmates and all will bark and run in the direction the first dog is running. This is not imitation, rather another example of contagious behavior. One dog in a farm neighborhood barks and the outside dogs over a five mile radius may soon all be barking. The bark of a strange dog in a neighborhood evokes barking. A dog howls at some noise and many other dogs lift their heads straight up and howl. Whether this is communication or singing we do not know; a dog will do the same when certain musical notes are sounded. The other sounds dogs or puppies make are too familiar to warrant discussion.

That dogs communicate by gestures cannot be doubted. A dog wanting to play dances or frisks about another making no sound audible to human ears and the play begins. He may roll on his back, or gently bite the ear of a companion.

A dog wanting to draw the attention of another dog or a man to a certain direction will bound up to the other dog or person and then run a short way in the direction he is trying to coax the other. I have had dogs perform this way many times. Coonhounds which have caught raccoons before the coons could climb trees, and killed them on the ground, have, on several occasions, led me right to the coons. They have come to me in the woods and beckoned me to follow them. I have observed one dog trying to entice another which was chained to a dog house and the antics were most interesting to watch.

Bitches communicate the fact they are in heat by either playing or raising their tails and vulvas. This excites male dogs too far away to realize from the bitch's odor that she is in heat.

Dogs learn to scratch a door gently to gain admittance. One will look at the refrigerator or toward his box of crackers when he wants food. He may push his head against his master's hand when he wants his ears rubbed.

If only dogs could talk, use words and not simply make noises, their progress up the scale of mental evolution would be rapid. But only man can use words. Because he learns that things have names, he uses the names. No dog can use words. Without words no dog can reason.

TALKING

Many dogs have been taught to make sounds which correspond to words used by human beings. But this is not talking. One very remarkable dog actually mimicked sounds made by his trainer. This is called "acoustic imitation"—a phenomenon often met with in birds. Yet this dog had no true language and failed to understand the significance of the sounds he uttered.

RESPONSE TO MUSIC

The dog which sits by the piano and howls does not, of course, understand music, and we are not sure what elicits such a response. Several explanations have been offered including that of aural pain when certain notes are struck. Others have thought the dog's sensation was pure pleasure. There is some basis for it in pack howling as all dogs will indulge in it if they are allowed; howling at the moon we are told it is, but packs of dogs will howl on completely moonless nights. One dog starts it, holding his head almost straight up and emitting long moaning sounds, with never a bark. This is what the dog does when the piano is playing. One old Shepherd dog I know would sit and howl when one certain note was struck and not when others were played.

Dogs can and have been trained to respond to a complex of three tones in order. At first they responded to each component but as training progressed the individual components did not elicit a response. The effective agent was the complex of sounds in a given order and not a pure correlation of tones.

Another group of dogs was trained to salivate as a response to pure musical notes. This study demonstrated that these dogs responded to a frequency range of 50 to 2,000 d.v.s. The same dogs could distinguish between air-borne sounds and tactile vibrations.

PLAY

Dogs seem to have a need to play. But as a need, it slowly disappears with age. Puppies love to play. The dog's desire for play can be used by the trainer in several ways. As I have pointed out previously, in the dog's consciousness you constitute to him the pack leader, the companion, because as we saw, dogs are at times at least, gregarious. Most dogs have no other dog with whom to meet in a natural manner. Puppies are taken away from their litter mates almost before they are old enough to do any rough playing. So your children can elicit play desire very easily.

Play in dogs occurs most naturally after eating but seldom when they are hungry. Puppies as we have seen, while young, simply roll around chewing on each other but as they grow older, they will play at fighting, tusseling, growling, rolling over each other, snapping, snarling, but seldom actually hurting one another. Playing at being mad at each other and having a wonderful time at it! This form of play may persist throughout life. One of my dogs now 10 years old plays with his younger companion, a bitch, and neither ever loses his or her temper.

There are dogs which never in their lives had had an opportunity to play with other dogs. Some will find ways to play by themselves. They may carry sticks about or toss the food pan into the air. Some will dig and bark as if they were actually digging after something. This amounts only to scratching at the soil. It might be interpreted as a dog "letting off energy" but it is a form of play as the whole happy attitude of the dog suggests.

No study seems to have been made on the importance of play with other puppies on the temperaments of dogs when they are mature. Puppies in homes love to play with children or their owners. They tug at leashes, play with toys, chew on milady's bedroom slipper and toss it about. Will dogs grow to be morose if denied these opportunities? Surely they will be to that extent less self educated. In children's lives, play has an important part in development of character. Group play develops good sportsmanship and the children learn how to get along with others. It would seem that dogs must learn something from play which is of permanent value. Play should probably be encouraged. And when no other dog is available the owner can fill the need by being a playmate.

HOMING

Whether or not dogs have any homing instinct is much debated. Raccoons seem to have none and when taken to unfamiliar country miles away, seldom return to their old haunts, as tagging experiments have demonstrated. Hunting dogs unable to backtrack themselves because of weather changes, when they are lost, seem unable to go in the right direction to find the camp from which they started. If a hundred dogs were all kept in a kennel for a year and then all were taken ten miles away and liberated at 100 different points, some of them in wandering would get back home. These would be given credit for homing instinct. But would they really possess it? Many of the others might be picked up ten miles in the opposite direction from home, to vitiate the actions of those which came home.

Many dogs shipped long distances have gotten to their old homes. But how? Three dogs of which I knew, were sold and shipped long distances but all came home. Upon tracing them it was found that they had been resold to persons in their old neighborhoods and naturally went to the first owners, who gave the dogs credit for having returned on foot.

Hundreds of instances of apparent homing, when investigated turn out to be dogs taken in autos, on boats or other means of transportation and fortunately returned near their old homes. So far as I can gather and so far as I can learn from study, no authentic study exists of true homing instinct, and its demonstration.

Students of homing in birds have demonstrated that it is not instinctive but that the birds navigate by the sun. When no sun is visible random scatter results. There are 360° in a circle. If 1000 homing pigeons are released from a point and all start out in different directions, if 10 per cent happen to fly in the general direction of home and rely on landmarks to guide them when they are perhaps twenty miles either side of home, then 100 birds would return promptly. But this would be because of random scatter. Probably the same phenomenon applies to dogs.

Liberated only a few miles from home dogs came home by ear, recognizing familiar whistles and other sounds or by smells which they identify. But this is not homing instinct.

How many dogs change home locations every year? A hundred thousand? How many, by random scatter, should get to their old home? And when one does what happens? Although it is as rare as a case of "man bites dog" the rare instance is heralded as a case of "homing instinct." Is it? May it not well be that the dog leaves the new home, becomes lost and wanders until by a happy coincidence he finds himself in a neighborhood with which he is familiar and is soon back at his old home.

How does the dog know his home grounds? Probably by memory of a succession of landmarks just as a man does. By the use of sense perception.

How does the dog find his way home when off his home grounds? By rambling maybe, which takes him as often in the wrong direction as in the right. Dogs with probably no homing instinct must rely on their endurance and luck and other influences. What are they?

One is sound. We have seen how closely dogs can place the origin of a sound (to within 5 degrees). Some observers are sure dogs have a homing instinct, and a few experiments in Germany led the students, who liberated dogs in strange environments, to conclude that dogs did use some sense unknown to us. But all of the explanations are not in. I have seen a pair of yearling puppies get home from three miles away faster than seemed possible, but they followed a river which ran past their homes.

Dogs which returned home in homing experiments can be explained on the basis of luck the first time, and, having found their way home that time would naturally start out the same way when liberated at that place. The German dogs were liberated from the same place each time and each time reached home more quickly than the time before.

RESPONSE TO HYPNOTISM

Dogs may be hypnotized and some hypnotize themselves. A Boston Terrier which I knew frequently stood staring at her owner, especially when he was talking on the telephone. The dog would end by becoming rigid and then tipping sideways in a convulsion. This never occurred at other times.

Hypnosis is simply the production of reactions by the use of associative reflexes. Reflexes will be considered in chapter VIII. Hypnosis is the eliciting of a state. It is my idea that dogs with inherited behavior patterns can be hypnotized in certain ways easier than those whose behavior patterns do not incline them to such actions.

Several theories have been advanced to explain the pointing of the pointing breeds. In these dogs the tendency is to be interested in flying things and to delay the customary chasing most dogs exhibit after moving objects of interest. It is an inherited behavior pattern. Training can lengthen the time pointing.

My explanation of pointing is that it is a form of hypnotism.

A French scientist's explanation is much more complicated. He calls it somnambulistic effect of hallucinating images. He says the preservation of the dog's response is due to a projected image of features of the training situation which are no longer present. The pointer, he tells us, lacking the intelligence to "reduce" his image (that is, to subject it to criticism) , must ordinarily depend upon man's assistance.

AGING

The chief changes noticed by those who have made studies of aging have been in the excitatory and the inhibitory processes. In old age dogs lose their normal ability and inertia appears. The inhibitory process suffers most from inertia. This too explains why old dogs which have been trained so that their normal tendencies are inhibited, tend to revert and lose the inhibitions.

This has been demonstrated by careful work. It is almost impossible in extreme old age to train a dog except by the training methods which are quite severe. Even conditioned salivary responses decrease, sometimes by two-thirds.

This explains why hounds which in youth ran rabbits or deer, were trained not to, and did not for many years, "reverted" as it were to their puppy behavior when they got old. Their inhibitions slowly disappeared. Perhaps this is a form of senility. These functions of the brain's cortex weaken, but the sub-cortical functions do not diminish with old age.

Chapter VII

THE EARLY LIFE OF EVERY DOG

THERE ARE BOOKS used as texts which are educating students to believe that the mature natural dog behaves as he does almost entirely as the result of training. One quickly observes from a perusal of the statements in those books that the authors have had little or no connection with dogs, nor had a chance to watch the natural, normal, uneducated display of behavior patterns. We might say standard development on which we could count, as the dog develops from birth on through maturity.

Of course education enters the picture and the first experiences of any dog or puppy are more important to him than later ones; they make greater impressions. And for that very reason we should be most careful about subjecting our pups to certain frightening or disturbing situations. One sees this principle in our own kind. As young children everything we see or hear or do leaves a much greater impression, one longer remembered than a similar experience in later life. We say we become blasé. Dogs show this principle in a marked degree as everyone who has worked with them realizes.

So it is important to know when, in the life of puppies, the times occur when they are first able to receive impressions for from that time onward, up to maturity, the experiences of the pups leave the most lasting impressions. It has been amply demonstrated that the effects of the earliest and also of the most recent impressions are most difficult to eradicate when such eradication is desirable. The results of impressions between the earliest and the most recent—the intermediate that is—are easiest to eradicate. This is another reason for greatest care that the early experiences are of the right sort. Not that all behavior is the result of these early impressions. Certainly not, for as the brain grows the inherited behavior patterns manifest themselves.

Some experiences are so vivid and stunning that psychologists call them *traumatic*. A trauma is a blow; a psychological trauma is a mental blow. One example often cited is that of a child who became locked in a dark closet. As the individual ages what would have been traumatic in youth, is less noticeable.

Puppies, according to the Bar Harbor group of students working with dog psychology, have four distinct periods of social behavior. The following, in italics, are their conclusions. My own observations are printed in ordinary type.

1. Neonatal: *or the period from birth until the eyes open. During these ten or eleven days the only senses puppies use are the thermal (temperature) and tactile (touch), smell and taste, but the later two are of less importance. When cold, they tend to pile up together.* Experienced puppy raisers have long used this fact to prevent loss of puppies. When a clumsy bitch or poor mother lies down, she may flop on any puppies which are spread out and smother them. So the proper bed is one saucer shaped so the puppies will roll together in a pile and where the temperature is cool enough so they want to stay together. When the mother lies down, if she is a good natural mother, she will nose the puppies into a pile and lie down around the pile with her udder and teats available. *Puppies in this stage seem unable to learn to solve problems. Their ears are not yet open so they do not hear clearly. They can crawl and turn right side up if they are turned on their backs. The wink reflex is present even though the eyes are closed. Puppies twitch while sleeping.* Although it is not mentioned in the report of the study, dog breeders know that this twitching is a sign of health; puppies which do not twitch are not in proper condition. They seem to sleep a good deal, and often cry.

During this period puppies appear to feel pain much less than later in life. Tail shortening should therefore be done at this time. I once had a Great Dane bitch which partially chewed her puppies ears off and they seemed to feel the pain but little. One was so artistically cropped by her that the puppy had a beautiful even pair of pointed ears when it was grown. This observation leads me to wonder why studies have not been made in early cropping because if they were and it proved a satisfactory procedure, humane societies would not object to ear cropping any more than they do to tail docking in the first few days of life.

When puppies nurse they push against the udder with their forepaws and push forward with the hind legs. This makes the body almost pivot on the umbilicus which is not yet healed. Thousands of puppies die annually because the floor under them is rough. This prevents the umbilicus from healing and it becomes infected so the puppy dies—as the direct result of puppy behavior and of ignorance on the owner's part. Even a layer of cardboard on the floor prevents navel infection.

While the puppies are nursing the mother licks the under side of them, removing their urine and feces. Actually the puppies hold their urine and feces until the mother laps them; a most important fact in puppy raising especially when bottle feeding. Before the puppy is permitted to suck, it should be held up and its penis or vulva and anus stroked with a soft brush or a piece of cotton, which will cause it to urinate or defecate. If this is not done, the nest will become fouled. If it is done, the puppies will stay clean.

Puppies cry when cold or hot. They also emit a plaintive cry when infected with diarrhea. There is also grunting sound emitted at the time the bitch from which they are nursing "lets down her milk." Few persons realize that at first puppies suck, but obtain little milk.

When the bitch becomes tranquil she suddenly seems to produce a pressure in the udder of such intensity that the milk flow is abundant and the puppies get it in large quantities. At this point one can hear a chorus of grunts as the little things swallow. Soon after this point they fill quickly. Some overfill and vomit the surplus which the dam laps from their faces.

2. The second period *is arbitrarily set as the time from the opening of the eyes until the time the pups leave the nest, or from eleven days to nineteen days of age. Almost as soon as the eyes are open, puppies tend to crawl backward. It is suggested that at this tender age, only touch causes winking and moving objects near the eyes do not. Therefore the supposition is that the puppies have to be conditioned for visual images. Pupillary reflex is present as soon as the eyes open.*

Not until the pups are twenty-one days old could they be startled by loud noises. Some puppies show it by withdrawing and flattening of their bodies (in a wolf-like motion.) Some puppies merely erect their ears. By nineteen days all the sense organs are functioning, but now most important are the visual, the hearing and smelling (olfactory) senses.

Throughout this period, the report shows, puppies are not suitable objects for conditioning or problem solving.

Puppies can be taught to eat quite easily by the time they are fourteen days old. In my studies of puppy foods I have removed half the puppies of a litter, had them eating gruel at fourteen days. They do better at sixteen days.

Puppies walk unsteadily at eighteen days and some as early as twelve. This seems to depend on the breed, the rate of growth and the degree of fatness. In my puppy food studies I found the puppies of our Redbone Coonhounds would walk through a hole too small for their mothers when they were twenty days old when food was placed for them. But where only two or three pups were left with a good milk producing bitch they became so fat they wouldn't try to walk until they were a month old.

In this second period puppies sleep less and are more active when they are awake. The teeth start to erupt and they tend to chew on each other.

Toward the end of the period the mother sits up more often when she nurses them. Some bitches have never been seen to nurse their pups in this fashion. *The pups take their first solid food at three weeks of age.* I have mentioned above that they will take solid food at fourteen days. To return to the wolf's habit of partially digesting food and vomiting it for the pups, this is also the normal practice of bitches which can get away from their puppies. Most of them begin this procedure at the twenty-first day of their puppies' life, the pups swallow it avidly and the bitch cleans them and eats what they couldn't finish.

By the time they are old enough to crawl away from their beds they begin to eliminate outside of the nest but the mother still cleans it up and still laps them while they are nursing.

Here is an observation of mine basic to housebreaking: Up until this point the puppies have eliminated from the feel of their mother's tongue. Now they wander out of their nest and eliminate nearby. But they are still being conditioned. If the area near the nest is dirt, they eliminate on it. If it is grass they become conditioned by the feel of grass to eliminate on grass. If the area is newspaper covered, newspaper will be what they are conditioned to use. If the pups are reared on wire buttom pens they will search for some place which feels like woven wire on which to eliminate. Suppose you buy such a pup and you live in a house heated from a floor radiator over a one pipe furnace! But more about this in a later chapter.

Puppies are less sensitive to cold but still tend to crowd together. Wolf litters are generally raised in dens of not large proportions. The puppies have to crowd together for the mother to be able to lie around them. Not until they are large enough to get about fairly well do they cease piling up.

Puppies play crudely during this period, pawing and biting at littermates. Growling is occasionally present but not barking, the report states. Perhaps not in the breeds studied but I have often witnessed puppies barking during play in the latter part of this period.

Toward the end of this period the pup shows his first consciousness of an attendant or observer and shows its first behavior which indicates timidity or fear responses.

3. Period of Social Adjustment. *It begins when the pups first notice the observer and ends at weaning time.*

All the sense organs are functional and the pups apparently learn to recognize and differentiate objects. Sensitive to loud noises, they crouch down in recognition of them. By the age of six weeks they try to follow scent trails and they investigate new objects. Puppies may be conditioned now, they have learned to run, they chew coarser food. Their teeth are so long and sharp that their mothers are often hurt by their nursing, which may be one of the factors which keeps the mother away for longer and longer periods. When the pups are even a month old *the mother often stands while the puppies nurse.* They learn to look up and catch teats. Sometimes they sit on their hunches while nursing, placing their front feet against the udder.

By the time they are eight and one-half weeks old puppies may have developed the tendency of defecating in one area and too they show interest in feces. Some pups never use a restricted area but defecate wherever they happen to be in their runs.

When frustrated the puppies whine. They may lick the face of another puppy or dog and paw at the face, the reaction occurring more often when the puppy is hungry. This may have been learned from watching the mother vomit or it may be instinctive. The pups of a good natural mother will often jump at her mouth, lick and paw her in anticipation of a meal of regurgitated food. Sometimes they seem frenzied, if we can judge by their actions.

The pups tend to sleep farther apart but pile up if the temperature drops. They play hard. In fact they seem almost to be fighting. Which they may be primitively, because they growl and the loser becomes submissive. *When the door is opened, usually all the puppies rush toward the observer unless they have been conditioned to fear him.*

During this period puppies bark and unless discouraged the barking tendency increases as they age.

Puppies sometimes mount one another during play when they are alone, in an attitude of sex. The report states that this becomes more common with age *apparently as the testes descend in the male.* The testes are descended at birth. *By the time this period has ended, most social relationships have been established.*

4. The Juvenile Period. *It runs from weaning to sexual maturity. At first puppies are too little inhibited to give attention long enough for certain training or learning such feats as running a maze, but attention develops with age. They become more agile and at sexual maturity are as capable as adults.* Some investigators state that male pups start to lift their hind legs at from five to eight months when they urinate. This is so with many exceptions. I have owned sexually vigorous dogs which did not lift a leg until they were two years old—trained hunting dogs, not kennel dogs.

By this age dominance and subordination develop. A bully develops in almost every litter of certain breeds. Nearly always a bully remains a bully only in the litter or group with which he is raised. Put him in with a group with a stronger dog and a serious

fight usually develops. If he has been bullying long enough, the
fight may be almost to the death, other members of the group
joining the winner. Some valuable dogs have been killed in this
way. Breed differences are clear in this matter. The fighting breeds
and terriers need to be kennelled separately from a fairly early
age. Moreover this bullying temperament, especially around the
food pan, can be modified greatly by the attendant. I have often
had four powerful hounds in one run together, each of which
would dominate an ordinary group of dogs, yet had them all eating
out of one large pan without a single growl.

The Bar Harbor scientists give us their opinion that the most
crucial period in the behavior of a puppy is the early part of
Period III when the puppies are establishing new relationships.
Another—earlier—observer states that the period from the seven-
teenth to the forty-fifth days is that of greatest importance in the
life of the dog.

Anything new entering the domain of a group of puppies is
at once the signal for a burst of energy. A rubber ball produces
the will to play and to carry it about, often with what seems an
attempt to create jealousy in the companions. The possesser will
hold the ball in his mouth, and in the case of retrievers, for hours.
A puppy of another breed may mischievously drop the ball before
his mates and before one can snap it up, snap it himself and run.
Sometimes there is a great deal of tosing of the ball. I have seen
one puppy throw it five feet in the air and others try to gain
possession, often successfully.

A puppy will pick up a stick and race to keep it away from
his companions. Single puppies and dogs throw sticks and stones
and amuse themselves by the hour. And they will do it with
companions. In the open, puppies will race for sheer joy with no
idea where they are racing. This is a form of play.

Some puppy play is useful to the dog in its adult life; racing
strengthens muscles, playing at fighting educates. Psychologists
call this preparatory play: it helps prepare the pup for adult dog-
hood. It teaches the dog control and, he learns as he plays.

Play also helps use up surplus energy. The more the puppy
plays the greater his appetite. Some psychologists make a distinc-

8-week-old German Shepherd Dog being trained to harness as a guide dog.

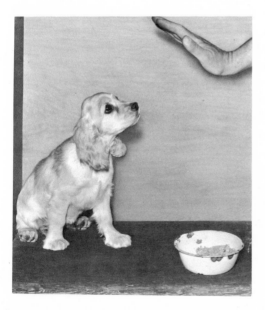

Young Cocker Spaniel being trained to hand signals.

10-week-old Labrador Retriever pup being taught to fetch pheasant wing.

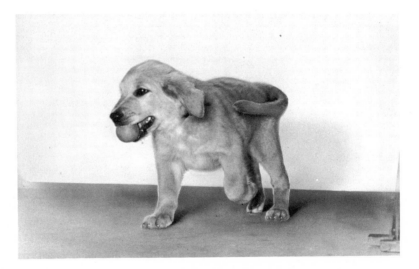

11-week-old Golden Retriever pup learning to retrieve a ball.

tion between preparatory play and sportive play, the latter being only an overflow of energy.

An old bone, a stick of wood—anything new brings on a desire to play with it. But two materials far above anything else I have ever seen excite the play response. These are clean straw in the bed and new sand in the run, or a pile of sand on which the pups can romp.

When a puppy at any age walks into its house and finds it filled with new straw, he becomes greatly excited and will even throw himself about in the straw, even bumping against the sides with resounding thumps. Years ago, when dog food manufacturers used flour containing agene in their dog biscuits or kibbled biscuits, such food produced running fits. There were and are other causes of fits but it was interesting to see the way in which a new straw bed evoked fits. Pups inclined to have them from any cause would enter their houses and, finding new straw, would become excited and a fit would result. I have seen five puppies with fits all at once, caused basically by agene, yet evoked by new straw.

A new sandpile in a dog run will give not only puppies entertainment, but the observer as well. Their behavior is reminiscent of that of so many children and the result on the sand pile is practically identical: it is soon spilled over a wide area and reduced to half its height or less.

On one occasion, there were two large new sand piles left at our kennels. One was in an acre run where I observe and train my hounds. The other was the other side of the fence. Both piles simultaneously caught the eye of some youngsters. The former was attacked by five Redbone pups about six months old, the latter by three of my grandchildren and a friend. The children ranged from four to nine years of age. With no obvious thought or purpose, both groups seemed determined to spread the piles as wide as possible. After watching them for half an hour I left and returned later to find that Grandpa had to do a lot of shovelling to save the grass which would otherwise have been killed by smothering by the sand.

Puppies can be counted on to behave in pretty much the same

patterns at various ages. At first they react to a specific situation with their whole bodies. A puppy reacting to a buzzing insect does not act as does a mature dog but with its whole body. Once it becomes accustomed to an environment, when it is placed in another, it may crawl about on its belly, reverting to an earlier age.

Puppies play much more than older dogs, but I have many times observed that a young dog, not past the playful age, will often evoke playful action in an older bitch with whom it is kept. I never saw one six year old Redbone bitch play at all until a young bitch was put with her and then the pair played roughly by the hour.

In attempting one-generation domestication, the age at which the young animal is transferred from its mother to human care is of vast importance. And this applies even to dogs gone wild. All of the wolves which were kept as pets, of which I have any knowledge were taken close to or after the weaning age. Few of these took to their human companions so they could be trusted like dogs and be "handled without gloves." But had they been removed from wolf dens at two or three weeks of age, then been raised on a bottle held by a human being, more than likely the results would have been different.

I have had some intimate experience with two litters of wild dogs. One lived in a den on the edge of the Yale Golf Course in West Haven, Connecticut. The mother was a skulking long haired mongrel who lived from garbage pails of neighbors living near the course. The pups were born under a bank and protected by roots from a tree.

Like a wolf, the bitch was almost never seen. She would slink away from her den and stand in the distance ready to flee but showed no protective instinct toward the pups. We let her raise the pups. Two of us took the litter when we estimated they were five or six weeks old. One man kept a kennel, put three of the pups in a run, and attempted to tame them. Perhaps if he had spent more time he might have done so, but by the time the pups were three months old they were still suspicious, resented being picked up and snapped on slight provocation. The other pups were given to homes for pets. Every one eventually was destroyed. And is not this much the same experience which those who have tried to gentle wolf puppies have had?

A close parallel of a distantly related animal can be had in the raccoon. I have raised many and my friend and co-author with me of *The Raccoon,* Acil Underwood, raised many more. Both of us have attempted to gentle coons' cubs in many instances and this is what we have found: If we start with weaned babies, gentling is a wearisome and unsatisfactory task. But if we start with two week old cubs and bottle feed them, the job is greatly simplified despite the inconvenience of five bottles of milk a day. One season Mr. Underwood removed thirty-six cubs from their mothers and bottle fed them all to make more reliable pets of them. He says they were practically domestic animals in contrast with others which he sold at weaning, only a small percentage of which were domestic.

A young wild animal, which grows up with no fear of human hands from the time it is able to appreciate its surroundings, is far easier to domesticate than is one which has to learn that human hands are friendly.

Many years ago I developed a formula for a canned liquid puppy milk which was marketed under the name of Fobilac (a contraction of Foster Bitch's Milk). Hundreds of puppies were used in the study. Many types of feeders were made, many types of nipples tested, optimum temperature for brooders, frequency of inducing urination and defecation necessary for cleanliness and the temperature of the milk which induced puppies to nurse.

I learned that little puppies will not try to suck on anything which fits the mouth, which one scientific study says they will do. Even two-day-old puppies would spit out certain nipples unless there was milk accompanying the rubber. Hungry puppies are much less discriminating than well fed pups.

Puppies given milk which was too hot would spit it and the nipple out, but they seem not to have become conditioned by the heat and would try again as soon as milk of the proper temperature was offered. Cold milk was always refused, by even hungry puppies.

One study on the sucking reflex in puppies concludes that non-nutritive sucking where pups will suck one's fingers or the body of another puppy is intensified by early weaning when the puppies are under nineteen days old. In older pups, sudden weaning produces less frequent non-nutritive sucking. The investigators tell us that there is also a deliberate non-nutritive sucking in older puppies which are not permitted to nurse the mother and which are on rigid feeding schedules.

In another study the early sucking behavior of puppies was investigated in relation to dropper feeding, bottle feeding and nursing from the dam. Non-nutritional, that is, sucking on something when no milk comes, was found to be common with the first two, but was almost never exhibited when puppies nursed from their mothers.

Dog breeders would contradict these conclusions because it is very common to see puppies sucking on parts of the dam's udder where there is no teat, and trying their best to get milk. We often find one sucking on the tip of its mother's vulva. Indeed, there is much non-nutritional sucking by young puppies which have always nursed from their mothers.

When the pups observed, which had sucked from bottles and droppers were returned to their mothers, they sometimes sucked non-nutritionally but this habit soon stopped—"became extinguished." The researcher concludes that in puppies a sucking need exists.

I have frequently observed in litters of puppies, the propensity of some to suck on some part of a litter mate's anatomy. It is not unusual to see a puppy sucking another's ear, or foot, or loose skin.

It has been demonstrated by experiments, that conditioned reflexes in newborn puppies cannot be formed, but after twenty days they may be readily established. Puppies can respond to odors at birth but the ear canals do not open until they are 18 days old. They react to contact by feeling from birth onward. This is demonstrated by the fact that they urinate and defecate when their mothers lap them. But, we are told, it is mostly a waste of time to try to condition them to anything but eating before they are twenty days old. That conclusion is wrong; I start puppies eating at sixteen days and they learn quickly not to dunk their noses and inhale liquids. In this respect they can become conditioned. And for this reason thick gruel is best to feed instead of milk to hasten their ability to eat.

Ch. Stella, Norwegian Elkhound bitch of the Runefjell Kennels, with four of her puppies.

Shih Tzu puppies, 12 weeks old, owned by the Chumulari Kennels. The Shih Tzu is the newest recognized (1969) of the 116 breeds accepted by the American Kennel Club for registration.

PART III

Open trailing Beagles. These are trailers, not trackers in the modern sense of the word, and their method of trailing is more efficient than that exhibited by non-trailing breeds.

Chapter VIII

REFLEXES AND CONDITIONED REFLEXES

MANY, IF NOT MOST, of a dog's actions are the result of his unconditioned and conditioned reflexes which we shall discuss now. Better that we should consider him in this light than that we should talk about his mind. Mind admits to a dualism. Some would have us believe that because someone once said or wrote that the dog has a supernatural mind, he must have one. One can't disprove ghosts but that gives no one the right to invent them in the first place. We should not think of a dog's mind as being distinct from his brain. He has personality surely. Personality is what we see and comprehend which makes one dog different from another. His appearance, his actions; these constitute his personality. These are what endear him to us, what makes him seem to live in our memories. But without our comprehension and memory, they would cease to exist when the dog dies.

A reflex is the dog's reaction to a stimulus, a completely unlearned reaction. To illustrate: If one scratches almost any dog on his back or side, the dog will squat and scratch at his shoulder with a hind leg. This reflex is much more prominent in some breeds than in others. Scottish Terriers probably manifest it more exaggeratedly than dogs of any other breed.

Shine a light into a dog's eyes and the pupil closes; this is another reflex. A dog is a bundle of reflexes. The medical dictionary calls a reflex "an involuntary, invariable, adaptive response to a stimulus," and goes on to list and describe 250. Many reflexes bear the names of persons who discovered them in human beings. Dogs exhibit most of these reflexes and also others which we do not possess. Some dogs exhibit reflexes which other dogs lack. One is the smile reflex which I described many years ago. Have you ever seen a dog smile? At any feeling of pleasure the dog draws up the lips and appears to smile. Another reflex, which so far as I can determine is confined to species closely related to dogs, is the "thrust" reflex. Behind the bulb on the penis there is a sensitive area which, when it feels pressure, causes him to thrust the penis forward. By pressing on this area with one's thumb and forefinger any dog can be made to demonstrate it. Another which I first reported is an area within the vulva. When a bitch is whelping, pressure on this area by the puppy's head or rear end, whichever presses against it, causes the bitch to strain to help expel the pup. I often use this reflex to assist a bitch in labor when she seems unable or unwilling to strain. By inserting a finger in the vulva, bending it and pulling backward, she will almost always strain powerfully.

This reflex which sets up peristalsis or wave-like movements of the uterus probably is helpful in insuring fertilization. The bulb of the male pulls against this area when the two are tied. This pulling, which is extremely powerful, helps to set up peristalsis and carry semen to the ovaries.

The untrained reactions of dogs to all stimuli are *reflexes,* not to be confused with *instincts,* which we consider in Chapter IX. Here we must now understand the *conditioned* reflex.

Much of what we know today about the reactions of our dogs, we owe to the great, late Russian, Ivan Pavlov. Today, everyone should understand what a conditioned reflex is. In fact, Professor Pavlov did not himself appreciate the tremendous significance of his discoveries at first and was not proceeding to study these things as such, when he made his initial discovery.

Pavlov's fame grew until he was about the most important professional man in Russia and was the one man who could speak his mind about the new order. But even despite criticisms of his work, it was so greatly appreciated that the government went so far as to set him up a laboratory that is second to none in the world, for the study of psychological principles. He was not interested in exploring the mechanics of the brain when he began his studies. Rather he was working on digestion. He had noticed many things about the saliva of a dog. It was primarily suited to the kind of food in the mouth. It varied in texture and the amount secreted varied. For swallowing, a thick lubricating saliva was excreted, for ejection of food from the mouth, a watery saliva was secreted. For dry food a great deal of saliva appeared and for moist food, very little.

No thought is required to control these actions. They are simple reflexes, acting in response to the signals given by sensitive areas on the tongue and in the mouth. You and I don't have to think when we eat a cracker, "My salivary glands must hurry and secrete an extra lot of saliva." They work without thought. But, and this is extremely important, they work with thought, too. You and I can sit in a chair and just call up before us a mental picture of a piece of luscious cake, and our mouths begin to water. Even before we touch food to our teeth, our mouths begin to water. Well do I remember the whipping I got as a boy by a German who was a member of a band which roamed the streets in Brooklyn, playing under street lights and then going about taking up collections. We boys used to get lemons and put sugar on them and then stand around close to the band and suck the lemons. The bandsmen would watch us and soon their mouths would begin to water and the saliva would get in their horns and make funny noises. Then they would chase us.

In the same way, if you offer a dog meat, his mouth will water with a *thick* saliva. He doesn't have to eat it, his mouth will water anyway. But if you offer him something that he has learned from experience tastes bad, his mouth will water with the *thin* saliva indicative of explusion. He remembers what has happened before and, it is memory that helps him to react. For some time I trained dogs to stop barking by putting a small teaspoonful of epsom salts in their mouths every time they barked. I taught them that instead of calling for food when they barked, they were calling for bitter medicine. Before long when they saw me coming with the spoon they would begin to water at the mouth. I learned that while this was not the best way I could devise to stop the barking— it was not sufficiently unpleasant—it did accomplish results in time.

Pavlov called the world's attention to the conditioned reflex— although he did not coin that term—and the unconditioned reflex. He was not a psychologist, but he gave us our best basic knowledge of psychology, like Pasteur who was not a bacteriologist, but a chemist, and who gave us our basic knowledge of bacteriology. Pavlov started by using a metronome and food in combination. In a room where a dog would have no distraction, he placed a metronome which could be started from outside the room. A food pan could be pushed through the wall for the dog while an observer watched through a peephole. When the metronome began its monotonous ticking, the dog knew nothing about it. But he would notice it. Then when the pan of food came in and he ate it, he at first discerned no connection between the two. Gradually he learned that when the metronome began to tick, the food followed directly and surely. Then after he had learned this, if the food was not sent in directly, he began to secrete saliva just the same. What was an ordinary unconditioned reflex—the secretion of saliva when food was set before the dog or put in his mouth—now became a conditioned reflex. In short the ticking of the metronome caused the saliva to run just as effectively as though food were set before the dog.

Pavlov made a slight operation on the underside of the dog's cheek and brought a salivary gland duct outside where he could actually watch the saliva drop from it or catch it in a container. Then he went further and operated on dogs and sewed off a portion of the stomach and dropped a tube from the pouch which he thus constructed, so that the tube could be watched too, and he found that the stomach juice was also secreted at the sound of the metronome.

Soon after Pavlov began his studies, an American, John B. Watson, began to learn a good deal about human behavior. Watson burned a baby's fingers ever so slightly. Holding a lighted candle before that baby's eyes, he found that the child reached for the light just as a moth is drawn toward a light that will kill it. As soon as the baby's fingers reached the flame she found it hot. But that didn't stop her from reaching toward the flame or the light. She would reach but instead of putting her fingers in the flame, she would double them up so her hand could get so much nearer without being burned. When she felt the heat there was a reflex action. Watson found it possible to condition the reflex and we have his words, "conditioned reflex" in common parlance today.

The warped reflex is the conditioned reflex as contrasted with the reflex that is natural and does not have to be learned. The conditioned reflex is less powerful in its effect on the dog than the unconditioned, and sometimes the conditioned reflex becomes unconditioned. For example, Beagle owners often remark that a certain hound which they have taught never to run on the track of any animal but a rabbit, will, as the dog gets older, seem to outgrow the training and run foxes and deer, much to the dismay of the owner.

We can establish conditioned reflexes in dogs, some with great ease and others with great difficulty. These may be established by punishment as well as by rewards, but we shall see that the two can be used together most effectively.

So much for Pavlov's and Watson's fundamental work. If I were conducting a class in dog training, I would first show all of the persons how a conditioned reflex works by taking a session to condition themselves. An easy way would be to use the unconditioned reflex of the dilatation of the pupils of their eyes in darkness and the contraction of them in light.

Each person would look in the direction of a light. When the light was turned on, a buzzer would sound. The pupils of the eyes would contract. Then each person would be given a switch button to push which would turn on the light and sound the buzzer. Then I would add a further stimulus. I would say *smaller* and let my students turn on the light and hear the buzzer. This I would repeat over and over again for say thirty or forty trials. By that time I would be able to say *smaller* and without the students turning on the light, or the light lighting or the buzzer sounding, their pupils would contract. Now I would have a power over them which would last for several weeks; I could say *smaller* and the pupils would contract—a power which nobody else ever had over them before. This is the basis of conditioning; the basis also for indoctrination in many forms. The only way my students could get away from it would be for them not to experience it for a long period of time. It is also the basis for dog training. And it is likewise the basis for hypnosis. But we shall consider that a little later on.

An unconditioned reflex is the *constant* connection between the external exicting agent and the dog; the conditioned reflex is the *temporary* connection. If a dog is hungry, he hunts for his food. Every action in this connection is a conditioned one, right up to having the food in his mouth. The physiologist calls all of these actions conditioned reflexes and the psychologist calls them *association,* but they are one and the same.

Some psychologists term the unconditioned reflexes *inborn* reflexes, some *generic* and some *adaptive,* some *stereotyped. Conditioned reflexes* are referred to by the several terms of *individual, acquired* and *learned.*

Lives of dogs consist of a multitude of conditioned reflexes superimposed on the inborn unconditioned reflexes. Since there are such a multitude of inborn, adaptive reflexes the number of conditioned reflexes is enormous because the inborn are often conditioned, each in several ways.

The inborn are connected with the lower part of the nervous system, the conditioned with the higher. If the cerebral hemispheres are extirpated, the simple inborn reflexes remain and the connecting reflexes disappear.

The relative intensities of the stimuli is important in conditioning.

The dog's condition is also important. I have found that dogs suffering from severe cases of intestinal parasites are poor subjects for training. Whipworms secrete so strong a toxin as to cause dogs, really keen at their work, to have convulsions. Tapeworms in large numbers make dogs highly nervous. Hookworms, because they cause so great a loss of blood, reduce the dog's sharpness very noticeably. Dogs with fever are sick and even if their early response may appear normal, will soon show a lack of enthusiasm and cooperation. Poor health is a distraction—internal stimuli are keeping the dog's attention away from the trainer.

External parasites exert a stimulus in themselves, sometimes so great as to be more potent than the one thing used in training. An itching dog has difficulty giving attention to the trainer. Irritating skin eruptions and manges will produce enough stimulus to scratch and chew at the irritated areas as to make training far more difficult if not impossible.

Establishing the first conditioned reflex in any dog is the most difficult. The more the dog learns, the easier it becomes to teach him. He pays attention better, he seems to sense what is expected of him and is more alert.

The new response has been so modified that a new condition elicits it. And the new stimulus is called a *conditioned stimulus*. This is most important to understand.

When a dog first responds to a whistle, he becomes alert and shows it in his expressions. This is a simple reflex and a simple stimulus. Now if the whistle is blown and the dog is fed every time he hears it, the whistle is a conditioned stimulus; if his saliva then flows before food is given, he is exhibiting a conditioned reflex. This you must understand as a basis for future discussion.

You see, any stimulus whatever, if it can be experienced by a dog can be converted into a conditioned stimulus; the dog doesn't have to hear the stimulus, it can be a taste, touch, balance, smell, sight stimulus or even a regular repetition at definite periods of time.

Another principle: The reflex action is established most efficiently when the conditioned stimulus preceeds the unconditioned stimulus by a second or less, preferably less. Even two seconds is too long.

A *secondary conditioned reflex* is established on top of an already conditioned reflex in this way: We substitute a new conditioned stimulus. The dog has been conditioned, let us say, to react to a whistle and he salivates. He receives food as a reinforcement. Now we want to substitute the word *eat* for the whistle. So we go all through the conditioning process again.

During this process we blow the whistle occasionally but give no food so the whistle response is extinguished. But if we want our dog to respond to both the primary and secondary stimulus we blow the whistle occasionally after our secondary stimulus has produced the conditioned reflex and offer food, the reinforcement, and we have a dog which will react the same way to both stimuli.

It has been possible to condition a dog to a third but not a fourth conditioned stimulus. This shows how very important it is that everyone concerned with a dog use the same word stimulus or no more than two for the same effect. In training my own dogs to stop barking I can say either *be still* or *quiet* and they respond equally well.

The strength of the conditioned reflexes tends to become weaker and weaker or to terminate themselves when the stimuli which trigger them are removed. Hunger—an internal need—is the stimulus for the behavior pattern we call feeding behavior. As the dog eats more his hunger is appeased and the behavior pattern disappears. Protective responses tend to terminate themselves. A good example is the scratching dog. His itch disappears with scratching so he no longer needs to scratch.

But this is short term extinction. What of long term? Extinction is negative learning. It is important to remember this: An acquired response may be completely extinguished one day but the next may be exhibited full strength. The older psychologists used to tell us that once we are trained negatively never permit an exception to occur; if you aren't prepared to carry the training through to completion, don't start it.

It is interesting to know that light work by dogs actually increases or reinforces the reflexes. When work, such as pulling a load in a cart, increases gradually, reflexes become augmented up to a limit. After that limit the reflexes decrease down to none at all in the case of dogs with recently conditioned reflexes. In dogs with old conditioned reflexes there was a decrease down to about 60 per cent.

Reflexes under work, when they do increase, do so in the same order: first reflexes to mechanical irritation such as a pin prick in the skin, reflexes to auditory (hearing) excitation, reflex to visual excitants. After rest the reflexes come back or become reestablished in the opposite order. Fatigue apparently is due to formation of chemical substances in the muscles, and these affect the cerebral cortex and spread to other regions of the hemispheres.

Generalization. Generalization is understood by realizing that if a dog is conditioned to a certain tone and then other tones close to it are sounded but not reinforced by rewards, in time the conditioned reflexes to them will become extinct and the real connection will become more precise.

Chapter IX

INSTINCTS

Now we come to a new approach to the study of dog behavior. Thus far we have considered the nervous system and how it reacts to influences and stimuli *from without*—from outside of the dog. Pavlov's work with conditioned reflexes dealt with the effect of stimuli on the animal. In this section we take up the subjects of instincts and needs. Here we find behavior which starts with some internal influence: hormones, a stomach movement, a pain, a need for a mate—and we shall see what these instincts and needs cause the dog to do—those things which influence *from within*.

An instinct is an inborn precise form of behavior in which there is an invariable association of a particular series of nervous responses from specific stimuli. It differs from a reflex in being compound.

Instincts of dogs are of interest and a knowledge of them is fundamental to anyone attempting to train dogs, because we can take advantage of the highly developed specialties we find in the breeds of dogs.

A good example of instinct is illustrated by the dog flea. A flea egg hatches one warm, damp day in August, in a crack of your living room floor. The little worm which emerges has never seen its parents which are probably dead from flea powder long before it hatches. No mother or father flea guides it to eat or tells it what its food should be. And when it has grown into a full grown larva and looks like a tiny worm, it has no parents to tell it when and how to spin a cocoon, nor when to chew its way out of the cocoon in its entirely new form. It crawls up the side of your davenport and stops climbing about a foot from the floor. Was it ever informed that it should wait right there? Did its mother or another flea say, "Little Jumper, if you stay here long enough something animate will come by and when it does, give a mighty hop in its direction?" If by luck it landed on a dog, nothing had to tell it how to hunt for another flea of the opposite sex and copulate so that more fertilized eggs could be laid indiscriminately so they would fall off the dog as long as the fleas were its passengers.

All of these acts of the flea are instinctive; they are inherited behavior patterns. There is nothing planned by the flea. The larva did not plan to spin a cocoon and pupate into a flea because it had never seen a flea, had not any way of knowing what a flea was, had no idea when it blindly did what its nature caused it to do, so that it would someday be a flea.

There is no knowledge behind instinct. It is a behavior pattern which does not need to be taught; like a puppy suckling, or a bitch making a bed in which to whelp, or a setter pointing. The instincts which are useful to each species have been fixed in the species by natural and some artificial selection.

An instinct is practically an inherited group of reflexes which involve the whole animal, not the reaction of say, one small group of muscles. In order to call one of these complicated reactions an instinct it is first necessary to be certain that the dog had no opportunity of learning it. It must be hereditary, not learned.

There are many actions which a dog performs, which, as we have seen, are the result of education, and there are others which he performs which are instinctive. He never has to be taught to suckle his mother's teats. He never has to learn to urinate and defecate when he feels her warm rough tongue rub against the external organs from which he urinates and defecates. He never has to be taught to copulate when he is grown, or to bring food to his mate and youngsters. He uses his nose to analyze odors without training and he doesn't have to be taught to deposit his urine on trees and other places where it may identify him. The bitch doesn't have to be taught to lap her puppies dry as soon as they are born, nor to mother them, nor to protect them when they are in danger.

The breeds which have been developed by gradual changes in their heredity consistently produce dogs which do not have to be taught to do the fundamental things for which they were selected. Thus the bird dog doesn't have to be taught to be interested in birds. The fighting bulldog doesn't have to be taught to fight for a throat hold. The shepherd dog doesn't have to be taught to want

The Newfoundland is one of the most natural water dogs, and has been used in the development of many water breeds.

Some dogs are such natural tree dogs that they never need training.
This dog, for example, treed the family cat from the time he was
three months old, and later developed into a great coon and
squirrel dog.

to herd. The hound doesn't have to be taught to follow a trail, baying as he runs, thus warning the foxes or rabbits that he is after them. He just can't help either the pursuing or the baying.

The terriers cannot help wanting to go to earth and to dig; they don't have to be taught. The sight hound can't help running after the fleeting object any more than a baby can help following with her eyes a shiny ball moved before her. The sled dog generally does not have to be taught to curl up in the snow and sleep, he just does it naturally.

What is the basis for these natural actions? We speak of them as instinctive. Instincts differ from learned ability in that the former develops with the individual naturally without the necessity of experience and formation of habits, while the latter is dependent entirely on training and habit formation.

An unlearned response is based on a behavior pattern which is independent of previous experience. Our job in this section is to try to assess some of the unlearned behavior in dogs which is useful to ourselves.

Many psychologists while using the word *instinct,* tell us that actually an instinct is simply an inherited behavior pattern. So we shall follow their lead and while using the term instinct, understand that we are discussing inherited behavior. And it is a very real phenomenon, this propensity to act certain ways in order to survive. Have you ever watched pigeons, for example, and observed their reaction to certain other birds? If a crow flies over their loft, one or two may glance in its direction but as quickly turn away. The same reaction is illicited by sea gulls, cranes and other large birds. But let a hawk of a dangerous species be aloft even so high that one must study the sky to find it, and every pigeon eyes it and watches until it is almost out of sight. And if the hawk flies low, the pigeons panic; crows do not panic them.

These reactions are hereditary and every pigeon exhibits them the first time it sees these harmless or harmful birds. No training is involved. The same instinctive behavior, is manifested by the hound's mane standing erect when it smells a bear trail, but this never happens when it smells the spoor of a fox, a bobcat or a raccoon.

Instincts can be used by man, can be altered by selective breeding and behavior patterns formed which are far more polished and exaggerated than those of the dog's ancestors.

These instinctive acts are the first of all acts; after the first, learning helps the dogs, so that most of his behavior through life is in some degree learned, not wholly instinctive. The central drive is hereditary, the modifications of the method by which the drive becomes action are changed by experience from which the dog has profited. A dog never has to learn what hunger is, all he has to learn is how to find the food so as to satisfy the hunger.

It is not always possible to say whether behavior is dependent on instinct or on acquired mechanisms. We should consider instinct as furnishing the foundations for learning. Learning helps to perfect inherited behavior patterns. Learning also may influence the direction that those patterns will take.

A well-known instinct, which can be demonstrated to depend to a large extent on glandular secretion, is urination behavior. We all know that all puppies squat to urinate, that males cease squatting, and lift a leg and urinate against a post. Some may wait until they are two years old and some begin when teething is completed at from five and a half to six and a half months of age. This depends on the rapidity of growth. The testicles are maturing at this time and begin to secrete testosterone.

If you want to see how testosterone causes an instinctive reaction, just inject some into an eight weeks old puppy and watch him, a few days later, lift his leg like a grown dog to urinate.

Guarding. One of these late developing behavior patterns is the guarding propensity, or instinct. This is exemplified by the fact that puppies seldom, if ever, chase and bark at passing automobiles. When the dog starts this behavior of his own accord, it is usually because of a drive. Shepherd dogs are more inclined to chase cars than any other breeds so within this action we probably have the manifestation of two drives—herding and protection.

The guard dog is more likely to stand and bark, while the shepherd runs just as he does to pass a fleeing sheep or cow and round it back into the flock or herd. The dog with both aptitudes strongly bred into it is the worst car chaser.

Circling Before Lying Down. Dogs usually turn around many times before lying down. May this not be due to the fact that their forebears lived in grasslands and they had to make nests in the grass by turning around trampling out a bed for themselves?

Packing. The packing instinct appears at times in dogs especially in those in the open country areas. Packs of hounds which regularly hunt coyotes together seem to be acting on the age-old canine instinct to keep intruders off their territory. Many instances are reported of the hounds running down stray dogs as readily as coyotes. Suburbanites can also tell you of dogs which guard whole blocks, driving all dogs away whenever they come near. The sight of another dog will almost always cause a dog to run in its direction, and only training will prevent such action.

Sledge dogs demonstrate the packing instincts and the territorial defense instincts which are related. Dogs from one village live in packs and act as one dog in driving trespassing dogs from their home territory, just as wolves do.

Sex Instinct. Sexual behavior, at first, is all instinctive. No one shows male or female what to do all the way from copulation through finding a nest and whelping the pups with all that goes with it. Hormone influences bulk large, in the causation of the bitch's behavior. Even so-called mother love is, we know, hormone produced. You can demonstrate this fact by injecting any female with prolactin.

This is a good illustration of the case in point. All of it is so much unlearned, so native that no one needs convincing. The male dog which has copulated successfully is little more adept at copulation than the male which has never seen a bitch. And vice versa, the bitch in heat which may have copulated many times is no more adept at raising her vulva and accepting the dog than is the bitch which has never seen a dog, provided that she is in the same stage of the mating cycle as the former.

By careless selection in breeding our forefathers have developed many unnatural mothers who are unable to raise more than a small part or none of their puppies without human help. The natural mother walks round and round her litter, pushing the puppies in a pile, and then lies down. But how many do this any more? Clumsy bitches often enter the nest box and plunk themselves down on top of puppies killing a large portion of their pups before they get the pups raised. But this fact does not necessarily indicate that puppy mothering is not truly instinctive in a natural bitch.

Barking. What makes dogs bark? For one thing it is an instinctive reaction to surprise. It can be a useful warning to other dogs as the wolf's bark is to a wolf family. But some dogs learn that barking brings them something desired. It may be food which the owner in desperation brings to quiet the dog. It may be human companionship he barks for, or just to be loose from a chain. He may bark from lonesomeness—a fact to be remembered.

Does he get satisfaction from hearing the noise he makes when he barks? Not at all. He has just as much fun but "no noise comes out" when he has been surgically debarked by a simple operation.

Leading Behavior. What we may call *leading* behavior by dogs has proved useful for mankind on many occasions. And in a way this is related to the behavior of the wolf which shows herself or himself to the hunter and then runs away, luring him after the wolf and away from the pups. The grouse shamming a broken wing to lure an enemy away from her brood leads too, but this behavior is away from, not toward. Only those of us who have had the privilege of observing the action of many dogs under nearly natural conditions are likely to have seen it. Examples:

The cow dog who, finding a cow has calved in a pasture, runs to the gate and by barking attracts the dairyman's attention. The dog repeatedly runs ahead of him and retraces his steps back to the farmer, then bounds on again seeming to express pleasure that he is succeeding in enticing his owner to follow his lead. This action is totally independent of training.

Many times my hounds have treed coons, then after barking for some time have run back to me and bounded back toward the tree leading me onward in the right direction.

Once, one of my hounds dug a coon out of a hole in the daytime. He came to get me and led me back to the dead animal.

A friend's little boy fell off a springboard and drowned. His companion was a shepherd dog. The dog came back to the house, barked and ran toward the lake, and no one in the family followed. He repeated the action until they realized something was wrong and followed him to the shore where they found their dead child.

Behavior in Water. The behavior of dogs in water and their reactions to it are most interesting. The first approach of puppies is marked by considerable trepidation. All dogs can be taught to swim at any early age. There is no doubt that dogs of some breeds go to water more naturally than do others. I have watched with fascination when I took Newfoundland dogs and Bloodhounds for walks together and later took cross bred puppies along with pure Bloodhound puppies. The Bloodhounds had no interest in swimming or even wading in a small river we crossed. On extremely hot days, they might flop down into the water near the shore to cool off. Newfoundlands are among the most "natural" water dogs ever bred. They seemed to delight in it and splashed about and swam with no urging. When the puppies from the cross were tried, the first time they saw the water they behaved like their Newfoundland parents.

How well a dog, not a natural water dog takes to the water depends on his drive or need. Hounds are not dogs which love water. It takes a lot of coaxing to call one across a stream even a foot deep, if he has had no previous experience. But let him be following a trail of an animal which crosses water and, if there is no current, he will usually dash across or even swim it so well one would think he were accustomed to it. He forgets or loses a certain amount of fear with his objective uppermost in his consciousness.

The instinct of going naturally into water differs from what some regard as the instinct of swimming. It is doubtful that swimming is instinctive. Watch a dog in the water for the first time; he exhibits fear and simply moves his feet and legs as if he were running. He finds this movement keeps him afloat and that he proceeds in the direction he wants to go. He gains confidence and gradually may come to enjoy swimming.

We are discussing the dog's natural entering of water the first time he is exposed to it, the same way a duck goes on water contrasted with the chicken which avoids it. A mature chicken forced to do so, will swim well. There are ducks and chickens among the breeds of dogs.

Killing. All dogs can learn to kill and some, more than others seem from puppyhood on to want to fight and kill. The terrier breeds were made by generations of selection to be brave and to kill. They not only dig but get into burrows and kill the varmints. Fighting bulldogs take to killing very easily. Certain breeds of dogs have inherited temperaments which incline them to kill.

The art of killing has to be learned, but the instinct is native. There are some dogs which learn to become excellent varmint dogs. How they learn it has not been explained fully. Their first attempts almost always result in failure. I have watched many a country dog stalk a rodent and lose it when it pops down into a different burrow from the one out of which it emerged. Some dogs never seem able to learn and quit trying. Others, like some shepherds and Redbone hounds I have owned, learned quickly. A good woodchuck dog learns where all the openings to the woodchuck's burrow are. When the chuck is down below, the dog walks to a location where it can watch its prey. The dog makes no move until the woodchuck is far enough from a hole so that the dog can overtake it before the chuck can reach one. One of my hounds caught 110 woodchucks one summer. A shepherd caught ten one week. These good woodchuck dogs almost always bring the game home and receive the expressed gratitude of the owner. Wolves depend on such behavior for food at times. Natural dogs have not lost the aptitude.

There are too many instances of dogs and cats or dogs and raccoons and squirrels having been raised together without any animosity, to permit us to feel that this was not the native behavior rather than trained. Studies with cats and rats raised together showed that the cat had to learn to kill the rats. When kittens were raised in a rat killing environment most of them became killers, but when they were raised in isolation only a few would kill a rat. Only three out of eighteen cats raised with rats killed rats and then not their cage mates. This was independent of hunger.

The fact that I raised my coonhound puppies around my raccoon pens did not make them killers nor detract from their killing propensity. Sometimes a puppy must be taken with killers before he will touch a coon which has been shot out of a tree, yet once he has learned to do so the pup seems to enjoy catching and shaking the carcass.

Maturation. Another principle—maturation—is one, a knowledge of which may save you time and trouble. Every dog trainer needs to understand it. *Maturation* is the name given to the development of instinctive behavior. We dog people depend on the hereditary instincts and behavior patterns of dogs to a great extent.

We know terriers love to dig, hounds to trail, setters to point, retrievers to retrieve, sight hounds to pursue their quarry by sight. Now suppose we take puppies of one of these dogs—Greyhounds for example—and start with a litter. We divide the litter of eight puppies into two lots. One lot we simply allow to age. The other lot we take out into the open fields and train to run after anything which moves—rabbits, cats, even other dogs. By the time the pups are ten months old we feel we have done an excellent job and have accomplished a great deal in the way of training. So now we tackle the four which had aged without training. To our amazement, we find that they do almost as good a job with no training as our trained four did with our long effort. Spontaneous development took care of the puppies and we see that much of our time was wasted.

This principle shows us the futility of expecting that young puppies will profit by training where inborn hereditary instincts are concerned, to a sufficient extent that our efforts will be repaid. I have learned this over and over with my trailing hounds. It has hardly paid to work them as puppies to trail because that instinct has been developing without training, and when I have tried it with part of a litter, the other pups were nearly as good trailers by nature, the first time they were given the opportunity to trail. One of the greatest Bloodhounds ever to work at trailing, Red Trailer, never was given an opportunity to trail until he was two years old and on that first chance, followed a boy's trail accurately. Before he died he had successfully followed twelve trails over seventy-two hours old and many other easier trails.

Many tales are told of retriever puppies trained to swim out into ponds and retrieve sticks, and of their brothers and sisters who without training at a year of age or older, performed just as well with no training at all.

There is always a good deal of debating about whether such

and such action is instinctive. To be certain, it is necessary to show that it is a part of the behavior pattern of a dog who has never had an opportunity to learn it. If you start a Beagle hound on the track of a rabbit, he will show you almost immediately whether or not he is a mute or an open trailer. I did the first experiments in this field in studying the inheritance of the open and mute trailing instincts. All of the scent hounds, Springer Spaniels and some English Shepherds when purebred, bark on the trail. Most of the other breeds are mute trailers. Even the long bugle voice is instinctive, as is the chop voice.

Instinctive need and enjoyment go hand in hand. Only man seems able to separate the two so that pleasure becomes an end in itself; dogs certainly cannot or do not do it, and are thus protected from excesses.

Tropism. Besides instincts and needs, psychologists talk about tropisms. A tropism is the result of the interaction between the inherited structure of the nervous system and environmental stimuli. It is the involuntary orientation of the dog toward or away from a stimulus.

A reflex is blind, spontaneous, unreasoning. It is the invariable response to a stimulus. It differs from a tropism by being sudden movement of one part of the body like the quick withdrawal of a foot from a hot ember; whereas the tropism is more of an inclination or movement of the dog's body as a whole.

Needs. A need goes from inside out, as does instinctive behavior. To satisfy a need the dog acts on the environment *before* it acts on him. Conditioned reflexes are the opposite; the environment acting on the dog.

Modern dog training should capitalize on the volition of the dog. This can hardly be sufficiently emphasized. He needs something, he uses his sensory apparatus and he acts. When the need is satisfied he ceases to act.

It is strange how most of the native behavior patterns become temporarily terminated by themselves. The stimulus pattern which starts them disappears. And this is true of nearly all of them, too. When the sex drive has been satisfied, the stimulus disappears. The food drive is gone when the appetite is satiated, the sucking

The true shepherd dog is one of the oldest and most useful of man's canine creations. His inherited behavior patterns of heel driving, shepherding, alertness and ready response to signals make him ideally adapted for his work.

This dog was a cross of a large farm shepherd dog with a Redbone Coonhound bitch. He combined most of the best features of both— open trailing with sharp loud bark, great endurance and tractibility, but his scenting ability was not above average.

response likewise. The maternal drive, and vomiting of food for the puppies both fade when the stimulus disappears.

A dog stops scratching when the itch is relieved. This fact of disappearance of the pattern is of great importance in training where various stimuli are used, particularly hunger.

An American, B. F. Skinner, studied animals to determine whether they could realize that their actions could result in consequences. Instead of hearing a sound and salivating, could the animal press a lever and observe what occurred after this action. He found they could. Learning, he showed, depended on success; those actions which produced happy results were perpetuated while those which produced harmful or no results tended to be eliminated.

In dog training, we shall use both forms of behavior. When we give a verbal command, the dog is taught to react just as he reacts to a buzzer or metronome or bell. Of course we shall use this first form of behavior. But as you will see, the second kind has been greatly neglected by dog trainers in the past.

Chapter X

NEEDS

IN THIS CHAPTER WE consider the dog's needs and how he satisfies them. Some of the needs are: 1. to escape from danger; 2, for food and water, 3, for companionship; 4, for play; 5, for shelter and to keep warm or to cool off; 6, for sleep; 7, for sex and a mate.

Needs vary with age. We have discussed puppies earlier and seen how they develop needs as they grow. The need for a mate does not appear until sexual maturity is reached. Food needs differ with age. The need for companionship changes. In old age sex needs may disappear as they do in states of illness.

The Need to Escape. The most dominant need of all animals is that of flight from danger. A dog is a modified wild animal, no longer threatened with dangers of the wild. Our domestic dogs lead instinctive lives; they need not even find their own food. When the dog resorts to its natural bent and roams the neighborhood eating from the neighbor's garbage pails, stealing butter left by the grocer on a back porch, we may think of the dog as abnormal. Yet it is far more abnormal for it to eat from the same dish every day. Not that it needs variety; wild dogs often live on a monotonous diet of rodents day after day.

All dogs which have learned to be shy and suspicious of objects and other animals are shy of men and are ready to escape from them but few dogs need to be shy. The preventive method is very early handling as we saw in the chapter on puppies. Some shyness may be inherited.

While the purpose of one study was not to investigate the inheritance of shyness, the fact came out as a by-product, one might say. An abnormally large number of dogs in a behavior problem turned out to be shy; far more than the expectancy. An analysis of the data (82 shy animals out of 178 in the study) revealed that forty-three (52%) were descendants of an exceedingly shy Bassett hound who was a "fear biter." So fifty nine descendants of this dog were traced and inquiries made about their temperaments. Forty-three or 73 per cent of these were shy and unfriendly.

According to the researcher who conducted the study, the trait of shyness would seem to be a Mendelian dominant and "not susceptible to modification through learning and training."

To this many dog breeders would say Amen; others remembering how shy dogs have come from normal parents would question that here is a simple dominant. At least the dam's shyness is not alone to blame, and there seems no doubt that it has an hereditary basis. It is more likely to be a matter of multiple Mendelian factors.

Among my dogs I have had timid bitches which raised entire litters of temperamentally sound dogs.

Gun shyness is a form of flight from danger. It is most interesting to witness its development and even more to see how the very stimulus of gun fire can be used not to cause fright and flight but rather become a signal for happy expectations.

Tall Boy, one of my Redbone coonhounds heard his first twenty-two gauge rifle shot, close to his ear, when he was nine months old. He ran away into the woods in panic and was not seen again for three days. What good was such a coonhound? Even the sight of a gun might cause him panic I decided, so next time I took him hunting I carried a pistol which he couldn't see. When he and an older dog treed a coon, both barked tree. They could see the coon in the apple tree where he had taken refuge. Tall Boy was securely chained and while he was excitedly jumping up and barking, he heard the pistol's shot and jumped back. But the chain held and he couldn't run. He also saw the coon fall out of the tree dead, and jumped in and shook it.

The same evening they treed one they couldn't see. Again a leash was fastened to Tall Boy's collar. He was held on the far side of the tree to be not too close to the pistol. He heard the report, jerked back a little but not so much as before. He witnessed the coon fall before him and jumped and shook it. Now Tall Boy associated the gun's report with a coon falling from a tree. What had caused fear now became a signal he liked. And this practical application of change-over can be used in practical training as we shall see in the next section.

Fear reactions, once they have become established, are difficult to overcome by simply treating the dog kindly. A point may come when it hasn't the slightest fear of the man who cares for it, yet the dog having developed the kind of response and behavior which we associate with a frightened dog, will continue to exhibit the characteristic behavior, long after - perhaps permanently - it has lost its feeling of fear. Many dogs which greatly fear human beings can be trained to fear them no longer.

My own work in nutrition when hundreds of puppies have been weighed once a week only, in some cases starting at birth, demonstrates the value of manhandling on the behavior of dogs. In some cases only one male and one female of a litter were weighed. In other instances all the males and none of the females, in others, two males and two females. The dogs of that part of the litters not weighed and not handled developed differently from those which received only this moderate amount of attention. The unhandled lots were shyer in general, not so friendly.

Our interest in shy dogs is that they are apt to retreat far more quickly from what they conceive to be danger than dogs which have learned which objects are harmless.

We read about "escape from boredom" in connection with human behavior. Perhaps dogs exhibit it but if so I have never seen a demonstration of it. Dogs raised and maintained all their lives in wire bottom cages do not try to escape, nor do they show boredom by any actions; they have never learned any other form of existence. If one suggests the escape of well conditioned hunting dogs from their kennels as an illustration of escape from boredom, a better explanation is that their escape is due to a desire to satisfy the drive to hunt. In house dogs, the damage dogs do to furniture, is sometimes attributed to boredom when it rightly is a domonstration of frustration.

Hunger and Thirst. We do not need all the information which a large book on canine nutrition contains to appreciate certain salient facts about a dog's need for food because we are interested in the dog's behavior. Few realize how important is the right kind of food and what effect it has on the animal's actions.

Physiologists break food down into the essential components: Protein, carbohydrate, fat, vitamins, minerals, water. Proteins are further broken down into amino acid and fat into fatty acids. No longer do we say that protein is essential to a dog's well being, but we know that if one of its building blocks, one certain amino acid is missing or in too short supply, the dog will show it in appearance and actions. Among the fatty acids there are essential ones too. And if vitamins are missing, the dog may develop eye weakness, nervousness or general debility and thus exhibit his need. Some of the minerals such as calcium, if missing from the diet can cause abnormal actions, even convulsions and iodine shortage affects the behavior as much as too much thyroid secretion can in the other direction.

A dog needs enough food as measured in calories and all the water his system craves to appease his thirst. And, important to behavior is the requirement that the diet should form firm but easily voided stools. Some diets cause constipation with attending anal troubles and some cause such laxation that dogs have to defecate too frequently. All these factors must be taken into consideration. A puppy with liquid stools is almost impossible to housebreak, a mature dog whose diet has too much salt will be so thirsty and need to relieve himself so often that he is a poor subject for training. A constipated dog which strains and cries from pain had best be cured before training, because his needs must focus his attention on his ailment, not on the trainer.

These however are medical matters but they illustrate how the need for proper food is important in our work of training.

For the sake of those who feel pangs of remorse at the mere thought of a dog fasting, please forget your qualms. Remember the wolf and his frequent feast-or-famine feeding. Remember also that the researches with human starvation during the war when conscientious objectors submitted to these investigations: they were in no pain for many days after their ordeal began. And don't forget the many dogs used in the same way. One, Oscar, lived for 117 days on water and on the 100th was still able to jump in and out of his cage three feet from the floor. A few days fasting is not only harmless, but often highly beneficial especially to overweight dogs - and most of our pets are grossly overweight.

Where the best results are obtained by using food as a reinforcement, training cannot be done every day. The schedule is on this order: Monday, dog is fed in early morning. Tuesday, No food, training in evening after which enough food, in addition to his re-inforcements, is given to supply the normal ration. Wednesday, dog is fed in early morning. Thursday, no food. Training in the evening.

If one prefers to train in the morning: Monday, dog is fed in evening. Tuesday, no food at all. Wednesday, training in morning after which enough food, in addition to reinforcements is given to supply the normal ration. In evening dog is fed normal ration. Thursday, dog is fed in evening. Friday, no food. Saturday, dog is trained in morning.

In working with some species of animals, students have found that quick results in training can be achieved by underfeeding the animal for some time until its weight drops to three quarters of normal. Thereafter the subject is hungrier than he would be if up to normal weight, and is ready for work on normal daily intake of food. His needs impel him to eat more than normal to make up his weight, which he can't do when fed a normal meal - one which gives him sufficient for his daily requirements but does not permit gain.

Few owners of pets or hunting dogs would care to use this method. Nor is it necessary if the dog is fasted twelve hours beyond his normal feeding time of once a day. The advantage of the above method is in the fact that a dog can be worked every day and not every other day.

In books on animal psychology written forty years ago we find such statements as, the greater the hunger, the greater the value of the food as a reward. Or, the more food fed to equally hungry animals, the greater its value as a reward. But this was in the days when food was called a reward, before the idea of reinforcement was propounded. And there is a difference between reward and reinforcement. It was also often stated that food for reward should be much tastier and tempting than the usual food the dog knew.

It is only partially true to say that the hungrier a dog is the harder he will work for a reward. The statement would have to be qualified with the words *up to a certain point*. This point has been found to be thirty-six hours fasting. After thirty-six hours the dog is less and less eager to work.

Nor does the dog do better work for a huge meal than a tiny

one. In fact he may stop working. Small reinforcements keep him working and attentive. As for the food being tastier, it has been found by some experimenters that small amounts of the food to which he is accustomed are more valuable than more savory tidbits.

Under some circumstances, thirst is an excellent reinforcement. When a dog is hungry, he will work better for food; when thirsty for water. And here is an interesting observation. Thirst and hunger are two needs. When a dog is both thirsty and hungry, he will learn quicker when one need is gradually satisfied than he will when he has only one need to start with and it becomes gradually satisfied.

Rat studies demonstrate clearly that hunger is associated with much greater physical activity and ordinary observation of the activity of hungry dogs attest to their activity also. This fact adds weight to the use of hunger need in training. Not only is the dog more eager to obtain the reward, but he is much more active.

It is thought that once a dog's appetite is satiated, he lies down and sleeps or becomes lethargic. Mature dogs do tend to do this, but the act seems to affect puppies differently; they want more activity and generally get it in violent play. One might think that a growing puppy would need to conserve his energy even more than a mature dog, but his actions belie him.

Contrariwise, it has been found in other species that starvation greatly increases activity. Even a diet deficient in protein made animals much more active. Rats, fed insufficient protein when tested in a cage attached to a revolving drum, increased their activity 177 per cent over rats on a complete diet. Fasting for three days increased their activity 44 per cent. When the blood sugar level is low (it is always low in fasting animals), there is greater activity.

Activity in dogs can be stimulated by short periods of rest. Sometimes only two days rest will increase animal activity as much as 25 per cent. This and the other facts above have a bearing on training. Two days is plenty of rest and an animal can definitely be given too much for best performances.

Some animals, horses, for example, when they are offered larger amounts of food than they can eat, eat much more than they need. The longer food is withheld up to about four days the more most animals will eat. How true these facts are for dogs we do not know for sure. Wild dogs are feast-or-famine eaters and manage very well.

They exercise considerably hunting for food and when they finally kill their prey, gorge.

A dog will act differently in the same situation as his needs differ. He is lying on the front porch; another dog runs up the other side of the street. In this situation, if he is very hungry and his mistress calls him to supper, he may turn and go through the door and eat. If he is excessively thirsty he goes in when he hears the door open and drinks. If he feels the need to investigate the strange dog or perhaps to guard his neighborhood, he dashes across the street and the two dogs smell each other. All this is patent, you say. I agree, but the older psychological conceptions held that the situation described would evoke only one pattern of behavior. A dog's behavior in any situation depends on the total of all its needs, and some needs at some times, are stronger than others and thus determine the dog's actions.

How much can one change the natural behavior of dogs by feeding them? This depends to some extent on how hungry the dogs were when the tests were made. One observer wanted to see what he could learn in a kennel of 178 dogs which were not very hungry. He tried offering food through the wire of the fifty-foot runways and measuring the distance of the dog at his closest approach to the investigator. He also tried squatting in the doorway and offering food, and standing inside the runways offering food and trying to pat the dogs' heads.

By the end of the experiment the percentage of those fed through the wire increased from seventy-seven to eighty-five; those fed from the gate from sixty-four to seventy and those submitting to petting from forty to fifty-six. Incidentally, the training did not influence the response of the dogs to other persons. There was also an attempt by the experimentor to force the dogs to submit to petting. This succeeded with only twenty out of fifty-four on which it was tried.

These must have been an unusually wild lot of dogs. After reading this account, I tried my own dogs, numbering fifty-two, in outside runs. Every one would accept food through the wire.

That a part of the brain and not "the glands" is concerned with obesity has now been quite well ascertained. For many years it was held by some physiologists that hunger was due to a lowering of the blood sugar (glucose). This hypoglycemia was supposed to act on the brain which in turn produced hunger contractions of the stomach and when satisfied caused the deposition of fat when the calories were not used in exercise. But the theory was vitiated by a scientist who removed a dog's stomach and found the dog continued being hungry without it.

The brain is now known to produce the hunger symptoms by governing food intake, and this center has been demonstrated to be situated in the hypothalamus. It appears that when the difference between the sugar in the arterial blood and that of the veinous blood exceeds 15 mg. per 100 cc., there is no hunger, but when there is very little difference, hunger is felt. So neurologists now talk about *glucoreceptors.*

This has a practical application in training when food is used as a reward (reinforcement). What, we ask, makes a dog hungry? The answer is, the reduction of the glucose in the blood to a level where the glucoreceptors are affected. How shall a trainer induce hunger in a pupil? He can exercise the dog and cause him to burn up the glucose or he can simply allow the dog no food until he reaches a point of real hunger.

Does the dog suffer pain when he starves? Probably not until he has exhausted his fat. Research into the starvation with human conscientious objectors during the war revealed that so-called hunger pangs are mostly simple pangs of habit. Many expert animal men allow their charges to go without food one day a week, which is the same as allowing a forty-eight hour interval between feedings. Research with dogs indicates that a starving dog will suffer no pain, so far as the observer could determine, not for many weeks, at least. Remember Oscar and his 117 days! If you have any qualms at getting a dog forty-eight hours hungry so that his brain hunger regulator makes him keen for food, allay your fears; it neither pains nor harms a dog at all. And if you still feel it does, try it on yourself. Be objective and honestly analyze your feelings. Can you say you suffer pain? Are you not keener? You are. I know because I have tried it many times.

Hunger is a much stronger drive during the first few days than it is later. You yourself may already have experienced the fact if you have ever tried to lose weight. During the first two weeks you found it much harder to refuse food than later on. In several species of animals, it has been found that after four days of starvation the need (and thus the stimulus) is much less.

In the case of hunger, it has been found that up to thirty-six hours the greater the hunger, the quicker the learning and also that the larger the reward the more it reinforced the action. The difficulty of giving a large portion of food is that the dog's hunger is satisfied too soon and when it is even appeased, training must stop. It is also possible in teaching some lessons to make the taste linger in the dog's mouth and whet his appetite all the more so that one training session will seem to him like a generous reinforcement.

Thirst. What makes dogs drink interests everyone. When a dog pants the average owner at once offers water. If he shuns it, the owner will often think he is sick. A dog pants to reduce his temperature. In doing so, he evaporates some of the water in his body and it is lost in expirations. Of course he needs a little to replace this water. He drinks when hot to help reduce his temperature. The swallowing of a pint of water at 50 degrees F. by a 50 lb. dog whose normal temperature is 101 degrees F. will help a trifle, but very little, compared with the evaporation from the throat. When water evaporates, it becomes very cold and, this is what reduces the dog's temperature.

Water drinking, when a dog is not overheated, has been studied. When the water loss is $\frac{1}{2}$ of 1 per cent of the body's weight, the dog becomes thirsty. The amount drunk at each draft is more or less proportional to the body's water deficit.

Dogs operated on so the water they drank ran out into a container on the neck showed that they also drink simply to obtain the temporary satisfaction of water moistening the mouth and throat. This they did even though water was introduced into the gut through an artificial opening. So dogs are like persons in that they enjoy fluids besides their own saliva in their mouths and they do not always drink to replace body water lost.

When a dog eats dry food his digestive juices have to moisten it. Food then is considered outside of the dog: it is in a tube (the digestive tract) going through him. The dog will drink to replace the water loss in the food. Surplus water is eliminated through the urinary tract.

This does not hold in the case of over-heated dogs. I have seen them drink so much water that they looked like pregnant bitches - far more than enough to make up for the water loss. The water sloshes about inside of them as they walk, like water in a tank and it will be an hour before the water is absorbed and eliminated.

Thirst can be used as an excellent incentive and water as the reinforcement. This has not seen much usage because food is so much more convenient to use.

Sex. The question of drive, it seems to me, while it is toward an end does not need consummation in all cases to keep the drive established. Let us take some examples: The sex drive - a hormonal process and a powerful incentive. In the case of a male dog, the realization that a bitch is in heat will keep it in force. The dog may never have bred a bitch, yet every time a neighborhood bitch comes in heat he will leave home and camp in front of her house. He may try ever so hard to reach her - climb fences which he otherwise never would think of trying to climb, break windows, attempt to crawl through narrow openings, lose so much fear he will push past strangers and enter strange houses.

Then there is the case of the bitch. When she is in the early stage of her heat she becomes goaded by her drive to roam, to go far from home, to deposit her urine far more frequently than she does when not in heat.

Being Left. The drive to be part of the pack is a far more potent one than any psychologist has ever mentioned. A dog tied to a tree in the woods while he sees his companions leave him, or left home in the kennels is filled with a most potent drive to get to them. A potent incentive is thus available to us.

A hound which follows a game trail has a drive he cannot resist. After a few chances to trail, the hound's drive becomes a passion; another powerful incentive. And though he never sees the game he pursues, his drive does not diminish. This drive can be used to excellent effect as a basis for future study and as I have used it. Few beside hound men know how potent a drive it is.

Being left home from a hunt will keep a hound barking all day or night until the hunter returns. The hound may become frustrated, tear a door down even chew a hole in the roof, dig under a fence, break a collar or chain to get to hunt. And a hound must be very hungry to be willing to stop to eat when there is the alternative of going for a hunt.

Drive is strengthened by having it consummated occasionally. The male who has copulated will be more persistent than one who has not. The hound who has heard the gun's report and shaken the fox, the coonhound who has seen his owner climb the tree up which the hound has barked and has "gotten his teeth" into the dead coon probably is more persistent. I say *probably* because dogs I have trained to know the hunt is over when I caught the coon alive seemed just as persistent tree-barkers as those which fought a coon or chewed on a dead one.

Once the man-trailing Bloodhound has been trained to differentiate scents, he needs no more rewards; his drive keeps him trailing with zest. He works for the joy of working. Letting him give vent to his drive is all the reinforcement he needs.

Sleep. "A dog never sleeps" is an untrue, very ancient proverb. Persons observing dogs curled up note that they move their eyelids when there is any movement about them. Dogs do sleep and soundly. The movement of eyelids is one of the best criteria of the fact. When the eyelids move, at least part of the dog is not asleep. Careful studies show that sight decreases with the duration of sleeping. Sleep lowers the threshold of response to sound. A dog can awaken quickly but he can also sleep soundly too. Wild deer are easily killed by their enemies because they sleep so soundly. I have come across them so sound asleep that I could walk within a few yards and stand watching them. But I have never seen even an exhausted dog so sound asleep that he did not move an eyelid when I approached.

The habit of sleeping and waking at regular intervals - the usual daily sleep - is regulated by the brain's cortex. Dogs who lack the cortex as a result of experimental surgery sleep soundly and are difficult to rouse.

Some students have suggested a hormone influence, some a vaso-motor cause but a purely nervous action is the probable base of sleep. This was determined by first a brain operation and then by slight irritation to the dog's infundibulum (part of the brain) which produced sleep immediately.

Puppies must have sleep in order to live. In a study it was found that even three or four days of sleeplessness proved fatal to some pups. Measurements revealed that the only noticeable result was muscular weakness. The pups' temperatures remained normal. A slight drop in blood cells occurred. No neurological changes occurred. No brain changes could be observed either; there was no enlargement nor shrinking of the size of blood vessels.

Older dogs seem able to remain awake for many days without developing any serious deficiencies.

In studies to determine how long a dog could live without sleep, it was found that the period varied with condition of the dog and other factors. Dogs lived anywhere from fourteen to seventy-seven days without sleep. At the conclusion of the study the dogs' brains and organs were examined, and the only changes found were in the cortex which resembled a psychotic brain. The question arises whether the method used to keep the dogs awake might not have brought about a psychosis.

Sleep is induced by excitation of one point in the brain, does not spread, but acts invariably on the one point, then sleep is induced. The stimulus must become monotonous and without consequences. Pavlov suggests that sleep ensures rest and that it prepares the brain for a new expenditure. Sleep is quite easily induced by repetition of sounds and in various other ways. Dogs often get sleepy in experiments when no variety intervenes and there are no consequences of an act.

Does a dog ever "play possum?" Indeed he does. The wolf which drops and "turns himself into a bush" is behaving much as the dog does when he is held powerfully until he lies and relaxes, completely immobilized. Generally his anal glands will have discharged. Some dogs will lie as if paralyzed for minutes on end. Actually they are exhibiting a self protecting reflex of an inhibiting nature.

Sleep and hypnosis are both manifestations of inhibition. We must keep in mind that we as well as our dogs are under the control of excitation and inhibition. When inhibition gains control, the dog goes to sleep. Sleep can occur in parts of the body without the whole animal becoming unconscious. This depends on the area of the brain which is affected.

When most of the stimulations to a dog are abolished, the dog falls asleep; this is passive sleep. When inhibition controls sleep, inhibition being an active process, it gives rise to active sleep. When dogs had most of the nerves carrying a stimulation to the brain destroyed by surgery, a not too difficult task, the dogs fell into sound sleep and remained asleep until shaken (ordinary petting failed to waken them.) Some slept twenty-three hours a day but got up to defecate and urinate and eat, then went back to sleep again.

We must constantly keep in mind that even sleep is not a neutral state as I pointed out earlier; the nervous energy does not rest. Even the so-called passive sleep is the result of inhibition which does not have to counter-balance stimulations and thus produces a sounder, longer lasting sleep.

When a dog is asleep, he is not conscious. When his hearing, sight, smell are taken away from him, he is asleep. But so long as he has one faculty acute his apparent normal behavior is not too badly disturbed. The question is, which is the normal state, sleep or consciousness?

The Need to Investigate. One of the weakest but most used drives is the dog's *need to investigate.* It has its basis in survival behavior. All dogs will approach strange dogs, will sniff places where other dogs urinated. Males will sniff to determine whether or not a bitch is in heat. Any new object within the area of a dog's ken must be approached and investigated. Watch your dog and see how often he exhibits this drive.

Chapter XI

DRIVES

DRIVES ARE THE dogs' dynamos which galvanize them to action. The dog trainer can often use them to advantage, these compulsions of his pupils. Satisfying a need, often temporarily, may satisfy drives at the same time. The poet asks, "Frets care the maw-crammed beast?" A dog, having satisfied his appetite may curl up for a long nap oblivious to every drive. A combination of drives makes the best basis for conditioning.

Those unreasoning drives which seem to force a dog to do certain things are *tropisms*. When a gang of dogs is encamped about the home of a bitch in heat, they are driven there by a common tropism. When a bitch knows that her puppies have been moved to a new location, she will surmount many difficulties to get them: tropism. It affects the action of the whole body.

The instincts, needs, tropisms, drives, urges and the learned or unlearned responses do not always occur in the mature dog in pure form. Many of them are mixed, combined some instinctive, some reflex and some learned.

A most interesting behavior in all dogs which seems to have interested a number of psychologists is dogs' behavior when urinating. In studying the papers and conclusions one realizes how many patient hours the observation has continued.

A male dog lifts his leg instinctively; the behavior is unlearned. Sex hormones such as testosterone are directly related to the leg lifting male pattern, injections of female hormones can cause the pattern to disappear. Some dogs lift one leg more often than the other, early castration (before the fourth month) of the male prevents him from ever lifting a leg to urinate, injection of testosterone into castrated dogs or young pups will cause them to lift their legs.

Practical dog breeders may be able to add to the conclusion of psychologists and such observations will be welcome. One of my hounds had sired two litters of puppies and was at least twenty-four months old before I ever saw him lift a leg to urinate.

Elimination, by either defecation or urination may be construed as a need. A need it is, so far as the actual elimination is concerned, but the way the dog uses the result of the need is a drive—he is driven by a compulsion.

When bitches are castrated early after they are grown they squat in the usual bitch position to urinate; the operation does not make them lift their legs like male dogs. This finding will relieve those who often ask it about spayed bitches.

One of the interesting facts about female micturition is the greatly increased frequency just as the bitch is coming into heat. When such a female goes for a walk, she leaves urine at many places, possibly to help males to follow her and locate her even a day or two later or possibly longer.

Another is the behavior of bitches not in heat and normal in every way, to act as nearly as they can like males in sprinkling on previously sprinkled bushes and tree trunks. Some, in fact many, agile type bitches will lift their rear ends as high as possible and sprinkle where males have left their urine. In car hunting, some bitches bother as much this way as male dogs. Some urinate this way in kennel runs, not squatting down in the appropriate feminine fashion.

Exercise. If you own a single dog or a kennel of dogs, try to calculate how many yards or miles each tends to run during a day. You will find that the distance may be amazingly small. Apartment house dogs may not move a hundred yards a day. Or if you take your dog for a walk on a leash you may walk him a quarter of a mile. If he lives in a kennel run and he is an inactive dog he may move 100 yards in a day. If he is one of those dogs which trots back and forth until he has the sand piled up at the ends of his run, he may move ten or twelve miles a day. These are artificial conditions. How far would his drive impel him to travel daily?

We clocked one of our circling dogs. He ran in a circle slightly over ten feet across which meant that every time he circled he covered a little more than thirty feet. He would make about forty circles a minute in the morning and was down to twenty-five by later afternoon. The presence of a person watching him made him speed up. Sometimes the track he made would be ten inches deep. If he made an average of thirty circles a minute, he traveled nine hundred feet a minute or ten miles an hour. To watch him and compare his speed with that of a dog trotting in front of a car, one would conclude that the circler was going very much faster. He circled always over five hours a day so he traveled fifty miles a day and kept up in good flesh doing so.

Female animals of almost all species normally exhibit more activity than males. This is even true of human beings. In rats where they were permitted the use of an exercise wheel, female rats showed 7384 daily revolutions of the wheel, whereas males showed 4138.

Castrated males show even less activity than normal males. In rats the effects are particularly noticeable. Normals ran in an exercise wheel 48,000 feet daily but castrated males ran only 10,000 feet (9 miles vs. less than 2).

Spayed bitches do not show so great a difference. A study of spayed Greyhounds brought to light the fact that they ran as fast in track racing as unspayed litter mates but were somewhat less active about the kennels which is to be expected since they lacked the hormone which produces restlessness during the heat period.

A hardened Foxhound on a trail will travel, even after the twentieth hour, six or eight miles an hour. Foxhounds often run over twenty-four hours in a single chase—144 miles a day is a minimum. How many miles does a hound travel when he stays behind the fox for two days? Some fast hounds have been estimated to have covered 500 miles in one chase.

A lot of dogs in an exercise run get a little exercise but let no one who is using exercise in dog training consider that a short walk is exercise for a dog—not even for a lazy dog. We have come to use the word *exercise* so often to mean *a chance for elimination* that we have lost the true meaning as applied to dogs. Both lazy and active dogs stay in good health—an appraisal of their adaptability.

The staying power of hounds is exemplified by reports of foxhound and wolf hounds. B. B. Titus of Fairlee, Vermont, started his long eared Black-and-Tan hound on a fox on Mt. Cube in

New Hampshire at seven one morning. That night the fox had not come near enough for Mr. Titus to shoot it. The next morning the hunter went back and could hear his bugle-voiced hound still running. All during the day the fox stayed out of gunshot and again Mr. Titus went home unable to call the dog off the track. Next morning the hound was still running, but slowly. So was the fox which Mr. Titus shot and carried, together with the hound, to his car. Many hunters believe that an exhausted hound will eat and then sleep but old Pokey refused food for twenty-four hours. His feet were tender but in three days he was again ready for a hunt.

A pair of Canadian foxhounds trained on wolf ran one from 1 P.M. on a Thursday, starting at Rankin, Ontario. Two days later the wolf was shot in Pickford, Michigan and both hounds were then ready to sleep which they also did for twenty-four hours before eating.

Circling, pacing or ranting, as zoo keepers often term it, in wild animals which let off energy by pacing back and forth at the front of the run, tail chasing, jumping up in corners repeatedly might all be considered neuroses. Actually they are only habits developed slowly at first and generally by overly energetic dogs. Can such habits be broken? Yes, but not in a short time.

Sex Drive. While there is some deviation from the sex behavior of the wolf, in the average dog which is not permitted his freedom, the behavior is not too different from that of his ancestor. Perhaps I should know much more about it than I do because I admit to having had over 12,000 puppies whelped in my kennels and I made the matings and witnessed almost all the copulations which produced all those puppies.

The first noticeable physical manifestation of the approaching mating cycle, before the vulva swells perceptibly is an increase in appetite and an increase in restlessness. Her vitality is at a high peak. The luteal hormone elaborated by the luteal bodies on the ovary is disappearing and with its disappearance there is no longer any "keep away odor" to repel male dogs. The follicles are starting to grow. Greyhound owners know that if they can detect a bitch at this point (it is illegal to race a bitch in Greyhound competition while she is in heat) they often find she will win a race.

How does the dog know she is in heat? First, by the absence of a keep-away odor in her urine and probably in her anal secretions. Stories have been written based on the popular notion that the bitch secretes or excretes a positive odor which can be smelled for miles by dogs in the neighborhood. Moths can detect some odor over great distances, but dogs definitely cannot and do not.

Dogs do not even know a bitch is in heat when as little as five feet separates them from the bitches. Among the hundreds of observations I have made, I have observed no undue excitement, no refusal of food, when only one vacant pen separates a stud dog from a bitch in heat. If she is in the next pen and the two are not permitted to copulate, the dog may pace up and down, refuse food, lose five of his sixty pounds in a week. If he is permitted to copulate and the bitch is placed with one pen between them, the dog knows and acts accordingly.

As in the case of wolves, the bitch is impelled by an insatiable drive to wander. Something of the same activity impels women to walk many more miles a day during parts of their sex cycle, too; it may well be a common female phenomenon. Certain it is that the bitch naturally covers a wide territory letting all the dogs know she is in heat and possibly, if permitted, of choosing a mate.

If she escapes she may run all over the countryside, often a mile from home, or, if a city dog, wander about her neighborhood but returning home for food. But suppose we observe a bitch confined with an experienced stud dog in a half acre run.

After getting acquainted, the dog will not seem to be especially attracted to her. Next step is swelling of the vulva and a slight reddish discharge. Some bitches "bleed" more freely than others. She still is restless, active and more alert than at other times. She still urinates many more times a day than is her usual habit. And now the dog begins to show some interest in following her about and sniffing and sometimes lapping at her deposits of urine and vaginal discharge.

This period lasts about a week or nine days from the start of vulva swelling. And here is an important fact to remember: We are discussing a dog and bitch left together from the start of the cycle. And we should also consider the dog as an average, not a highly sexed unusually vigorous dog. So we should digress here to consider the behavior of the usual mating procedure when dogs are bred.

If a bitch has reached a time in her cycle where she wants to play with the male, a vigorous male may force her to copulate by what we might call his strength of personality. With an ordinary dog she might not copulate until several days later. Some of my stud dogs would growl and attack any bitch which would not stand and copulate, and almost at once, without any play, but these were dogs which were used to having "ready" bitches brought to them for mating. They became frustrated and showed it.

Some of the errors in working out the canine mating cycle were made by those who had no opportunity for determining when the first day of acceptance actually was. One study reported that the day of ovulating corresponded with the first day of acceptance. Had those investigators had the opportunity of observing what teasing and growling by a vigorous stud dog would accomplish they would have set the day of acceptance much earlier, or the day of ovulation several days later.

But to return to our dogs in the enclosure. The discharge of the bitch appears to change from bloody to creamy color and it is less abundant. The bitch becomes more playful and by the seventh to ninth day she could be teased into accepting the dog. But copulation generally is not attempted. If it is and the dog's penis is even partly inserted in the vagina the bitch may cry and jump away in apparent pain.

A few days after the first day of acceptance the vulva quite rapidly loses its firmness and swelling; it softens. Studies indicate that this softening is a good sign she has ovulated. The amount of follicular hormone has reached its peak. Now with the rapid growth of the corpora lutea an antagonism results; one hormone acts plus and the other minus on sex behavior. As the follicular hormone disappears the luteal will gain the ascendency and behavior correlates with this chemical change. At this time copulation almost always occurs naturally. And this may be anywhere from the tenth to the twentieth day of the cycle. Bitches vary considerably. Matings which occur on the first day that the bitch can be teased into copulating are usually sterile and those which occur just before or after the vulva softens result in maximum size litters.

Natural Time of Copulation. There are many instances of male and female dogs having been raised in homes together. They did not copulate until the owners thought the heat period was over. I could site a dozen owned by my clients.

End of Cycle. Another debatable point about the mating cycle is its end. Thousands of bitches have been kept under close surveillance or penned in escape proof runs until the owners were certain the cycle was over, and then have been released. Meeting with a vigorous dog which tried hard enough to copulate and was persistent enough, a bitch will surprise her owner and cooperate with the male. Curiously enough these late matings are almost always fertile. A bitch seems not to be over her heat until a day or two after the owner is certain she is. In her blood there still remains some follicular hormone. The whole process requires about twenty-two days.

Pseudo-Pregnancy. If a bitch fails to ovulate she will often come in heat again in approximately twenty-five days and sometimes fifty. If she does ovulate but is bred so early that she fails to conceive, or isn't bred at all, we expect her to have what formerly was described as a pseudo- or phantom-pregnancy. When I first contradicted the old observations of veterinarians and others that this condition was abnormal, and I declared it always occurred and thus was normal, my findings were received frigidly. But I have never seen an exception.

Bitches with pseudo-pregnancies even produce milk. Some have enough prolactin to make them try to adopt puppies. They refuse food, make nests and deceive owners who are sure from their actions that puppies will arrive momentarily.

Effect That Raising a Litter Has on Bitches' Timidity. Producing and nursing a litter of puppies, many a timid bitch has lost her timidity because of the handling by the owner who cooperates with her in rearing the puppies. Overactive, flighty bitches quiet down and lose their hyperkinetic activity to a marked degree. In many ways it makes a bitch "grow up" to have whelped and raised a litter to weaning age. After that she fails to recognize her puppies as her own unless they have been with her almost constantly as they grew.

Frequency of Copulation. Male dogs which may show no compulsion to copulate, after eating a meal will be eager. This is common knowledge among many experienced dog men, who use the fact effectively when they own shy breeders.

The bitch in heat will willingly copulate as many times during the day as the dog is able; the frequency of the pair is within the male's province entirely. He is limited by the previous day's experiences, the number of times he has copulated, that is, and by his physiology, age, condition. One of my hounds which had not copulated the day before could copulate five times with a willing bitch the first day she was put with him and then three times each of the next few days.

Diminution of Sex Drive with Age. It is rather surprising to find that the sex drive does not diminish as much as most persons expect. The dog mentioned above was seven years old when we kept track of his sex behavior. As a hunter he had no more drive than many others which were content to copulate twice a day. The great Cocker Spaniel stud, Red Brucie bred seven bitches during one week—one a day—and all conceived, when he was thirteen years old.

A stud dog left with a bitch may have copulated twice and that will be his seeming capacity or drive for a day. If a new bitch is substituted for the former he will usually copulate with her.

In the field of sex behavior and sex physiology in dogs, I have done considerable work and, I hope the following observations will prove useful to those having difficulties with their dogs.

Unnatural Dogs and Copulation. In the case of male dogs there are dogs which never seem to have trouble copulating. Those who are not well acquainted with kennel problems may wonder that in such a natural act, any dogs ever have any difficulty. Actually so many breeds have become unnatural that they would cease to exist as breeds or certainly many strains would die out, if the males did not receive human aid in copulating.

Many of the giant dogs would be helpless. Of all the heavy

English Bloodhounds I have owned only a few were ever able to copulate without help. I have been called to help St. Bernards, Mastiffs, Great Danes. Some of these dogs were anatomically unable to copulate, the penis hanging so low it was sometimes several inches below the bitch's vulva. Some, in making the necessary motions to copulate never came close enough to the bitch to make contact.

Helping such dogs it was necessary to hold the penis up and to press on the reflex center behind the bulb which thus causes a thrust and once inside the vagina the penis was thrust all the way and the dog held the bitch to him with his front legs until the bulb had swelled sufficiently to produce a tie.

A bitch after the first experience copulating generally indicates to the dog her desire to copulate even when he makes no positive move in her direction. But how?

*Escape Behavior in Bitches.*The sex drive is a powerful compulsion in the case of some bitches. They are reported to have gone to extremes to escape and male dogs have also achieved unusual feats in breaking into their isolation quarters to copulate. From the stories clients have told me the feats have been about equal. Windows are often broken, screen doors scratched or chewed through. Sound oak doors have been gnawed through. Ladders have been climbed by dogs who had no training in that art. One bitch was kept in a barn attic. Stairs led up and a flat door, even with the floor, barred the entrance. The bitch gnawed a hole from the top to get downstairs as was obvious from the chewed wood she left upstairs and a dog gnawed from downstairs and was seen doing it. They were obviously trying to get together.

Oddities in Male Sex Behavior. There is a wide difference among dogs in respect to their sexual behavior. Some will lick the bitch for an hour before making any attempt to copulate and no efforts on the part of the owner seem to be able to shorten the period. Some will play for half an hour. Some won't make any effort unless the bitch plays or at least bumps into them and plainly exhibits a desire to copulate.

Many inexperienced dog breeders have not observed a useful fact and should know this: If a dog in breeding a bitch permits the penis to slip out of the vagina and an erection occurs with the bulb swelling, it may remain swollen for half an hour. Most breeders wait until it subsides naturally and then let the dog try again. This is entirely unnecessary; if the dog mounts a bitch at once again and makes copulatory movements his penis will at once shrink to normal size and he can copulate.

Stud dogs quickly become trained to wait for help. Several of my Bloodhounds would make no attempt to copulate with bitches placed in runs with them. Instead, they would stand or jump up at the gate waiting for me to enter the run and help them.

Some stud dogs of small breeds expect to copulate on a table and make no effort in any other location, refusing even to play with a bitch which attempts to attract them into play.

Then there are dogs which are trained to copulate anywhere and want no preliminary play, often growling at a bitch which does not stand and elevate her vulva at once.

One of my hounds would kill a bitch which did not respond at once. He actually killed two, one before we knew he was so inclined and another which jumped a six foot fence and got into his run during the night. Yet he was kind with all human beings.

Cooperative Efforts of Bitch in Copulation. The length of time dogs remain tied is mostly a matter of male virility, but I think from many observations that the bitch plays some part. Once tying has occurred, a pulsation can be observed in both dog and bitch. It can be clearly felt also by touching the penis and the vulva. This is peristalsis which is moving sperm and semen along from testicles through the length of the penis to the bitch's vagina. And peristalsis which is moving the sperm through the length of the uterus, the Fallopian tubes and into the sac surrounding the ovaries. A bitch in the latter part of the mating cycle shows this pumping effect clearly. One can observe the tightening and re-laxing of the vulva and the muscles around the anus. It is probable that this movement of tightening and relaxing of the uterus on the dog's penis plays some part in keeping his penis enlarged.

In the same way, a bitch which digs her toenails into the soil of the run and pulls against the dog, also helps. A dog copulating with a bitch which simply stands limp and does not pull against him does not remain tied as long as when the bitch behaves normally.

Few realize the strength of a dog's penis. When the pair pull in opposite directions the strain on that organ is far more than the weight of the bitch. I have often lifted a dog and bitch off the ground, have even put the pair over a fence by holding the dog up by the shoulders and letting the bitch hang on his penis. And since the dog knew me and was not afraid this disturbance did not cause him to become "untied."

Effects of Fright on Tying. Persons frequently are embarrassed by finding dogs tied in their front yards or other conspicuous places and wish they knew how to separate them quickly. I received many calls from clients who asked what they should do. Even pouring water over the pair had failed. Scolding did no good. The remedy is to produce fright. Think of wild dogs. If they were copulating and there was no mechanism to quickly separate them, they would be easily overcome by enemies. Fright very quickly produces the desired effect. Slamming two boards together close to the dogs' ears startles them and they will separate. Shooting a revolver will also do it. Two dogs in New Haven were tied and a large crowd of children were observing. The police didn't know what to do. An officer phoned me and I told him to get a short board, hold up one end while the other was resting on the pavement and step on the board so it slammed with a loud noise against the pavement. He did and kindly phoned in a few minutes to thank me for the help.

Duration of Tying. How long do dogs remain tied? The longest I have timed to date was one hour and fifty minutes. The shortest tie which resulted in pregnancy was sixty seconds. The average is in the vicinity of twenty minutes. The longest ties seemed to be in the middle sized breeds. I have known a Great Dane to be tied seventy-two minutes. The longest in a midget breed was twenty-eight minutes. The duration is influenced by frequency of mating; the males which seldom copulate will be tied longer the first mating than they will at others during the day.

Frequency of Copulation. In no other realm of dog breeding, unless it is feeding, is there more foolish information extant than in this field of reproduction. Here dog owners seem unable to separate their dog's behavior from that of their own kind. One hears it is cruel to permit dogs to copulate more often than once a week, for example. Obviously such persons know little about human sex habits and should read Dr. Alfred Kinsey's great book on the subject. It would shock those who anthropomorphize domestic animals to learn that a ram has been known to successfully impregnate sixty ewes during one twenty-four hour period. Dogs are not rams nor are they human beings.

How many times I've been asked whether permitting copulation of a male dog was of benefit to him, I do not know. But it is a very commonly asked question. There appears to have been no controlled study in dogs but if rats are any criterion the answer seems to be that it has little or no effect on the male. One rat copulated thirty times one day and the next day ran his usual distance in an exercise wheel. Female rats do decrease their activity but small wonder when one considers the change in physiology due to hormones.

Effects of Castration on Males. When an older, already trained dog is castrated, the effects of castration are most pronounced during the first two to three years following the operation. Old conditioned reflexes are retained after five years; coarse discrimination also, but they are more or less inconstant. Thus, we say, castration causes an instability of the excitatory and inhibitory processes.

New reflexes are formed with greater difficulty soon after castration than they are six years later. It appears that alterations of cortical activity depend not only on the absence of sex hormones but also on inter-glandular disturbance due to the influence of castration.

Castration, whether of dogs or bitches, produces marked changes over the normal. The earlier the operation is performed the more marked are the changes. It is definitely preferable to wait until the dog is sexually mature, not necessarily in heat, in the case of a bitch, before having the operation performed. One study showed that it was very difficult to form conditioned reflexes in very early castrates because—the author tells us—of insufficient excitability of the nerve cells. Even in the late castrates, there is a weakening of conditioned reflexes and differentiation ability. Many stimulations which, before castration, produce strong lasting impressions are not effective afterward. Animals' interests diminish. Administration of testosterone or transplantation of testicles completely restore the normal function of the cerebral cortex.

Castration weakens all dogs to some degree. The process of inhibition is most affected and that of excitation to a lesser degree. Dogs of different types of nervous systems are affected differently. The age and even the temporary state of the nervous system have to be considered. Rest after the operation restores most dogs of the excitable and well-balanced types. Weak animals belonging to the inhibitive type can give a more efficient and energetic reaction but only as a temporary state, followed by a deep depression.

Almost all castrated dogs display a cyclic work ability and hypnotic susceptibility. Bromide and rest seem to partially substitute for the sex hormone and restore natural and normal activity. There is a great difference in the amount of bromide needed before and after castration.

Dogs castrated at one month of age show a wide difference from whole dogs by the time they are six months old, and a wider difference at nine months. Memory and attention of castrated dogs are not affected but watchfulness is diminished. Castrated dogs according to one investigator are less mischievous, more easily disturbed, less jealous, more fearful and of a more even temper.

When several normal and castrated dogs are placed together, the castrates tend to play together at quieter games. Normal dogs possess more love of liberty, a taste for adventure, a personality having powerful interests, while castrated dogs show much less volition.

We know that castration produces a definite effect, the tying off and severing of a portion of the spermatic cords, including blood and nerve supply produces a different one. The testicle remains in the scrotum and slowly degenerates. Two weeks after the operation all forms of inhibition become absent and all negative conditioned reflexes which have been previously successfully established become passive. The scientist who made these observations had previously successfully transplanted testicles into sexually mature males. He found that this present operation produced similar symptoms to those in his dog with the transplanted testicles, due, the scientist thought, to the greater amount of testicular hormones.

Adoption of Puppies. It is sometimes difficult to get a bitch to adopt foster puppies. Once she does however, her behavior toward them is the same as toward the bitch's own. To her, they are her puppies, just as she fails to recognize her own after they have been weaned a few weeks. In my experience color of such puppies is of little consequence, rather it is chiefly a matter of smell. To get a bitch to adopt and suckle puppies in addition to those she already has sometimes presents a problem. She may kill them, become excited and root them away from her pups or rarely appear not to care once she has sniffed the newcomer. Then there are those bitches which will steal puppies from other litters to increase the size of their own.

Many dog men know that the most important basis for getting the bitch to adopt strange puppies is to make the pups smell like the rest of the mother's. Some smear the bitch's vaginal discharge on the orphan pups, some rub the bitch's milk on them, An easy way is to remove a few of the mother's pups and permit the orphans to lie in a pile with them for a few hours. When the pups are again placed with the dam, each orphan pup is held up to her separately to let her lap its external organs of elimination and clean it up. Once a bitch has acted that way toward a puppy, it is almost always safe to leave it with her.

We are here considering the problem of pups added to a litter. Getting a bitch which has lost her litter to adopt an entire new lot of puppies is simple by comparison. In my studies with Malucidin, I have aborted many bitches at close to term. These dogs have an adequate supply of prolactin and want to mother puppies. Each of those we tested, even three days after they had lost their litters, cuddled around the new litter regardless of the puppies' odor and mothered them as her own.

In years past I have had bitches which have lost their puppies sometimes refuse to adopt any others. Most of these dogs, I found, had retained placentas; in other words they were sick and only healthy bitches can be expected to behave normally.

When bitches have pseudo or phantom pregnancies they may

do strange things: make nests, sometimes steal puppies from other bitches, and behave much like bitches which have whelped. Some will even adopt stuffed animals and one psychologist reports the adoption of a rubber toy like a ball, curling about it and uneasy because it didn't nurse. He reported another virgin bitch which, while she did not mother the toy, assumed a protective attitude toward it.

Female Behavior Differences. The observable differences in a large kennel in the behavior of fertile unbred bitches at the normal time of whelping are wide. They range from no apparent change to a complete picture of an ideal mother. And it is a simple matter to see which bitches have ovulated and which not by observing the udder development. Bitches which have not ovulated do not show udder development nor have any, which I have observed, ever shown the least maternal behavior.

Protection of Litter. A mother grouse, when her brood is threatened, shams a broken wing to lure a marauder away from the chicks. It is instinctive. A wild bitch, hearing or smelling a possible enemy sometimes acts in a similar manner. From my own observations of two wild bitches which whelped in the woods near our home, I can attest that each bitch tried to lure me away every time I approached the places where they had whelped. Keeping within sight of me these dogs barked and ran away. When I approached the "dens" they followed barking vigorously. They showed no inclination to attack me to protect the litters but rather seemed to be trying to draw my attention to themselves.

Monogamy in Dogs. Over the past years I have observed the sexual actions of dogs during the heat periods in many hundreds of matings. My findings in dogs coincide with what others have learned from wolves.

Darwin records an observation regarding the selection of a mate by a bitch and how she chose him from among the dogs of a neighborhood. My first observation along these lines was of a farm shepherd dog of a neighbor. As everyone knows, a bitch in heat attracts all of the dogs in a neighborhood but in the case of this shepherd dog, bitches in heat often came to him and my friend would find them tied somewhere on his property, often surrounded by other males. On several occasions, pursued by a pack of males which sometimes included my friend's shepherd, bitches were seen to have eluded the other dogs and permitted copulation with this special dog. Further observations could not be made and it was not known whether these bitches permitted any other dogs to copulate.

On a number of occasions I have tried an experiment of putting two pairs of dogs together in a half acre run, sometimes by themselves and sometimes with several other bitches. Each bitch of the pair was in heat and was bred to the male of the same breed. I always used a dominant male and the other of a more retiring or smaller type. In no case has either male attempted to mate with the female of the other pair, even though they were allowed to stay together during the entire heat period. Several dog houses were available and the pairs stayed mated and each night the pair occupied the same house.

Artificial Insemination. For many years I have had excellent success with artificially inseminated bitches. These have ranged in size from St. Bernards and Great Danes to a two pound Yorkshire Terrier, and of crosses between breeds.

There are few points necessary to know in making this operation successful. A knowledge of physiology and psychology helps. To review what has already been said:

Within the vagina of the bitch there is a reflex area, which when stimulated seems to initiate peristalsis. I discovered this when assisting bitches to give birth. When the puppy is moved along to the pelvis and starts to pass through, the pressure on the vulva causes the dam to strain and more quickly expel the puppy. When I am assisting a sluggish bitch to whelp, I insert two fingers into her vulva, bend them toward her tail and pull hard. She at once begins to strain.

When the dog's penis swells inside the bitch's vagina, what holds it in is the vulva. Pressure of the penis bulb against this tissue—and the pressure is greater when the two dogs pull in opposite directions—encourages peristalsis.

In order to obtain semen from the male, he can be permitted to mount the bitch, if he is of a proper size, and when he begins his motions, it is only necessary to slip the penis out of its covering, grasp it behind the bulb, apply pressure to the reflex area and the

bulb will swell and at once ejaculations will begin. The first discharge is clear liquid. I do not use it but wait until the ejaculant is
milky from the millions of sperm in it, catching a few cubic centi-
meters and transferring it to a syringe.

If there is too much discrepancy in size of the dogs, the male
may be mastabated quite easily until the bulb swells.

Many who tried artificial insemination simply introduced
semen from a male into the vagina. They often failed. The
method I developed simply entails inserting the end of a long,
blunt pointed canula into the opening of the uterus and then
hooking two fingers into the vulva and pulling with that hand
while I slowly pushed in the syringe plunger with the other. I
always continue pulling until my fingers are too tired to pull any
more. When dogs copulate, the sperm are moved in less than ten
minutes up the long Y-shaped uterus, through the Fallopian tubes
and into the sac about the ovaries. I say *moved* because most
persons have an idea that the sperm swim up. They do indeed
swim and at a rate which for them is fast. However, they are so
minute that at the rate they swim they could not negotiate this
distance in less than a matter of hours, certainly not minutes.

Chapter XII

HORMONES AND THEIR EFFECT
ON BEHAVIOR

THE DOG'S PERSONALITY and his behavior are not alone the result
of the anatomy of the brain and nerves and stimuli, but they are
also the result of chemical influences—hormones. In several parts of
the body there are glands which discharge chemical substances into
the blood, each of which is capable of producing definite and pre-
dictable results.

The Pituitary. This is called the master gland of the body.
Not only does it produce hormones which are effective directly,
but hormones which act on other glands, causing them to produce
their hormones. It has two main divisions and in a sense is two
glands joined into one: the anterior lobe and the posterior lobe.
Whereas it might appear that the effects are physicial, which they
are, these physical effects give rise to or are accompanied by changes
in behavior. For example, a hormone - prolactin - which stimulates
milk flow also causes a bitch to become maternal. Another which
initiates birth may result in a certain bitch becoming temporarily
ferocious if her puppies are approached. If she had not whelped
her behavior would have been lacking in ferocity.

The Anterior Lobe. The *luteinizing hormone* (also called
LH) produces *corpora lutea* on the ovaries which in turn secrete a
hormone which terminates the desire of a bitch to mate.

Follicle stimulating hormone (also called FSH). In males it
causes the testicles to increase in size and they in turn secrete testosterone which produces maleness and male behavior. In females it
causes the ovaries to increase in size and to form follicles which in
turn secrete a hormone, *estradiol,* which induces the desire to mate.

Prolactin produces lactation and maternal behavior.

Thyrotrophic hormone regulates the thyroid gland which in
turn produces *thyroxin* which controls the rate of metabolism (the

rate of food burning in the body) and also the general activity, energy or laziness of the animal.

Andrenotrophic hormone regulates the part of the *adrenal gland* called the Cortex.

The Posterior Lobe. This interesting part of the master gland secretes what are called the *posterior pituitary principles.* Their effects are to produce a rise in blood pressure which naturally somewhat effects behavior, to hasten whelping and to speed up the whelping process, and has an effect on the quantity of urine secreted which is of considerable importance to both male and female dogs.

The Adrenal Gland. This remarkable controller is composed of the gland proper - the *Medulla* - and the covering or *Cortex,* mentioned above. While it is the larger substance, the hormone the medulla manufactures has fewer functions than those produced by the cortex.

Epinephrine also called *Adrenalin.* If an animal goes into shock, epinephrine is often injected by the doctor to stimulate circulation because it causes the blood vessels to contract in size and it also stimulates the heart. In mild doses its effects are short-lasting, but it has a dramatic effect on behavior. When a dog is angry or frightened his blood has considerably more adrenalin.

Behavior and adrenalin are definitely related. In a quiet starving dog, adrenalin causes hunger contractions to occur. On the other hand, when a starving dog has hunger contractions in his stomach, adrenalin produces a relaxation and dilation. Adrenalin does not affect digestion contractions of the stomach.

The Cortex. The hormone from the cortex is more like those secreted by the sex glands and is of a similar chemical structure. The hormone influences the rate of burning of carbohydrates, protects against stress and some poisons, heat and cold, effects muscular efficiency.

Parathyroid Glands. Located just over the thyroid glands, these small tissues control the use of both calcium and phosphorus in the dog's body. These minerals are of great importance in canine behavior and a lack of them, especially of calcium, can produce serious effects. Bitches whose puppies are draining her system of calcium via milk, if they do not consume enough calcium or if their parathyroid glands are not functioning properly, develop eclampsia which results in violent trembling and prostration. Calcium is concerned with proper nervous functioning, so parathyroid glands are of the utmost importance.

Thyroid Glands. These glands located in opposite sides of the neck and joined by a connection called the *isthmus,* control the rate of living through their hormone *thyroxine,* half of whose constituents are iodine. Dogs without sufficient thyroxin tend to be slower and phlegmatic. Injections of the drug or feeding it in the diet may result in a general speed-up of activity.

Testicles. Testosterone produces maleness in dogs and, as we have observed above, is controlled by the pituitary gland.

Ovaries. Estrone and *Estradiol* are both ovarian hormones whose action is to cause bitches to exhibit the behavior and reproductive changes which we call being in heat.

Progesterone is secreted by the luteal bodies of the ovaries which develop after the eggs (ova) are liberated by the ovaries. This puts an end to the willingness to mate.

Placenta. The placentae are the tissues developed during pregnancy from which the embryos derive their nourishment. Blood from the mother flows through them and the blood supply of the embryos take up the nourishment and carry it to them via the umbilical artery and vein. The placenta also helps dispose of wastes from the embryos which pass through and into the mother's blood. The placenta secretes several hormones of great importance to behavior.

PMS. Because so much of it issued in medicine PMS hormone (stands for *pregnant mare serum*) goes by that name although it may be a combination of the same hormones LH and FSH secreted by the anterior lobe of the pituitary and its action is the same.

The placenta also produces estrone, estradiol and progesterone.

While a bitch is pregnant she often acts calmer than when not and her behavior toward males, her activity and, toward the end, her nest-seeking propensity are all the result of her placentas. Then, with the approaching birth and the placentas becoming detached from uterus probably cause a liberation of the hormone prolactin if it has not already been secreted, as we have seen in the section on maternal behavior.

Chapter XIII

THE RIGHT DOG FOR THE JOB

THE VARIOUS WAYS in which dogs of different breeds react to external stimulii is quite definitely inherited. When I first began to study this interesting field, I called the traits mental aptitudes. The first study ever to report on "the inheritance of mental aptitudes" as I called it then concerned the dog's reaction to smelling the scent of an animal he trailed. Dogs of a majority of the registered breeds follow it mutely, not even barking occasionally like the wolf. Dogs of the hound breeds all bay on the trail. When I crossed still trailers with trail barkers or "open trailer" as the hunter calls them, the progeny barked on the trail, usually with a choppy voice of housedog quality, the drawl or bay of the hound's voice was missing. Psychologists have since corrected me saying I should have called the reaction "behavior patterns."

Everyone should understand that behavior patterns are inherited, that some breeds are truly remarkably efficient and capable by inheritance, "cut out" as some would say for certain jobs, while others are incapable. The sad fact is that because so few persons know the characteristics of several breeds, they conclude that the one they fancy is capable of doing anything that any breed can do!

To me it is incongruous to see persons trying to make trackers of dogs with inferior natural ability, to call guard dogs shepherds, to expect bird dogs to be guard dogs, to expect bull dogs to retrieve, or Doberman Pinschers to hunt ducks, Beagles to hunt bear, or Cocker Spaniels to draw sledges.

It is possible to train dogs to do any of these things. An old fashioned lantern gives light but who uses one any more to light the way when modern flashlights are available?

Through all the years while the 150 odd breeds were being developed to be what they are today, each was fulfilling better and better some specific purpose. Man had jobs for them to do - hunt ducks, guard, herd cattle, fight, trail, sit in women's laps, haul heavy sledges. By constantly breeding from the most efficient at each job, and discarding the least efficient, the various breeds were developed into the most useful for each job. Moreover, the degree of specialization is truly amazing. Of this, the best illustration I know was my own Bloodhounds. When I began breeding them many years ago, most of them bayed on human trails as they did on the tracks of game animals. Some were mute on human trails. By rigid selection of the mute trailers I developed a strain, none of which "gave tongue" on a man's track. But every one, if trained on game animals, bayed like any scent hound.

The Pointer dog is another good example. Because hunters have destroyed all of them in the past which dropped their heads and tended to trail with their noses, the trait of hunting with head up became fixed. Now, even if one is crossed with a scent hound, the pups will still hunt with heads up.

It does not pay to start training dogs to do jobs for which they are not fitted by their hereditary backgrounds. It is a waste of time. Millions of dollars have been wasted by police and defense departments training non-trailing breeds to trail.

Another fact every potential dog trainer must know is that there is no such thing as an all purpose breed, a jack-of-all trades. A person wanting such a dog might as well buy a wolf pup and raise it. Wolves can do every job dogs can do, though most of them not as well. The dog that hunts birds by pointing does not trail, the Newfoundland so naturally at home in the water is of little use hunting upland birds, the German Shepherd, so good at guarding is inefficient hunting foxes. Each has its own realm of maximum usefulness and is not a general purpose dog.

Perhaps you have been deceived by the way in which many new breeds have been introduced - the Airedale, Doberman Pinscher, German Shepherd, German Shorthaired Pointer, Weimaraner - all were proclaimed general purpose breeds but not one is. Each has its own specific field of usefulness.

Knowing what the field for the dog you own is, makes training so much simpler. We don't even need aptitude tests for dogs; we know by understanding his breed, what any typical representative's behavior patterns are. Human beings are now being given aptitude tests. No longer do parents expect their boys to be musicians when tests show they lack musical ability. Or artists when the predictions indicate small likelihood that the boy has artistic ability. And in the case of dogs the differences have been segregated into breeds and are not found scattered throughout dogdom in the same degree. In popular parlance it doesn't pay to try to put an oyster into a slot machine, when a nickel just fits.

To describe the 150 odd breeds of dogs and detail their hereditary behavior patterns would require a large book. We must therefore be content to group them and mention the outstanding behavior patterns of the group.

DOG BREEDS CLASSIFIED ON THE BASIS OF THE PURPOSES FOR WHICH THEY WERE BRED:

Upland Bird Dogs
Griffons (Wire-haired pointing)
German Shorthaired Pointer
German Wirehaired Pointer
English Setter
Gordon Setter
Irish Setter
Pointer   Vizsla
Weimaraner

Retrievers
Chesapeake Bay Retriever
Curly Coated Retriever
Flat Coated Retriever
Golden Retriever
Labrador Retriever

Spaniels
American Water Spaniel
Brittany Spaniel
Clumber Spaniel
Cocker Spaniel, American, English
English Springer Spaniel
Field Spaniel
Irish Water Spaniel

Sussex Spaniel
Welsh Springer Spaniel
Sight Hounds
Afghan
Basenji
Borzoi
Deerhound (Scottish)
Greyhound
Saluki
Whippet
Wolfhound, Irish

Scent Hounds
American Long-eared Black & Tan
Basset
Beagle
Bloodhound
Foxhound, American, English
Harrier
Otterhound

Tree Dogs
Black-and-Tan Hound
Bluetick Hound

English Hound
Plott Hound
Redbone Hound
Rhodesian Ridgeback
Treeing Walker Hound

Terriers
American Fox Terrier
Dachshund, Longhaired, Wire,
   Smooth
Airedale Terrier
Australian Terrier
Bedlington Terrier
Border Terrier
Cairn Terrier
Dandie Dinmont Terrier
Fox Terrier, Smooth, Wire-
   haired
Irish Terrier
Kerry Blue Terrier
Lakeland Terrier
Lhasa Apso
Manchester Terrier
Norwich Terrier
Schnauzer, Miniature,
   Standard
Scottish Terrier
Sealyham Terrier
Skye Terrier
Welsh Terrier
West Highland White Terrier

Shepherds
American Farm Shepherd
Belgian Sheepdog
Belgian Tervueren
Border Collie
Briard
Collie, Rough, Smooth

English Shepherd
Great Pyrenees
Komondor
Norwegian Elkhound
Old English Sheepdog
Puli
Shetland Sheepdog
Welsh Corgi, Cardigan,
   Pembroke

Sledge Dogs
Alaskan Malamute
Eskimo
Samoyed
Siberian Husky

Guard
Bernese Mountain Dog
Bouvier des Flandres
Boxer
Bullmastiff
Chow Chow
Dalmatian
Doberman Pinscher
German Shepherd Dog
Great Dane
Keeshond
Kuvasz
Mastiff
Newfoundland
Poodle, Standard, Miniature
Rottweiler
Schnauzer, Giant
Schipperke
Saint Bernard
Spitz

Toy Dogs
Affenpinscher

Boston Terrier

Chihuahua

English Toy Spaniel

Toy Fox Terrier

French Bulldog

Brussels Griffon

Italian Greyhound

Japanese Spaniel

Maltese

Mexican Hairless

Miniature Boxer

Papillon

Pekingese

Pinscher (Miniature)

Pomeranian

Pug

Silky Terrier

Toy Manchester Terrier

Toy Poodle

Yorkshire Terrier

Fighting Dogs

Bull Terrier

Bulldog

Pit Bulldog

Staffordshire Terrier

As you will see, this grouping is based, not on the names given to the breeds, some of which are entirely misleading, but on the work they were bred for. For example, we don't place the common farm dog of Norway, the Dyrehund in the group with the hounds because it is in no sense a hound. Far better, place the Farm Shepherd in the hound group because some of them will do a fair job of trailing rabbits and hunting squirrels. Nor do we place German Shepherds in the Shepherd group simply because certain Americans decided to call them by that name. The man who developed the breed in Germany bred them to be guard and attack dogs. As we have seen, the English call them Alsatian Wolfdogs. What's in a name?

The Guard and Attack Dogs. Females are seldom used for guarding and attacking but the males are aggressive, tend to be somewhat cowardly in the presence of larger dogs, tend to attack smaller dogs, are one-man dogs. They are alert, quick to learn, attentive. When past the age of two, the males are in general not trustworthy with children because of inherent jealousy which is easily aroused. In the hands of women or of men who are not sufficiently severe with them, these dogs can be dangerous to other human beings. All are large and soon come to know their strength, so dominate their owners. Of all the dogs in this class, the Mastiff is the most phlegmatic and difficult to arouse.

The Sight Hounds. Bred for speed and vision, these dogs love to chase anything which moves. They are extremely alert, easily taught and do not drop their heads when coursing. They kill by holding and twisting their heads back and forth very rapidly; the rabbit or fox being very rapidly dispatched. Coyotes, too are killed by several Greyhounds in packs, the dogs attacking with great abandon and no cowardice.

Most of the best Greyhounds are strictly track dogs, bred for rabbit coursing and chasing artificial rabbits around tracks, and some show real competitive spirit. Some of the breeds in this class are strictly burst-of-speed dogs - Whippets for example - and others, like the Wolfhounds, will run for miles without quitting.

The Scent Hounds. This group of dogs, despite the difference in size and form, all bay on the trail of animals they follow, whether it be squirrels or human beings. The nose is usually held close to the ground. Among the various breeds most show a great propensity to follow the trail of deer. Bloodhounds seem most fond of rabbit and human trails. Coonhounds follow trails to trees and when they have been well trained sit barking at the foot sometimes for twenty-four hours. Redbone Coonhounds seem to have an aversion to foxes; so few of them ever follow fox trails naturally. Bloodhounds bay on game animal trails but my strain was selected to trail mutely on human trails. Scent hounds have remarkable determination and stick-to-it-iveness. We do not know whether their olfactory ability excells that all other breeds or whether their degree of passion to trail and not quit (determination) is responsible for the results they achieve.

The Upland Bird Dogs. In this group we count the breeds which exhibit more natural interest in things which fly, than do any of the other breeds. Puppies soon after weaning will try to catch butterflies to which dogs of other breeds may pay no attention. The Setters and Pointers hunt with heads high, finding it difficult to follow a ground scent. Some of the dogs in this group - spaniels for example - also hunt with noses on the ground - and are useful in trailing pheasants and Springers are sometimes used as rabbit dogs.

All of the group are natural retrievers, some having been bred with mouths so soft they will not crush a baby chick; they return the retrieved birds without a toothmark. The early Cocker Spaniels

Retrieving for the Springer Spaniel is as natural, because of selective breeding, as trailing is for a hound or herding for a shepherd.

Afghan Hound, Ch. Sandhihi Joh-Cyn Taija Baba. Sight hounds are bred for speed and vision.

Ch. Merrelea's Vetter of Dornwald, C.D. The German Shepherd Dog's name is misleading—the breed has been developed primarily as guard or attack dogs, rather than as herders.

Ch. Fezziwig Ceiling Zero. The Old English Sheepdog is a natural herder, but has been little used in this work in America.

Eng. & Am. Ch. Cudhill Kalypso of Harham, Wire Fox Terrier.
The Terrier breeds were originally bred for "going to earth", but
are very rarely used in that purpose today.

Maltese, Ch. Aennchen's Shikar Dancer. The Maltese is one of the
more popular of the Toy breeds.

Sled team hauling mail, with Samoyed in lead.

were such dogs and until popularity caused careless breeding, seemed unable to bite - they could not kill a rat - in contrast to the many positively vicious untypical Cockers being bred today.

Many of the upland bird dogs are at home in the water, not to the extent of the retrievers bred for that purpose, but none refuses to swim to retrieve wounded birds. All the upland bird dogs have one special behavior pattern in common: They all tend to come to a stop before rushing at attack - pointing. All dogs possess this trait to some extent, but in these the pattern is considerably lengthened. Springer Spaniels can qualify in both this and the following class.

The Water Dogs and Retrievers. The Newfoundland is the most natural of all dogs in the water. All the typical specimens will spend much time swimming when they have the chance. Moreover, they dive like seals and can hold their breaths many seconds while they may swim ten or more feet downward to retrieve perhaps a water-soaked piece of wood. Calm and quite phlegmatic, this Adam of the Retrievers, so-called, the Newfoundland has his mark in all of the dogs used to retrieve game from water. Each is an excellent swimmer, a natural retriever, and all should have soft mouths. Most are much like the Newfoundland in that they are fairly phlegmatic and inactive when not working at their trades. It is said that the Irish Water Spaniel is not related to the Newfoundland but came by its love of swimming through selection just as the Newfoundland did.

Retrievers are easily directed by signs from the handler, in which respect they are like shepherd dogs. Indeed, a good retriever has many of the behavior patterns of both the Newfoundland and the Farm Shepherd, so many that one might almost think they were a cross of these two old types.

The Fighting Breeds. All of the breeds under this classification are quite reserved but when they fight are remarkably powerful in their jaws and the way they snap their head quickly from side to side to drive their fangs deeper. They are hangers-on, once they take hold. The females are docile and even the males are among the finest of human companions. Bull Terriers have traits in common with Greyhounds with which they were often crossed. Both tend to chase anything moving and attack it when they catch up.

My experience with many of these dogs and crosses I have made with them leads me to think that they actually feel pain in the skin less than other breeds. This is merely opinion; I know of no study to verify it. However, I have witnessed many dog fights between fighting breeds and non-fighters and have never heard a fighter cry from pain or quit in a fight as I have dogs of many other breeds. I once saw a Bull Terrier send a Great Dane kiyi-ing down the street after the Dane had attacked the Bull Terrier.

In treating fighters for wounds, suturing gashes, either the dogs have some grit which other dogs lack or I must conclude the fighters do not feel needle pricks to the same extent of others. And in crosses of fighters with dogs of other breeds, the behavior seems to be inherited.

The Shepherd Breeds. Here we find those dogs whose inherited behavior patterns makes them want to herd. The behavior shows early in their lives. I have seen a three-months old puppy herd 20 little pigs back to a barnyard at the mere command of his owner.

Ever alert, among the easiest of all dogs to teach, the outstandingly most useful dog in World War II, the natural shepherd, whether it be Border Collie, Collie, English Shepherd, American Farm Shepherd, Belgian Shepherd or any other natural herder, possesses the herding, heel driving behavior for which it is noted.

The dogs herd with head close to the ground, chin almost resting on it. Kicks from creatures the dog is herding go over its head. Alert to signals from its handler, it is easily taught to act on arm or cane motions when it is a quarter mile away, attesting to its excellent vision. Probably no breeds behave so cooperatively with their handlers, are so quickly and easily trained.

Not all of the breeds make good human companions because they have been so closely bred for herding and "sheep sense" that their temperaments have been neglected, along with their appearance.

The modern show Collie, however, has been selected in the reverse pattern, namely, it is excellent with human beings, less proficient at the work of herding than any other herding breed.

In fighting, all the shepherds slash and jump back. Collies are notorious for this type of behavior, so much that experienced dog men claim to be able to tell a Collie's work on another dog by the kind of wound he finds on the other dog.

The Terrier Breeds. "To go to earth" is the old English expression to characterize the forte of all terriers. But of course, many of the terriers are much too large to "go to earth" — follow animals like badgers or foxes into their dens or dig them out.

Terriers are scrappers, or should be to be typical. They fight at the least provocation. They "have a chip on their shoulder." Many Terriers are raised in individual hutches or stalls and when let out for exercise need to be carefully watched.

At the work for which they were bred, terriers are no longer useful because so few are used in that way. They have become pets and guard dogs. Like the fighters, terriers seem to feel pain less than most of the other breeds; they seldom quit in a fight even with a much larger dog. They are prone to attack large dogs as well as small as if unable to discriminate size. I have seen a Scottish Terrier attack a St. Bernard, another attack a Great Dane. Are they lacking to some extent in the sense a self preservation? In this respect, Pekingese dogs behave much the same.

My experience with terriers is that they are no more inclined to dig than are many other dogs. In my kennels, Fox Terriers, Scottish and Airedale Terriers raised in sand floored runs dug no more holes than did scent hounds. The Airedales I have known on farms spent no more time digging for woodchucks than did shepherds or hounds.

Inheritance Of Behavior Patterns. Now what can we say about the inheritance of some of these behavior patterns? For those of you who are not acquainted with Mendel's Law of Alternate Inheritance, following are the main features:

Each simple character of the dog is governed in the germ plasm by *a pair* of genes.

When the male sperm cells are formed the many partner pairs split up, half going to one sperm, the other half to the other.

Approximately the same thing occurs when the female eggs are formed but one half of all the genes are discarded, not put into another egg.

When the sperm meets the egg, the pairs of genes match up again, but each gene has a different partner now.

Some genes differ from others. When a pair or different genes get together, one will dominate the other, and the end result will appear like the *dominant* gene. The one which hides is called *recessive*. For example, a dark-eyed white German Shepherd is mated to a grey dog. The pups will all be grey. Why? Because each received one gene for white and one for grey and the grey-producing gene dominated the white-producing gene.

But when this hybrid grey grows up, if he happens to mate with another of the same germinal constitution, both will be carrying white-producing genes. Figure it out for yourself: Each supplies 1 white and 1 grey. How could they pair up? There is one chance a white will pair with a white; one chance a grey will pair with a grey and two chances a white will pair with a grey.

The pair of whites will produce dark eyed white pups, the greys will produce pure greys and the grey with white produce greys which carry white recessively.

So you see what dominant and recessive mean and how it is that a character can skip a generation.

Of the behavior patterns of dogs the following have been studied to greater or lesser extents with the designated results:

Trail barking ("open trailing") dominant over silent trailing.

Hound drawl recessive to chop voice of the still trailers.

Head up hunting of Pointer dominant over hunting with head to the ground - scent hound type.

Water going imperfectly dominant over non-interest.

Interest in flying things dominant over non-interest.

Smiling behavior is dominant over non-smiling.

Besides these a number of characteristics have been paired for contrasting purposes:

Independent hunting vs. packing in hounds.

Backing vs. non-backing in bird dogs.

Staying behavior in trailing vs. early quitting.

Use of the eyes when hunting vs. use of the nose.

Mouthing prey vs. quick killing.

Retrieving vs. non-retrieving.

Pointing vs. non-pointing.

Inhibited behavior vs. non-inhibited.

Slashing method of fighting vs. tenacity of grip.

Fighting mutely vs. fighting noisily.

Digging for game vs. non-digging.
Pugnaciousness vs. docility.
Energetic behavior vs. lethargic.
Horse wisdom vs. lack of it.
Sensitiveness of nature vs. coarseness.
Stubbornness vs. cooperativeness.
Herding behavior vs. lack of it.
Quartering in hunting vs. straight-hunting.
Flock responsibility in shepherds vs. non-responsibility.
Liveliness vs. phlegmatic behavior.
Sensitiveness vs. undersensitiveness.
Propensity to carry articles vs. lack of this behavior pattern.
Passive defense reaction vs. active defense reaction.

As one might expect from the country of Pavlov, some excellent work on the inheritance of behavior patterns in dogs has been conducted in Russia, notably by Dr. L. V. Krushinsky. Noting that some dogs naturally carry things in their mouths while others do not possess that kind of behavior, he crossed those which did with those which did not. He concludes that the carrying form of behavior is hereditary and that conditioning them was much simpler than in the case of the non-carrying dogs.

Krushinsky studied cowardice and anger. Cowardice he terms, passive defense reaction; anger, active defence reaction. Each is a distinct component of the defence attitude, he says.

A Russian breed, the Giliatzki Laika, is a placid, unexcitable breed and seldom exhibits shyness. The Alsatian Wolfdog (German Shepherd) he says is excitable, shy. When he crossed typical representatives of both breeds, the offspring were usually shy. He compares the cross with the dog-wolf cross which shows a pronounced shyness.

Krushinsky's explanation of how individual behavior patterns and traits become enhanced in breeds is excellent. He emphasizes the necessity of using only a dog of the type best for a given task, to train, and the foolhardiness of spending time on types ill-adapted for the job.

Another Russian, Dr. T. Marchelewski noted that German Shorthaired Pointers often hunt with noses to the ground in contrast to the English Pointers which never did. Crosses carried their heads high. However, he found that the German Pointers "did a lot of yelping" when hunting and that the English did not. Crosses of the two produced mute hunters. This is contrary to my findings of crossing hounds with still trailers.

The characteristic of "backing" which is desirable in pointing breeds is dependent on specific genes, according to Merchelewski.

Iljin crossed Alsatians and wolves. Also Alsatians and Siberian Huskies. Normal dogs, he says, are lively but he finds that there is an inherited factor which depresses liveliness. Crosses of Alsatians and Siberian Huskies are seldom lively.

Humphrey and Warner in their book, Working Dogs, show that dogs with the characteristic of being easily startled by noises tend to produce few of their kind when mated to dogs with under-sensitiveness.

Even so nice a difference as the position which Dalmatians took, when they ran under the coach and behind the horses was hereditary. Some dogs stayed close to the horses' heels and some stayed farther back. So concluded Keeler and Trimble from their studies.

That behavior characteristics "run in families" can scarcely be doubted. My own experience with the reactions of thousands of puppies to the feeling of the hypodermic needle at the time of vaccination furnishes an excellent illustration. Doberman Pinscher puppies and Bull Terriers usually seem not to feel it. Many Cocker Spaniels usually yip once and as soon as the needle is withdrawn sit down and scratch at the area where the vaccination was introduced, but some strains exhibit the greatest discomfort and are the most difficult to inject of all the breeds. Many urinate and defecate in the struggle. Puppies of my strain of Redbone Coonhounds make no sound but scratch after the injection. Knowing the behavior of a previous litter from two parents enables one to predict the behavior of the next. Springer Spaniels are quite variable. Some even urinate, some scream in terror and some are quite unaffected.

Perhaps it can only be fully appreciated by those of us who have bred and known many breeds well for many years, but is not the story of the Cocker Spaniel a most extraordinary illustration of how, by careless breeding, one of the most dependable little dogs extant, with jaws they scarcely knew how to use to bite with, has been changed into a breed now composed of a majority of vicious, neurotic, piddling dogs? Having bred over 2000 Cockers and not having known of one of the vicious kind, it comes as a surprise to see how this money thirst has degenerated so fine a breed. At one time one out of every four dogs registered by the American Kennel Club was a Cocker. Over 7,200 were registered one month. As I write this, the number has fallen to 1,200 - the reaction of the public to those who had a part in the deterioration. True, the miserable temperaments are not all the story; the long, wooly coat which has developed at the same time is a large part, too. This, the public does not want either. Combing the snarls out of such a coat on a dog inclined to snap and urinate is too unpleasant to tolerate.

There are still thousands of basically sound Cockers with typical coats available. Many are in the hands of hunters and field trial enthusiasts and from them the old type Cocker will come back to reasonable popularity soon.

It is interesting to note how certain combinations of form and behavior patterns when mated to their opposites, tend to recombine in new combinations in the second generation. Dr. W. T. James crossed sluggish dogs with very active dogs. The sluggish was represented by a Basset, the active by a German Shepherd. In the first generation, the relationship between physical form and behavior broke up. But when pups of this mating were crossed, the ancestral characters recombined in new ways: Basset form and excitable temperament, German Shepherd form and sluggish temperament.

Those interested in following the studies on the inheritance behavior patterns are referred to the author's book: *How to Breed Dogs,* Howell Book House Inc., New York City.

The higher one goes in the scale of animals, the less the species acts as automatons, the more the nervous system and behavior can be shaped by previous responses. In the dog we acknowledge - indeed start with the assumption - that certain breeds react to definite stimuli differently. The hound cares little for the flying bird or insect, the Pointer or Setter is stimulated by the sight of one. We also assume that there are some behavior patterns, some times also called *mental aptitudes,* which are not subject to modification, and others which can be partially modified. We have observed how the brain cortex is capable of being modified. From here on, therefore, we shall study to learn the processes by which modification is possible and how to apply these processes to training.

The competitors at field trials put emphasis on behavior and improving ability, based on inheritance. They often develop dogs quite different in appearance from those which dog show exhibitors have set as their ideals.

PART IV

So far we have studied about the nature of dogs and the means of using their abilities and behavior patterns in our service.

From here on we apply what we have learned to conditioning dogs in specific fields of usefulness.

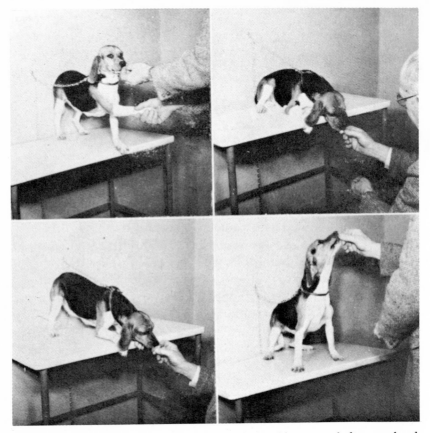

Upper left: To condition a dog to shake hands, get him to reach for your hand. As he does, give your signal and enforce it with a tidbit. *Lower Left:* To condition the dog to lie down, make him reach for the tidbit held below the table top. Give signal, and reinforce when he is down *(upper right). Lower right:* To condition dog to stand up, hold tidbit (reinforcement) high. When he starts to stand, speak the signal and reinforce when he is up. Each separate response will need thirty or forty repetitions before a dog is well-conditioned to the signal. After that he must be occasionally exercised in his responses to prevent their fading.

Chapter XIV

HOW DOGS LEARN

A DOG, WHEN LEFT to his own devices, learns by the *trial and error* method. A dog trying to get through a farm fence, the wires of which are spaced wider and wider apart as the fence is higher, will make every effort to get his head through the lower holes. Finally, in desperation, he may stand on his hind legs and find that the wires higher up are far enough apart so that, by turning and twisting, he can slither through. After several attempts at the same fence, he doesn't have to try, but stands up, pushes his head through a hole and jumps. And he finally learns not even to hesitate but to find a hole, twist sideways, and jump with his hind legs; he is through so gracefully, it is pleasant to watch him.

He learns, by painful reactions what he must not do. From early puppyhood he learns that his mother's growl means, *"No, stay away."* How does he learn? By hearing the growl and when he continues doing what he should not do, feeling his mother's fangs which hurt him and frighten him terribly. It is as though there were a fence made by the growl. The mother is eating and growling. If the pup stays his distance he is safe, but woe betide him if he crosses that invisible fence. And yet have you ever seen a puppy *imitate* his mother and growl to keep his litter mates away from food? Puppies are several weeks older before defense of their food begins to show. And this action is demonstrated even when a puppy is raised on a bottle.

How does a dog learn? Learn what? That barking will bring friendly companionship? That barking drives people away from his domain? To shake hands? That a flame will burn him? To drink from a pan? That bees sting? That porcupines are different from other animals? It is not easy to define the word—learning. It has well been suggested that the field of learning is equal to the field of psychology.

Psychologists are learning more about learning every day and

will continue to do so for some time. Without attempting to pro-
pound a definition we can say that dogs have now been studied so
thoroughly that we have tools and methods to influence behavior
profoundly and in a fraction of the time it formerly took to accomplish the same results. A dog's behavior shows what he has
learned. Our job is to influence the dog to behave as we want
him to. As we shape his behavior he is learning the elimination
of ill-adapted acts and the fixation of the adaptive acts.

It is most worthwhile to understand certain psychological
principles, even though learning about them may require considerable study.

As we have seen, *there are two kinds of behavior, the reflex
and the voluntary.* Many psychologists find fault with the terms
reflex and *voluntary,* for many reasons and have changed them to
respondent as a substitute for reflex, and *operant* as a substitute
for voluntary. In this book, we shall use the older terms which
seem to be applicable to dogs. Operant and respondent are mentioned here to make clear what the words mean when you may
see them elsewhere.

A good example of reflex action is the experiment employed
to teach students in psychology laboratories. When a buzzer
sounds, the student plunges his hand into a tub of ice water.
Naturally the blood vessels in the hand contract, its temperature
drops. The action also effects the left hand which is not in the
water. Every few minutes the right hand is dipped into the ice
water at the buzzer's sound. At about the twentieth sound, the
hand is not dipped into the water. What happens? The temperature of the hand drops anyway—a conditioned reflex.

Pavlov called his metronome a *neutral stimulus,* others call
it a *conditioned stimulus.* In the case above, the buzzer is the
neutral or *conditioned stimulus,* the cold water the *eliciting*
stimulus, the drop in temperature the result. The condition resulting from the continued exercise was a *conditioned reflex.*
When food entered the picture (some might call the food a reward), Pavlov called it *reinforcement.*

Reinforcers can be either positive or negative. Food or drink,
for example, are positive reinforcers; an electric shock or whip-

ping, are negative. Dogs' responses may slowly be strengthened
by no more than their owner's expressed approval or disapproval.
Most dog owners seem to think, judging from their conversation,
that this is all that is necessary, that showing approval or scolding
is the most efficient way to train. Two persons who have a mistaken attitude about the nature of dogs have written in books that
dogs are not seals which must be fed after every action. If expressions of approval or disapproval are all that is necessary, why
then are 99 per cent of all dogs almost completely untrained?

In a following chapter the most feasible reinforcements for dog
conditioning will be described.

I hope I have made it clear what a reflex is, what a conditioned
reflex is, and what a conditioned stimulus is. If not, recall then,
that food placed in a dog's mouth is a stimulus to which the dog
responds by salivating, which is an unconditioned reflex, inborn
and unlearned. A bell's ringing accompanying the food which
causes the dog to salivate without tasting or even seeing food,
becomes a conditioned stimulus and the salivating of the dog,
when he now hears the bell, is a conditioned reflex.

We can condition many kinds of stimuli, even time. A hungry
dog fed a little every twenty minutes, after a while will salivate
every twenty minutes whether he is fed or not.

Another principle which every dog trainer needs to know is
this: *The conditioned stimulus must come shortly before the
eliciting stimulus.* If there is too great a time lag between the two,
conditioning may not result at all, or if it does, the condition
will take much longer to accomplish. Seconds only should separate
them and the reinforcement should be attained by the pupil very
shortly afterward—the principle of togetherness. A more accurate
word it seems to me, is *concurrence*. What we do in training is to
effect a new response to a new stimulus. This works either positively or negatively.

Still another principle was that suggested by Thorndike, an
American psychologist: *Any act may be altered by its consequences.* If a dog jumps up and puts his paws on a table's edge,
and an empty tin can falls to the floor with a bang, the dog will be
startled. If he jumped and a whole box full of cans came falling

down on his head with the clatter accompanying them, our dog would be so impressed by fright, that he would be much less likely to jump up again than he would if only one can fell down.

If he attacked a dog and received a little bite, he might not be much deterred by the bite. But if the dog he attacked was a Bull Terrier and this fury "chewed him up" and left him a bleeding wreck, he would not likely attack another Bull Terrier.

Reinforcers (or reinforcements) are negative as well as positive. And whether positive or negative, they *strengthen* the behavior they follow, and they suppress the wrong kind of action.

This brings us to the problem of unlearning or, as psychologists call it, *extinction.* In plain terms, the dog owner calls it breaking bad habits. A dog unlearns a bad habit through extinction—by our withholding reinforcements. But this may take time. If the reinforcement is withheld long enough, the bad habit or wrong kind of action will disappear. Some call this *brainwashing.* It is, but by a slow process.

Brainwashing. We frequently hear a person say of another, "Oh, he's been *brainwashed."* What they really mean is that the person has been *conditioned,* not brainwashed at all. Brainwashing is the process of erasing the learning which an animal has acquired. One way it is accomplished is by creating a situation so terrifying that the animal finally all but loses its mental capacity. The great evangelists used it to remarkable effect without understanding the basis for the effect. On a high plane, John Wesley converted a large proportion of the people of England to Methodism through its use. He would make hell so vivid to his audience, that they gave up all hope. They were lost, sunk in horrible dejection. When he finally put them there with his oratory, he would then tell them that the way out of depravity and sinful condition was to believe in Jesus. And they did, and rejoiced.

Pavlov learned the basis for modern brainwashing through a near accident. A flood came to his city. In the basement of his laboratory was the room containing the dogs he had patiently educated to react in various ways, dogs of tremendous value to him in his work. The attendant had forgotten to move them to safety.

The flood water crept in to the laboratory slowly. Up and up it came until the dogs were swimming. The cage walls were constructed up to the ceiling. As the water rose, the dogs rose closer and closer to the ceiling in terrified fear, fighting for their lives. The area above them slowly was decreasing. Then someone remembered the dogs. He swam underwater into the room and one by one the dogs were rescued.

When they had recovered from the shock, not one dog remembered any of its past education; they were cleanly brainwashed. But what an experience it took to effect that result!

When dogs which are trapped in burning buildings escape after having been sufficiently terrified, they run away oblivious to commands to which they previously responded. It is not necessarily the terror they feel which accounts for their actions, it may be that the experience brainwashed them.

This method which can and has been duplicated many times in psychological studies can account for complete brainwashing, or milder experiences can account for lesser degrees of this effect.

But to return to the milder way of brainwashing, namely to remove the stimuli for a long period of time, so that the conditioning wears off. I mentioned Red Trailer not recognizing me by sight or hearing six months after he and I had parted company when I sold him. He was brainwashed in these two areas—sight and hearing—to a small degree, but memory of smell persisted.

Bad habits may be broken in the same way: there's just no need to completely brainwash a dog to break one undesirable conditioning. It may be negatively reinforced by punishment, or it may be allowed to wear off by cutting off the stimulus. If a dog learns to bark every time he sees a horse, if he is kept where there are no horses for a sufficiently long period, in time the sight of a horse will not evoke the same response. He may bark, but not as much.

The practical way to brainwash is to see that no satisfaction is obtained by the dog for his action. Or as a psychologist would put it, if the stimulus is presented repeatedly without reinforcement, the response will be extinguished. Whether this effect is permanent will depend on how well conditioned the dog has been. Extinguished reflexes have a way of reappearing and must be extinguished repeatedly. "Punishment"—negative reinforce-

ment—can be a secondary conditioned reflex. A barking dog which
has had his barking reinforced by frequent dishes of food given
to keep him quiet and which is punished *every time* he barks, instead of being given food, has received a secondary conditioning.
It extinguishes the barking-for-food but a little time passes and
the dog goes back to barking.

Negative conditioning is the quickest way of stopping a bad
habit—of brainwashing it out of existence, if you will. It is simply
the application of the process of extinction.

*A negative reinforcer is a stimulus which weakens the response
that follows.*

The effect of a strong negative reinforcer, whipping, a shock,
a bucket of water thrown on the dog, such things decrease the
frequence of its occurrence. The harsher the punishment, the
greater the effect upon that rate. Note that I said *rate;* the dog will
misbehave less often.

The effect of the punishment—the negative reinforcement—
will wear off if the dog is left in the old situation and not
"punished" on every occasion of misbehavior and in a short time
he will be as bad as before.

Emotional responses which are associated with the punishment stimulus are conditioned in a reflex fashion. To illustrate:
that dog which is sloshed with water, the water is the negative
stimulus, but the sight of the pail which holds it comes to be
associated with the "punishment." Or suppose a dog has a habit
of jumping up on persons. You break him by saying *No* or *Down*
and stepping hard on his hind toes while he is standing against
you. The negative stimulus is a pain the feet, but he associates
the word *No* or *Down* with it. After a while *No* or *Down* is
enough without causing a pain in the feet and the habit is extinguished.

One of the best illustrations I know is the way simply bending
over and touching the ground will stop many dogs barking or
make them run for cover. This fact indicates that ever so many
dogs have had something thrown at them. Perhaps it was a snow
ball or a stone or a handful of soil. In a northern kennel, barking
dogs are often silenced by their owners who throw snowballs at
the barker and say *Quiet!* at the same time. How quickly the dog

becomes conditioned to the sight of his owner bending over and hearing the word *Quiet!* And how long this simple conditioning lasts!

Another illustration is a certain dog which barks when tied to his dog house, but does not when he is put into the garage for the night. And certainly he never barks to be put into the garage for this reason: His owner is afraid of what the neighbors will say if they see him disciplining the dog out of doors, so he brings the dog into the garage where they cannot watch and applies negative reinforcements—"punishments"—when the dog barks. Let's say it is being left alone, which produces barking when he is outside: he seeks companionship. Why doesn't he bark while tied to a similar house inside the garage? Simply because he has come to associate the garage with the "punishment" and all by itself, the building is a stimulus. But this fear can become extinct in time, unless reinforced by punishment for remissions of good behavior.

Negative stimulus is really punishment whether we realize it or not. Much work had been done on the problem of extinction and its relation to reinforcement. One of the most memorable facts uncovered is this: *That it is more difficult to extinguish a bad habit which has been established by occasional or intermittent or irregular reinforcement than it is to extinguish one which was originally established by methodical regular reinforcement.* But the emotional upset is more severe in the latter case.

To illustrate again with our dog tied to a dog house in the back yard. He barks. At once the housewife rushes out with food to keep him quiet. She never permits his barking to go on for fear of incurring the neighbors' animosity.

And there's another dog, on a farm. It barks too, but there are no neighbors, so occasionally, not regularly, the barking brings some food.

Both dogs are sold to the same man who now has the job of breaking them from barking. He ties them to separate dog houses and decides on a water cure. He sets two pails of water, one beside each dog house. As soon as a dog barks, the man runs out and sloshes the bucket of water over the dog. In which dog can he "break," decondition, or extinguish the barking more quickly?

It will be harder in the dog which was rewarded occasionally and easiest in the dog whose barking was rewarded without exception, but this latter dog suffers the greater emotional shock.

It seems certain that a combination of positive and negative reinforcement together is considerably more effective than either alone. And so the question arises, should the two be administered from the start of training, or should we start with positive and begin negative reinforcement, later. Obviously we must start by letting our dog learn that for proper behavior he can satisfy his need. We can't start by "punishing" him. Studies with several species of animals show that the most efficient system is to delay negative reinforcement until the animal will perform correctly 75 per cent of the time, and only then to start negatively reinforcing for wrong behavior.

Just suppose that you have a Beagle which you want to train to run only on rabbit tracks. If the first tracks he followed were those of foxes and you punished him for making these wrong choices, the chances are you might "break" him of running tracks of any species. So you catch him off the fox tracks and perhaps take him to a brush pile and chase out a rabbit by jumping on it and letting the Beagle run the track as long as he will. And if you are lucky enough to shoot the rabbit so the hound can nuzzle it, so much the better. After he has become quite proficient at running rabbits, then, if you take him where fox tracks are and punish him for running them, he will not be spoiled for rabbit work.

Pavlov applied the word *generalization* to another most interesting phenomenon. *If a dog is conditioned to respond to a certain stimulus, he will also respond to another stimulus close to it and when he does the response will be less pronounced.*
Example: Your dog learns to bark when the door bell rings. If you should have the bell changed to one with a tone different from the old, he will still respond, but more weakly.

When the dog learns to bark when the bell rings, he may bark when any bell rings—cooking timer, telephone, alarm clock, etc. In time he finds that barking at any but the front door bell gets no response from you and he gradually stops barking at any but the door bell.

Here we have *discrimination. The greater the incentive, the more rapidly the dog learns discrimination.* I mentioned the actions of the morphine-addicted dogs and how they picked me out of a small crowd. Their need for the incentive was tremendous. They discriminated exquisitely for dogs.

In the laboratory, a dog is conditioned to salivate when he hears a certain tone. If a tone close to it is sounded, he will salivate, but weakly. Now, if he receives his food only at the one tone and never when any tone close to it sounds, he will soon stop salivating except when he hears the right one. He has discriminated. And as everyone knows, a dog learns to discriminate quite sensitively.

Pavlov's famous experiment in training a dog to discriminate between a circle and an elipse is often cited to show what happens when too much is expected of a dog. Pavlov made the elipse nearer and nearer and nearer in shape to the circle until, when it was very close, the dogs' discrimination broke down and they became neurotic. However, it is hardly likely that anyone, in practical dog training will make a dog neurotic.

Every dog must make thousands of discriminations before he can be said to be a well trained animal. Probably it accounts for the difference in intelligence between the two-year-old dog which has run unrestricted on a farm and the kennel dog if both are tested at the same age. The farm dog has been learning far more than the kennel dog, making many times as many discriminations. Thus we see that *discrimination is a matter of extinction or of unlearning some of the generalizations.*

To review a little and to clarify the subject: We've discussed reflex conditioning, and voluntary conditioning, then we have seen what extinction means, and discrimination. Each is a kind of learning. Even though at first thought, it may seem to be more a matter of unlearning, extinction is necessary to discrimination, a vital part of the learning process.

Differentiation is different from discrimination, but the two go along together, as it were. The Foxhound following a fox scent keeps to the one scent and does not change even though the trail is crossed by a fresher scent of another fox. The Foxhound *discriminates.* But what of the many other species of animals he might be tempted to trail, when he first enters the field: Rabbits, possums, grouse, pheasant, raccoons, deer, woodchuck, squirrel? He has learned to *differentiate* one species from another.

In fact, he discriminates the scent of the fox because sometimes it is wet and "hot" as the hunters say, sometimes dry (cold). It may cross a plowed field and disappear, but he may pick it up on the far side of the field. He must discriminate acutely to keep on the changes in that one trail, just as much or even more so than he must in not changing from a cold trail to a hot one of a different fox.

In the case of some dogs with tremendous natural drive it is a difficult matter to teach differentiation; much more difficult to teach discrimination.

The Principle of Chaining. This tells us that one response or reaction to a stimulus may be stimulus for the next response. A dog is trained that when he carries his aluminum bowl to a certain place, it will be filled with food by his mistress, who goes to work and feeds her dog when she returns at 5:30 p.m. As soon as the dog sees her, he fetches the dish. Her presence therefore, is a stimulus which evokes a reaction (the dog goes for his dish), which evokes another reaction (watching the bowl being filled) which is his reinforcement. But soon he comes to learn that the insertion of his mistress's key in the lock means she will enter. It is a stimulus (cue, if you will) which brings the dog to welcome her, her presence is a stimulus to fetch the bowl, etc. This is a simple chain reaction.

Dogs' lives are filled with chain reactions. When Nick Carter, the greatest man trailer ever to live in America, felt his master transfer the snap on his leash from his collar to his harness, he knew that meant to get ready to trail. He became keen to work. When he felt the tenseness leave his throat, as his master "dropped" his head, this was another stimulus to trail. The finding of the same scent which his first breath drew in on the garment he was over, was a stimulus to trail. But was this all?

Back of where we just began were more stimuli in this chain. First, the dog heard a long distance call come over the phone. In the days around 1900 a long distance call was a long, steady ring as contrasted with short, local rings. Nick learned to discriminate, and so the long ring was his first stimulus. He ran to where his harness hung, took it off the hook and carried it to his owner. When the harness was put on and buckled underneath, another stimulus had reinforced the former. Having learned that he was not to jump into the auto in the yard unless he had his harness on, he had another stimulus for a response. This in turn led to a ride which was further stimulus, and so on. The love of trailing, being permitted to indulge this passion, was responding to the stimulus. Eventually catching up with his quarry and sometimes receiving a reinforcement in the form of a tidbit was all part of a chain of responses and stimuli. Moreover, it illustrates:

The Principle of Secondary Reinforcement. A discriminative stimulus for one response may be the secondary reinforcer for a following response. As I pointed out, chains start first with the conditioning of the last response and going backward, a link at a time.

One of the most important of all principles is called *Secondary Negative Reinforcement.* We saw that negative reinforcement is, in a sense, punishment. Here is an example of secondary negative reinforcement: A hunter takes his rabbit hound into an isolated woods where there is, unknown to the hunter, a bear. The hound's hair on his nape stands up on end—a reaction which most hounds exhibit when they smell their first bear. Just then the bear bursts out from cover, whacks the hound with a paw, then pounces on the dog, chews him badly and is frightened off by the hunter before the dog has been killed. The dog manages to run out of the woods and is taken home where he recovers.

Next time he is taken hunting in the vicinity of that little isolated patch of woods, what does he do? He may not realize, in his zest for hunting, that he is headed for it but suddenly, he does realize. His hair stands up on his back again. He refuses to head into the woods. It was the bear which hurt the dog, but now the woods where the punishment took place is avoided as if it were "to blame" also. So the patch of woods becomes a secondary negative reinforcer.

Probably to dogs as well as to human beings, secondary negative reinforcers are of more significance than any other kind. It becomes clear that for the dog in our illustration, escape from the woods as well as from the bear is positive—reinforcing.

How may the dog be cured of his fear of the patch of woods? We saw that a stimulus loses its effect when it becomes a monotonous thing (the man who lives near the railroad track in time becomes inured to the sound of trains) so if the dog is led through the woods and finds no bear in them a sufficient number of times, this secondary negative conditioner loses its ability to effect a response.

Remember, your dog will learn faster in proportion to his having the proper need, when the proper incentive is present and the promptness with which he receives the reinforcement after each proper performance.

Besides these qualifications we must add the fact that *attention* is so exceedingly important. Some trainers, to keep the dog's attention, speak his name. There are better ways, however. After repetitions, the pupil becomes inattentive unless his need is kept unsatisfied.

And as important as keeping attention is to keep your dog free from all distractions. Noises, strange objects, other dogs, other human beings, had best be absent. A plain room or empty garage which the dog has had an opportunity to investigate is a good place to start him in. The atmosphere of obedience classes constitutes one of the worst possible environments in which to train dogs. Once they are well trained, the obedience class is excellent for further training and for exhibiting home training. It is also an excellent place where a trainer can explain to a group how to train the dogs at home. One of the reasons that classes need to be of such long duration, is that the new dog must first accustom himself to the many distractions about, and this requires much time.

If dog owners could treat their pets as scientists treat their experimental animals, they would learn some remarkable facts about the effect of distractions on behavior. The well-fed animal in fine condition is most easily distracted.

The degree of learning and the speed of learning hinge on the *number of repetitions* and the *recency* of the experiences. The dog is constantly finding that responses become linked with certain aspects of his environment. He soon learns to discriminate the many responses and the degree of his education is a matter of hundreds of differential responses. Some are conditioned reactions to outward stimuli and some are conditioned drives and needs which come from within the dog. We must use both kinds in increasing our dogs' repertories, or, if our dogs are hunters, to conditioning them in the behavior we want from them.

A dog need not be reinforced for every correct reaction, because of the fact that *anticipation can act as a reinforcement.* This is a memory phenomenon. For example, one of my newly acquired experimental dogs would not come into the kennel when I went out at night to close the dogs in. So I decided to make him very thirsty. I withheld water from him for twenty-four hours and that night snapped a little cricket to get his attention, then put a tablespoonful of water in the pan inside the kennel. After I walked away, he came furtively in and lapped the water. I went back, he ran out, I snapped the cricket and poured in more water. In a few trials he would come in when he heard the cricket. I had conditioned him quickly. For three nights I watered him and no trouble. But the dogs were watered outside by my assistant. And so was he. So now he would not come in and stay. Therefore, I starved him all day instead of feeding him in the morning. That night I fed a little and clicked the cricket. He acted almost as he had at first with the water, but his memory of coming into the pen to relieve his thirst changed to anticipation of food and now I could give him a small dog biscuit each night and close him in. The point is that his memory of satisfaction derived held, whether the reinforcement was water for thirst or food to relieve hunger.

In studying books on psychology, one frequently comes across the principles of *frequency* and *recency*. These scarcely need explaining to anyone who has trained animals or who has thought about his own learning. To learn, one must exercise the facility one is becoming conditioned to *frequently* and the most recent experience is uppermost in memory. Earlier psychologists used to say that things must be experienced together in order to be associated. It is quite well established that frequency and recency are necessary for learning, but they are not effective unless they are accompanied by *effect* and *concurrence* (togetherness). How does this apply to dog training? It is part of the answer to the question, How do dogs learn?

Suppose we place a dog in a cage in which there are several pedals. He is hungry and eager to satisfy his hunger. He touches the right pedal and a little door opens and in comes some food. Whenever he touches any other part of the cage or any other pedal, nothing happens, so he is becoming *conditioned to avoidance.* The correct lever becomes a *conditioned stimulus for food,* while all the rest of the cage is a *conditioned stimulus for avoidance.* Don't you see how this applies, for example, to housebreaking a puppy? He is actually responding to the need to relieve himself of urine or feces. The door to outside becomes a conditioned stimulus for relief, while all the rest of the house is a conditioned stimulus for avoidance. It *can* become that. The problem is, how to make it. Frequency and recency apply here as elsewhere in learning. If a puppy learns to let you know he wants to go out, in time the rest of the house becomes a conditioned stimulus for avoidance.

Another principle is known as the *phenomenon of least effort,* by which is meant that an animal takes the shortest route or selects those acts which involve the least effort. The dog won't learn unless he is stimulated to activity by internal tensions and finds appropriate incentives to release those tensions. You will remember that we observed that behavior is never uncaused. It isn't, and learning is based on this fact.

In some kinds of training, the avoidance of the dog of harm, such as electric shocks, cold water thrown on him, etc., can be a more potent incentive than satisfying his appetite. An illustration: You want your dog to enter your home only by the back door. You hear him barking to get inside. He may be expressing a need to get warm, to satisfy his hunger, or for your companionship. But though you have repeatedly blown a whistle at the back door and given him a tidbit when he came in, he still persists in barking at the front door, probably because he smells your odor from your having entered that way. He must stop it.

Now you already know he will respond to the whistle, but that behavior hasn't conditioned him to always come to the back door. What shall you do? Why, make coming to the front door distasteful. How? Condition him against it in one of a number of ways. For example—slosh a pan of water in his face every time he barks at the front door. This, you will probably find is more effective in half a dozen treatments than two dozen conditionings with tidbits as reinforcements. And it illustrates the above principle.

This brings us to the question of motivation. What makes the dog seem to want to do certain things? His needs or his instincts. Hunger is one need. A need to be satisfied. If hunger is used as the motivating need and the dog begins to learn, and if he receives the same reward each time with monotonous regularity, he will not try as hard as if he receives it somewhat irregularly. In any training session, you will find that he will be trying harder the fifth trial than he will the first. This is seen in dogs running mazes, or just working at learning a new trick. To be positively sure of a reinforcement for a successful performance, is not as effective as being reasonably sure.

The squirrel dog which trees a squirrel and expects the hunter's gun to fire, see the squirrel fall, and then to shake the paralyzed animal, may tree half a dozen squirrels which crawl into holes and are not shot, but this does not deter him from following squirrel tracks and treeing them. But this behavior is based on the fact that his first treeings were rewarded every time, or almost every time.

One of the most important facts learned about training, from the observations of laboratory dogs and other animals is that there is a happy medium between a long steady series of responses and infrequent opportunities for habit formation. If a dog is given a large number of lessons, he will make some mistakes and there is a strong likelihood that he will embody the tendency to make these mistakes along with the whole desirable pattern of behavior. But, if a little time elapses between sessions, he learns to avoid the mistake and to learn the proper response without errors. This is the happy medium. If the time is increased, the dog forgets the errors, but takes longer to learn to avoid them.

Experienced outdoor dog trainers have learned this fact, so it becomes second nature to them. When they start training, they keep at it every good day, but do not keep at it for long periods of time at first. Neither do they train once in two weeks and expect quick results. Errors are the unsuccessful responses. These, the dog should learn to abandon, while it continues to form associations between stimuli and responses which are successful. Thus, the dog learns to cope with its environment and to serve its owner as he wants to be served.

We have now covered the basic theoretical psychological knowledge which should be familiar to everyone who wants to understand dogs, and train his dog more efficiently. Now let's get down to the business of applying the information to practical dog education.

Chapter XV

SIGNALS AND STIMULI

In TRAINING, WHAT are we attempting to do? Simply tying up a conditioned stimulus with an unconditioned, so that we can, in time, make use of the conditioned stimulus to elicit the behavior we want from our dog. We use a drive (hunger), food (unconditioned stimulus), a whistle or other sound, (signal or conditioned stimulus), and permit the dog to partially satisfy his need by feeding him (reinforcement). When he is fairly well conditioned, we may punish misbehavior—apply negative conditioning.

The old fashioned kind of dog training was almost entirely by the use of the force system. A dog was forced into obeying a command, One book on training tells the reader to show the dog what you want him to do. To have him sit, you show him what you want by pushing him down into a sitting position. To have him "heel" you pull on the lead chain with a jerking motion whenever he gets behind or too far ahead. To teach him to stay, you push him down, hold up your finger, and say *Stay* while backing away. In each case you are supposed to have shown him what you want and he soon learns to obey. But does he obey for that reason? Of course not. This is simply an application of the force method.

The modern method involves the use of volition by the dog—getting him to act of his own accord and using some conditioned stimulus. Having based the action on drives or needs, the actions are then reinforced, as the psychologist puts it, by giving the dog satisfaction. The simplest illustration which comes to mind uses hunger for a need to be satisfied, a signal to be associated with the desired action and food as reinforcement. But there are other reinforcements, and in this chapter, we shall see what is known about the effectiveness of some of those we can use efficiently.

Every movement of a dog in training must be its own. You can modify the movement by training. When a dog is pushed over the shoulders and commanded to lie down, it is not the pushing which does any good; it is his own voluntary movement of muscles to escape the weight you are putting on his muscles, which you are educating.

Dogs placed in puzzle boxes in which pressure on a lever causes a door to open and food to fall out, are not easily taught to press on the lever. The student can take a dog's foot in his hand and press it on the lever many times and food fall out each time, then let the dog alone and he won't be able to solve the problem. But let the dog monkey around, pawing here and there to get it and have his foot accidentally strike the lever, and he will soon learn.

Have you ever tried to teach a dog to jump a high wire fence? Hunters—thousands of them—do it every year. The dog may be after a fox. He has never tried to jump a high fence. If he looks up he can easily see that its height ends only a little over his head. Does he stand on his hind legs and investigate? No. He runs back and forth. Suppose you go to him and lift him over. You have shown him the height. Will he try to jump over the fence? No, indeed. He will try less, but wait for you to lift him over to solve his problem for him. In short, he must try of his own volition and then, and only then, can you educate him.

The greater part of this book is about education. Here we have again pointed out one of the basic principles on which it must be based—voluntary movements, modified in the direction we want.

So now we consider first the signals that are practical for dog trainers:

Words. The sharper the better! Words are only sounds. They may be yelled at the dog or may be spoken quietly. One of the best trained dogs I have ever seen responded to a *chk* sound made by the owner with his tongue against the inside of his mouth. You or I would have had to be close to the owner to have heard what the dog heard distinctly. *Chk* was a word to that dog. Another man whose dogs obeyed quickly lost his job because the man for whom he trained disliked hearing the handler's voice above every other at the hunting field trials. The least volume which the dog can clearly hear is enough.

Words are only sounds to which you and I respond. If we had

learned that *up* meant to *lie down* we would respond to it just as readily as the other way around. And so would a dog. You can have him shake hands when you say *applesauce* if it pleases you. But why go out of our way to teach dogs other meanings for words from those used by ourselves? These come naturally. Furthermore, your dog may some day change hands and the new owner may not want to use your new vocabulary.

The inflection you use is also important. Imported dogs should be spoken to in the language they understand if you expect responses. I will always remember a Norwegian Elkhound that I imported. Her name was Finna. For a month we could not get her to respond to her name. Then one evening we were all in our living room and I tried different pronounciations of her name: Finna, Finnar and finally, Feena. She heard and to my amazement, jumped right into my lap.

Whistles. The sound of mechanical whistles carries a great distance so they are used by hunters and shepherds as well as by those who find their use an easy way to call a dog to come. But there are whistles and whistles. The so-called Galton, or silent whistle, is usually useless unless it is calibrated and set. We human beings can hear only a rush of air when we blow one. The dog can hear a variety of sounds, depending on where one is set. If you attempt to use one, have it set and if you educate your dog to that one and lose it, have the next one set at the same point on the scale.

An interesting trick with Galton whistles is to train each of a group of dogs to an individual tone. Have them sit about a room and have each respond to a different whistle, each of which would look alike and sound alike to an audience. In fact, one could pretend to be smoking different cigarettes from a package and each dog would seem to respond to a different cigarette!

Lights. Dogs can be trained to bark only when it is dark. In fact, most kennel owners train their dogs this way without realizing it. They punish dogs for barking when it is light because they are present. After dark, when no one is around to stop them, the dogs bark unless they are locked in houses. I learned that I could stop my whole kennel of dogs from barking by having a large flood light at one side of my kennels and lighting it at the first sound. If the barking persisted, I went to see the cause. For certain causes there was no punishment! A dog escaping, a wild animal—raccoon, or possum or fox—close by where the dog could see it. For other causes there was punishment. A light can be a wonderful signal in such cases. It can be used in trick training and occasionally in other ways.

Sounds Made by Hands. Clapping the hands, snapping the fingers, are sounds which can be used to good effect. Clapping can be heard from a quarter of a mile away and finger snapping is useful for close-up work.

Mechanical Clicks. A cricket is inexpensive and one of the most useful little devices that can be found. It is easy to use, too. Chief objection to it is the fact that many persons own them, especially children, and sometimes the imps, knowing your dog responds to one, will use it when he shouldn't and cause consternation to you as a trainer.

Odors. One of my first experiments with odors proved successful. I stationed a dog in a small room and blew odors to him via fans and a long pipe. When he smelled a raccoon's odor, he barked and received a tidbit. When he barked at the odor of a rabbit or porcupine, he received a shock. It was amazing to see how quickly dogs learned in this device. The method is described hereafter.

It is an odor which acts as a stimulus to a dog to start trailing. Sometimes a variety of odors trigger the behavior. The dog must then be taught to discriminate and follow only one.

Bells and Buzzers. The sound of a bell can be heard at a great distance. Years ago women often used crude triangles to call their men folks from the fields at dinner time. The dogs learned these sounds quickly and it was a common sight to see the farm dogs and hounds come romping in ahead of the men, responding to the triangle's sound.

House bells, telephone bells, fire house bells, school bells, bells of many kinds have been signals to which dogs have responded and still do.

REWARDS—REINFORCEMENTS

In a previous chapter, we learned about certain needs and drives and we have just sketched those conditioned stimuli which we can couple with the inherited reflexes. Now we shall consider some *reinforcements* which are useful in training.

Food. Small morsels of the dog's regular ration, constitute probably the simplest rewards, provided the dog starts the training lesson 36 hours hungry. If the day's ration is divided into 20 equal parts, it will prove adequate and if there is any left over, it can all be given as the last reinforcement.

There is much to be said for dog biscuits made of the same formula as the dog's complete ration. When I am training, I feed a complete kibbled ration and water and use small dog biscuits of that same formula as my reinforcements.

Escape. There are ways in which permitting a dog to escape from something distasteful to him can be a reward. Even letting him out of a dark closet into which you have put him for barking is, to him, escape.

Companionship Satisfaction. Dogs are gregarious animals. Like wolves, they gang up. Permitting a dog in training to satisfy his need for companionship can be used as a reinforcement in some instances. The fact that makes it less useful than some is that it can be used only at long intervals.

Investigation Satisfaction. As in the case just above, this need can be satisfied, but only infrequently.

Play. If your dog enjoys playing with you, permitting him to romp after each correct choice can be an excellent reinforcement. He must be tightly secured during training however, and almost instantly liberated when he performs correctly.

Shelter Satisfaction. This satisfaction or protection is often used without the dog owner being aware of it. Example: Your dog scratches on the door and obtains shelter by your opening of it.

Sleep. Despite the fact that we know dogs need it, it is fairly difficult to think of any way that sleep can be used as a reward in humane training.

The Attitude of the Trainer. To get the best of desired reactions from dogs a trainer can—should—adopt the attitude the research worker has found most productive of results, namely one of comradeship and affection, one which establishes the dog's confidence. This affords every dog satisfaction. Even without any knowledge of basic dog psychology, the English trainers who command in a quiet tone, who try to "bring out" the best in their dogs come close to showing the proper attitude. Have you ever watched a group of German or German-trained dog trainers commanding, shouting, barking gutteral commands at their dogs? If so, you know the kind of attitude for which several German breeds were developed and in which, with that kind of handling, they do not break down. But this training is force training, one of the least efficient forms. It may be necessary with the males of certain breeds—Dobermans, German Shepherds, Giant Schnauzers—to keep them docile, but dogs of most breeds and mongrels can be trained ever so much more efficiently by modern methods and a kind attitude.

Punishment can be administered in such a way the dog respects the trainer more, and even so that the dog does not associate it with his trainer. In training higher apes, these animals are treated as collaborators. "Good will, cooperativeness, optimism," were found more important than rewards and punishment in problem solutions. "Good dog" with a smile and pleasure in the voice comes to be quite quickly understood by the subject. And so does the opposite when dogs do wrong.

Negative Reinforcements. As we have learned, punishment is essentially a reinforcement for behavior just as reward is. Satisfying a need reinforces desirable behavior; negative reinforcement acts to eliminate undesirable. There are many kinds of punishment available to everyone, and some for which special equipment must be made or purchased.

Physical Pain. The laboratory psychologist mostly uses electric shocks for punishing his dogs—a most unnatural, but also a most efficient reinforcer. A dog's blood contains more salt than that of a human being and this possibly accounts for why a tingle that you and I can scarcely feel, is of considerable annoyance to a dog.

Electricity can be of great value to the dog trainer who works in the open, but in any case it must be used with great care because wrongly used, it can do more harm than good. In one of my juvenile books, *That Useless Hound*, I told how electricity was used by the young hero. After its publication, a number of enterprising and ingenious boys wrote to say they had rigged up similar outfits and "cured" their dogs of bad habits.

Physical pain can be inflicted in many ways. One of the most successful mountain lion hunters describes his method of "breaking hounds off deer" as follows:

"When one of my Blueticks finds himself a deer track and takes off on it, I let him go. Maybe a half mile, maybe a mile. It's flat country here and I know I can catch him, so when he's got himself a good track, I ride after him and when I catch up, I just let my horse trample that hound. Never say a word, but neither do I make any exceptions. It's not long before the hound knows that running a deer invites getting trampled by a horse. Never had any broken bones by this method, either.

"Another way we have of doing out here, I guess is quicker and it works, too. We ride after the hound and throw a lasso around his neck and pull him up over the limb of a tree hanging and then we just whip the _ _ _ _ out of him. It's an experience he won't forget. I've known of just one punishment to break him permanently off deer."

My own opinion of such brutality is that it is cruel and unnecessary, and we may ask, "How does the hound associate his punishment with the deer track?"

The other extreme of physical punishment is probably a slap from the open hand of a woman. Veterinarians are often asked how a dog may be trained negatively. Women will say, "I slapped him as hard as I could." When one replied in these words to a question from me as to what she had done to stop the undesirable behavior, I used to take one of my larger dogs out and ask the woman to demonstrate to me how hard she slapped her dog by slapping mine on the side. Only rarely did any woman slap the dog hard enough to elicit anything but a wagging of the tail to show the pleasure of being petted.

The Open Hand. In article after article, authors have written that the human hand should always be a symbol of kindness to a dog. To the dog, your hand should become a symbol of justice, reinforcing proper behavior and negatively reinforcing improper. Actually, a slap beside the cheek is excellent punishment.

Rolled Newspaper. The effect of this, properly used, is not to hurt, but to startle the dog by making an explosive, cracking sound. This can be and often actually is, used as a reinforcement for improper behavior. The blow must be really hard and frightening, in order to make this form of negative reinforcement effective.

A Whip. This is the principle punishment used by the outdoor man. It is efficient, quickly understood by the dog, and easily available. For little dogs, a switch which tingles the skin is enough. For big dogs like bird dogs, hounds and others, a limber whip, one-half to three-quarters of an inch thick and four feet long is heavy enough. It is applied by holding the dog by the nape of the neck just behind the head and whipping him along the side of the body, meanwhile saying, *No! No! No!* in a stern manner. Whipping a horse raises welts on the skin, but whipping a dog does not. This is a reinforcer which must be used with deliberation, never in temper, and invariably with justice.

The Dark Closet. Using the dislike of being left behind (lonesomeness) as the stimulus, a dark closet into which a misbehaving dog is unceremoniously popped when caught in the act of misbehaving, can be used to much better effect than most housedog owners know.

The Water Cure. A bucket half filled with water sloshed in the face of a dog as part of his misbehavior will often temporarily terminate it. It may require a dozen sloshings before your pupil learns that barking, for example, is asking for a wetting, but he will, eventually. Next day it may take but six dousings and each day fewer, until the habit is extinguished. Then, even the pail sitting where he can see it, will keep him quiet. Seeing the owner rushing toward him is part of the cure.

Scolding. So long as dog and man have been companions long enough so that the dog has learned to recognize voice inflections which denote pleasure and those which denote displeasure, the latter with sufficient emphasis, can be quite effective. But it is not the words you use, so much as the inflection. Many probably have seen the clown and the circus dog do their act. The clown stands and abuses the dog in the most emphatic language he can, and the dog just stands there and wags his tail. But when the clown switches to softly spoken kind words, the dog puts his tail between his legs and cringes. Which illustrates how emphasis, which the dog learns, is what motivates his behavior. You could punish a dog with kind words and reward him with abusive whichever he has learned.

A Broom. This is an instrument of training, wonderful in the hands of a courageous woman, and especially useful for puppies and small dogs. It inflicts little pain and accomplishes wonders if properly used. A worn out broom is better than a new one.

The Feet. Some outstandingly successful trainers have used their feet as indicators for desired responses and for disciplining too. There are those who say, "never kick a dog," but there are other observing persons who say, "tromp on 'em" a typical backwoods expression of dog men who have conditioned excellently trained canines. It is true that a dog tends to watch one's feet as an indication of one's actions. Properly used, feet can be used in training, but we shall not consider their use in this book except in training dogs to walk away from under them and in training dogs to stay on the ground and not jump against us.

Shaking. I doubt there is any more effective punishment for misbehavior than picking up a dog by the loose skin on his neck and back and shaking him hard. Or picking him up by the neck with his back towards you and shaking him that way. His anal glands may discharge and if they do, he is not much of a subject for conditioning for some time afterward. This is useful only for dogs small enough to handle.

Chapter XVI

SOME USEFUL RESPONSES

Here are some simple but useful behavior responses which every dog should be taught and can be taught with great ease: *Don't Touch, Take It, Shake Hands, Sit, Lie Down, Roll Over, Up.*

The feeling on the part of the shepherd dog that his flock is his pack, can be engendered in many, if not all dogs and should be one of the first things you try to accomplish before you start training, and while you are actively training; you are the pack leader.

No word better expresses the ideal feeling between you and your pupil than *rapport* (an harmonious and sympathetic relationship) . The way to develop it is not simply by feeding him but by doing something with him that he loves to do. If he is a house dog, and you are taking a walk in a park, and he trees a squirrel, throw a dead stick into the tree to show him that you are cooperating with him. If he digs at a mole, act so you seem to help him. If you want him to be a guard dog and he suddenly starts and runs to a window, act startled and hurry with him.

The guard dog won't guard unless he is guarding for you. He guards you as the shepherd dog guards the sheep. He guards your property only after he grows to feel it is his too, and you and he are of the same pack. This is a fundamental wolf characteristic.

Some call this playing with one's dog. If your's will play with you, great! Let him hold the leash while you swing him, or take it away from you and race with it. Make a simple game with him. Get him in the woods and hide from him. If he is inexperienced, call to him from your hiding place and observe how he must learn to localize the origin of sounds, how he may run in any direction, and how quickly he learns.

Suit the play to the dog's usefulness. You wouldn't let a retriever swing on a leash or you would find it difficult to get him to drop the retrieve; instead, he would hold it tightly as he did the leash in play. For a Bull Terrier or Fox Terrier such play is excellent.

Part of establishing rapport is having a signal to which your dog will respond by giving attention. His name makes an excellent signal. He is conditioned to respond to his name in the same way as to all other signals. If his name is Jim, the word *Jim* simply means *give attention.* He has heard it repeatedly and usually the sound has been associated with something good. It has been slow conditioning, to be sure, but sound. Sometimes it has meant reproval for misbehavior. A wise trainer would not permit that because one word should have only one meaning - evoke only one response.

Some owners call *Here Jim* when they want Jim to come, and Jim responds. *Jim* alone evokes the same response in most dogs. With careful training a dog can be taught to come at the word *Here* and to run away at the word *Go.* If that is desirable, the words should be reversed. *Jim, Here!* or *Jim Go!* Jim is the signal for attention and the dog responding seems to know his name. If a number of dogs are trained in a group, the name of each is recognized and each responds separately.

Don't Touch. This is a most useful command for every dog which is associated with human beings to understand. You may own a Dalmatian. When you come in from your car with an armful of groceries, he greets you and naturally sniffs the lowest part of a bag of frozen foods. The hamburger fat has begun to work through and he makes a grab for the bag. *Don't Touch!* you say, but he doesn't understand English. It's time he did.

After putting the meat and groceries away, you drive back to the butcher and buy a big knuckle bone with some meat on it and you have all you need to train with. You start by getting 'your pupil' thirty-six hours hungry. On a sheet of newspaper you place the tempting bone. It is so big that he couldn't possibly swallow it. As you put it down, say sharply, *Don't Touch!* and as he ignores your advice, slap his face hard enough so your hand stings. Or if you have an electric shocker described on page 239, use that. You will be surprised how quickly he becomes conditioned. Simply repeat the procedure, saying *Don't Touch!* as he approaches the tempting food. Keep on until he will stand and look, but not touch. One would expect that this negative training was all that could be accomplished at one session, but no, you can now teach him to respond to *Take It!* and he will learn both terms within twenty minutes.

Cut a small piece of meat off the bone, and drop it in front of him, saying *Take It* as you do so. He may hesitate. Wait until he eats and then drop another small tidbit, and repeat, each time saying, *Take It!* It is usually more difficult to condition any dog to the positive command because, as we saw, negative conditioning "trains" quicker than positive. After six or seven trials at learning that he may eat when you say *Take It,* you can now start combining *Don't Touch* and *Take It.* This is a little more difficult for him. Having been eating the tidbits, he may have momentarily forgotten your conditioning to *Don't Touch,* or he may have associated a small tidbit with permission to eat (Take It) and the big chunk with words *Don't Touch.* Therefore, you start *Don't Touch* again with a small piece, being ready instantly to slap his face and open his mouth and extract the meat if he does snatch it up. A few tidbits dropped accompanied with *Don't Touch* and he won't touch. So now you say *Take It* and very gingerly and uncertainly he may do so. Over and over, you drop a tidbit and say *Don't Touch,* watching him eagerly looking at it, and each time after a minute or less, say *Take It.* Even your first session will be successful.

But it takes several sessions to thoroughly condition 'your pupil' to all sorts of situations where *Don't Touch* and *Take It* are always reacted to precisely as you want. By the end of the second, you should be able to throw the tidbit from ten feet away and have your commands obeyed.

Each day as you feed him, fill his dish and make him stand back waiting for your *Take It* command, thus, by the principle of recency, making him a well-conditioned dog.

Whether you are a house-dog owner or a hunter, this command is one of the most useful you will ever teach your dog. The house dog waits like a gentleman for you to feed him, without hooking his chin on the dish and spilling food. The suburban owner, taking his dog for a walk at night, confronts a harmless skunk in search of beetles. The dog rushes at the skunk, the owner calls, *Don't Touch!* More than likely, just at that point, the skunk flips his greenish musk into the dog's face and eyes. Your *Don't Touch!* has been reinforced by the experience and your dog is far less likely to touch another skunk than as though you had not shouted *Don't Touch!*

at that particular moment. I should know, after the hundreds of experiences with my night hunting dogs. I always teach *Don't Touch* as the first command for all my dogs.

A really well conditioned Beagle will quit even a fox or deer trail at your words *Don't Touch*. And *Take It* will start him after a rabbit or even a rabbit's faint trail.

I have shouted *Don't Touch* at one of my dogs, starting after a flock of sheep which broke and ran, and had him quit instantly. You can do the same with yours.

In our Northern states and Canada, porcupines become a great hazard to hunting dogs and especially to spunky dogs of city persons who go to the country for the summer. How many thousands of quills I have pulled from Boxers, Dachshunds, Poodles, Chows, Dobermans, hounds, you might not believe. On one dog I worked three hours. These dogs had been quilled in Connecticut, where porcupines are not abundant: I always told my clients who were intending to go where porcupines lived to teach their dogs *Don't Touch*.

In their frenzy to attack the strange animal, some time about twilight, if the owner is with them and shouts *Don't Touch* and the dog does touch, he is much more thoroughly conditioned not to attack again and to avoid porcupines in the future than he is from feeling the pain inflicted by the barbs on the quills. The consequent pulling of the quills occurs too far from the attack for the dog to associate it with the attack, so that is not part of the learning process.

Night hunters purposely train their dogs to stay away from porcupines by shooting one out of a tree and letting their dogs attack it after the porcupine's tail stops twitching. The tail is filled with small quills which the porcupine drives into an attacker, and these are very difficult to pull, but the big back quills can be pulled easily. The idea is to see that the dog associates the attack and the pain.

Shake Hands. It is possible to teach this command to dog running loose in a room, but the simplest method and the most effective one I have found, is to use a table about 30 inches wide, a short chain, about 28 inches long with a swivel in it, a hook or ring in the wall six or eight inches above the table top, to which the chain is attached. You yourself may sit in a chair in front of the table and train without even standing.

With your hungry dog and tidbits of his regular food, you are ready to train. Place the dog on the table, attach the chain from his collar to the ring in the wall. This permits him to stand close to the table's edge, but he cannot jump down.

Hold out his reinforcement. His hunger is his stimulus. He sees the tidbit, smells it, but you hold it out of reach. He will strain to reach it, but can't do so, and he will reach out with a paw. As he does so, say, *Shake,* grasp the paw, and with your other hand, give him his reward or reinforcement. Step back while he is chewing it. Hold up another: he reaches, you say *Shake,* grasp his foot and feed him the tidbit. Repeat a dozen times and then, without showing him the food, say *Shake.* Twelve repetitions are not enough with all dogs, but they are with some. If he doesn't react to the word *Shake,* go back to showing him the tidbit and letting him paw for it as many times as is necessary to prove to you your pupil is conditioned. Try saying *Shake* without showing the food and immediately he reaches, grasp his foot and reward him. Repeat until he reacts as you want. The whole task will be done in fifteen minutes. Feed him his regular meal now as the last reinforcement.

At the next session two days later, go through this procedure again until you are sure your pupil is behaving as you desire.

Lie Down. This one is generally quickly accomplished. With hungry pupil on the table and you standing or sitting before him, let him sniff a tidbit, but not taste it. Now, holding it just out of his reach, lower your hand down, down, down, until it is below the table top. The dog will flop down and as he does, say, *Lie.* Presumably we shall reserve *Down* for another situation.

In a few moments, hold another tidbit up so he will rise and then lower it as before until he flops and say *Lie.* Repeat at least 12 times and try him by saying *Lie* without the reinforcement in front of his nose. If he flops, reward him and repeat until he is well conditioned.

The next session, start off with *Shake* and *Lie* and when he shows he still remembers, put him on the floor and try him there. You may have to hold a morsel at floor level to get him to respond to

Lie. If so, do it until he will lie down at the command, and reward him immediately.

Up. Put your hungry pupil on the table and make him lie down. Now hold his tidbit up in front of him and say *Up.* He may only sit up, but don't let him have his reinforcement until he is standing on all fours. Say *Lie* and every third time he lies down, let him have his tidbit, but every time he stands up, say *Up!,* and reward him instantly. Remember, in all your conditioning to let him obtain satisfaction as part of his responses, and don't delay giving it.

When he responds to your *Up* every time, go through the exercise again with him on the floor.

Sit. Put hungry pupil on the table, and holding your reinforcement in your hand, move it toward his face so that he backs up. As he does, he will almost always sit. As he sits, say *Sit* and let him have the tidbit. Now get him up again and repeat over and over until you can say *Sit* and he will, without your pushing out a hand at him. When I say over and over, I do not mean you will spend an evening doing this; it may be no more than ten minutes. Feed him his regular meal when the session is over.

Next session, do it again and when he responds well, put him on the floor and try him there.

The old way of training for this behavior was to push the dog down to make him lie or sit. This more modern way will accomplish results in a fraction of the time. One was is forced on him, the other is volitional.

Chapter XVII

SOME ILLUSTRATIONS OF THE USE OF THE NATURAL METHOD

IN THIS CHAPTER, YOU WILL LEARN how to apply what you have read and learned to elicit specific useful responses. Some of these are basic to desirable behavior of dogs used in various ways.

To Dance. I've put this first not because it is important, but because it illustrates so well the process of the application of the natural method.

In an empty room free from all possible distractions and noises, with our dog 36 hours hungry, a food pan, and a cricket, we begin our conditioning.

First, condition the dog to the sound of a cricket. Snap it and drop a morsel of food in the dish close to you on the floor. He will eat it. Wait for him to get his attention away from the dish, snap again, drop tidbit. Repeat as many times as it takes to condition him. This should be done in less than two minutes.

Watch your pupil and when he is standing with his head up high, snap and drop the food. Repeat only when his head is up high. You will soon note that the dog has learned that only when his head is high does he hear the click and get the food.

After a few minutes, he will be trying to get higher and higher, standing on his hind legs eventually. Hand him the tidbit.

Next, you want him to turn to the right and this can be done when he is up on his hind legs. Don't click until his head is toward the right. Repeat only as such times and reinforce. He will soon "catch on" and will stand up and twist to the right giving the impression that he is dancing. Reinforce less and less often.

Don't stop here. Your dog reacts as you want him to, but he hasn't yet been properly conditioned. Go through the performance at least twenty times and preferably forty. Remember the illustration of the hand plunged in cold water. One plunge would have had no lasting effect; it took many to condition the reflex. Just so with your dog. Repeat over and over no matter how monotonous, giving just a small tidbit for reinforcement each time. When you are ready to stop, you will probably have given about half the dog's daily calorie requirement in small pieces. Give the rest of his meal at his last repetition.

You can't train a dog by sitting in your living room reading this book, and imagining that you are training him; you must try it. Having accomplished it, you have got something to show your friends and will have derived a lot of satisfaction yourself. The above method was first devised by Dr. B. F. Skinner. It works.

In any kind of training, you had better exercise your pupil in what he has learned occasionally after he has been trained, especially if you have trained him in a form of behavior which is not based on an inherited drive. And if you have not kept your dog "practiced up" and want to give a demonstration, then "practice him up" once to recall the proper behavior pattern.

The same principles apply in conditioning a dog to respond to signals and jump over low objects set in a row, or in other words to broad jump. Only a rough floor surface may be used if the action takes place indoors. A few slips by the pupil on a smooth surface will make it very difficult to condition him to response.

To Jump In. Every dog, which accompanies his owner in the car should respond to some signal which is used to mean *jump in.* The same signal can be used to have a dog get into his bed or dog house, down cellar, through a door. It is imperative that every hunting dog know it, especially those taken in crates to shows or field trials or just hunting.

Few actions are easier to condition. A good signal is the movement of a hand or the use of the word *In* or both or either. Condition the dog to both at the same time. If you own a dog crate, place it on the floor with the door open. Get the attention of your hungry dog. Let him smell the reinforcement and toss a piece into the crate. He can smell it, see it go in. He hears the signal *In* and sees the motion of your hand. Thirty repetitions of the exercise and he is pretty well conditioned. You can teach him to go to bed this way too. Next session place the crate in your station wagon and go through the exercise again making him jump down each time after he has eaten the reinforcement. Twenty repetitions and you have him trained. Every time you take him hunting you are filling a need more compelling than hunger so no food is needed. On every occasion use your signal.

The same conditioning method is used for training to enter a dog house, jump in the car or go down cellar.

To Overcome Timidity. Timidity is one of the commonest of the undesirable characteristics of dogs. It often destroys all the value of an otherwise worthwhile animal. It is seldom cured by conventional methods and some dogs slink their miserable ways all through their lives. Owners who keep them feel they must make apologies for them. Nearly everyone assumes the dogs were "terribly abused" when they were puppies. Very few persons want them. What brings on this timidity? How did the dogs get that way? Is the condition hereditary? Were they all actually abused?

There must be some basis in heredity, but not in the form of inherited shyness and in a Mendelian manner because so few shy dogs are bred. That there is a kind of sensitive nature inherited in contrast to coarse nature, there can be no doubt. That there are kennels which turn out far too many shy or timid dogs and others which never have them, cannot be doubted. But may not the reason be in the wrong kind of early conditioning? Go back to Chapter VII and you will find the partial answer in the early handling of pups.

One of my old friends of years ago, never was known to have raised a timid Pointer, the breed he fancied. But I know some puppies of his strain which in other men's hands were gun-shy. My friend made it a practice of banging his food pans on the tops of his dog houses just before he filled them with food. He handled all his puppies a great deal and from their earliest puppyhood, never chased one to catch it, but made it come to him.

In the strain of Redbone Coonhounds with which I have done so much research, we have found that we could easily make puppies timid. In fact, we purposely made many timid in order to work out the cure you will read further on in this chapter.

Many of these dogs were weighed every week of their entire growing periods, or until they were about eight months old. Each was picked up, carried some distance to the scales, set on them and made to sit still while the weight was adjusted on the scale beam and then carried back to the kennel run. We found that of all of these weighed dogs, we never had a timid one.

Those we made shy, we kept in dog houses with small entrances. The puppies were driven in these houses while the runs were being cleaned. They were shut in at night. The food pans were filled outside and the dog houses opened in the morning by pulling a wire from outside the pen. Some, but not all of these dogs, became timid.

There are dogs terrified by thunder storms which no amount of attempted conditioning has been able to cure. Among my clients were owners of lightning-shy dogs which were given sedatives or tranquilizers at the first evidence of an approaching storm (dogs can detect storms before we can) and were also sedated during Fourth of July days to allay fear of fireworks, but this practical elimination of the stimulus for a year, did not extinguish any degree of the fear reaction so far as owners could detect; next year the dogs were as terrified of storms as they were previously.

Very likely, if the cause of fear could be detected early enough, something might be done to overcome it. I am not certain that it is noise alone which terrifies a dog in thunder storms. Lightning liberates ozone, which may effect a dog's nose differently from the way it does ours. The electricity may effect him with his greater amount of salt in his blood. Possibly he could have actually been struck by a fraction of a bolt and naturally become conditioned. Human beings have suffered all degrees of shocks from lightning. Perhaps it is all a matter of what the dog hears and not what he feels. Research will discover the answer and when it does, we shall know how to treat the lightning-shy dog.

Here we will discuss the gun shy dog and the man shy dog, and how to extinguish these reactions. What I advise is not "impractical theory" but is based on actual training or conditioning.

To cure a dog of man-shyness, we need a space without distractions - one with which he is familiar - and a stool or low chair. We need a neutral or eliciting stimulus, and a reinforcer. The reinforcer can be the food to which he is accustomed, dropped in a pan, the eliciting stimulus can be an electric buzzer or nothing more than a cricket, previously described.

In line with the findings that a dog works best when he is 36 hours hungry, take him after he has had nothing to eat for this length of time, and only water to drink, into the room with which he is familiar, or use his pen if there are no distractions. He retires to a corner as far away from you as he can get. Place your stool against the opposite wall or corner. Be nonchalant. Place the food pan on the floor close to him. Snap the cricket and drop some food into the pan. Retire and sit. Hunger and the smell of the food will entice him to eat. Repeat the exercise, but each time retire only as far as you need to, to let him eat. By a few minutes, the cricket's click will stimulate him to expect food, the reinforcement. When he has learned this, pick up the pan and move it closer to your seat. Click again, drop in the food and this time see that he has to stir from his original position, take a few steps toward you.

He will run back to his corner after eating. Get up and move the pan on the floor close to him. Snap the cricket and drop some food and sit down. When he has eaten the food and returned to his corner, move the pan nearer to you, click and drop more food in and go sit down. Each time he hears the click he will be less hesitant to hurry for his food.

Finally, move the pan between your feet, then under your legs so he has to move right between your calves to get the reinforcement. After he has done this three times, give him all the rest of his meal in that position and call it off until next session.

After thirty-six hours of fasting, he will be ready to work again. This time he will seem to have forgotten what he learned earlier, so you repeat the whole lesson. But it will be learned much faster than before and at the end you may experience a novel reaction in your dog, as I have with mine. Some, but not all, of the man-shy dogs I have worked with have turned from being shy to being "over affectionate" with me.

Perhaps for years a dog has been afraid of men. Now he seems to realize that he need not fear you and he may treat you as his protector and actually crawl under your legs or jump against you and lean. One of my dogs which was conditioned to lose his shyness was actually used as one of the hounds in *Midsummer's Night Dream* at the Stratford Playhouse in Stratford, Connecticut both summers of 1958 and 1959. This particular dog, when I am outside of the run, stands up and leans as tightly against the wire as he can to be as close to me as possible. In fact, the reaction of some of these dogs is almost pathetic.

Seldom does it require more than these two basic lessons of perhaps fifteen or twenty minutes each to extinguish the man-shyness as far as you are concerned. If you feed the dog and pet him while he is eating as further reinforcement, there-after simply supplying your presence is sufficient reinforcement.

Another method of overcoming man-shyness in the hunting or outdoor dog is to take the dog on a leash to do what he enjoys doing - going into the woods or fields. This is slower, much, than the first method.

What we have said so far applies to the attitude of the dog towards his trainer, not to other persons. To get him to lose his shyness of your friends, it is necessary only to obtain their cooperation and, in advance, have your dog fasted thirty-six hours. After the friend has sat in comfort awhile, bring the dog's food and ask him to feed the dog, using the cricket which the dog will not have forgotten unless a considerable time has passed. The meal can be divided into four parts and your guest will enjoy watching the dog "lose his fear."

To Overcome Noise-Shyness. Of course, the simplest but wholly impractical method of teaching the dog to overcome noise shyness is to tie him just outside the window of a drop forge factory or in a building where a huge Diesel engine is working. The sound which frightens will become so frequent and monotonous that it will not be heard. Thereafter, what would even a gun-shot discharge be in comparison? But since this is not possible, we must condition the dog so that each stimulus (the shot sound) is accompanied by, or quickly followed by, a reinforcement. Dogs have been broken of noise-shyness by having persons who lived close to busy railroad tracks keep dogs for their owners and give the dogs reinforcements every time a train roared by. Even though the stimulus is intermittent and not steady, the dogs lose their sound fear.

In extinguishing gun-shyness, naturally you will not fire a cannon nor a shot gun at first. A cap pistol is fired perhaps 50 times a few feet from the hungry dog who is fed a tiny morsel each time he hears the report. The food can be divided into 20 portions. Next lesson can be a series of .22 short discharges, the next .22 long, then long-rifle and finally, at a distance, where he will not feel the shot, perhaps a 410 shotgun can be used. The noise is his conditioned stimulus.

A friend of mine had a flock of Mallard ducks. He took his gun-shy dog to a field which sloped, but was surrounded by a five foot dog-proof fence. He used the ducks as the stimulus. When the duck he had planted was kicked out and the dog chased it, the duck flew straight, but the dog, going downhill and farther from the duck as he ran, heard my friend's shot. Every day my friend used a louder gun until he reached the 410 shotgun size, at which time he shot a duck. He advanced then to a 16 gauge gun and shot another duck. From then on the dog was no longer gun-shy.

To Bark. Those who own guard dogs, coonhounds, farm shepherd dogs realize the importance of barking. Then there are deaf persons who depend on their housedogs to bark when the doorbell or telephone rings. A bark they can hear, a bell they often can't.

How can a naturally silent dog be trained to bark at a signal? There are few forms of behavior easier to condition.

Here is where the incentive of wanting to accompany you or other dogs can be used. If you have another dog, use him; if not, you will have to do. Take some of your dog's food in a container and have him hungry. Go to a place strange to him, such as a neighbor's garage, out into the country, to a woods, to a warehouse —anywhere with few distractions. Tie him up and leave, letting him see you and his pal walk away. Be sure he can't slip his collar. Get out of sight and wait. When he barks call, *Speak* and run to him with a tidbit. Just keep walking away, saying *Speak* and going back every time he responds. After sufficient repetitions, so the dog is conditioned to *Speak,* stand in front of him and try saying *Speak* and see if he responds. If he does, go on from there and without walking away, say *Speak* giving the tidbit and repeating. After twenty repetitions give him the balance of his meal and lead him home. Next training period can be at home if he responds properly. If not, back he goes to a strange place.

Every year, hundreds of otherwise excellent tree hounds are disposed of because they won't tree bark. Field trial dogs must bark the instant they locate the tree at the end of the course, but a night-hunting dog can take his time. Indeed many experienced hounds will circle a tree to determine whether the trail leads away from it, the coon having climbed down, or, in the case of a bob cat, jumped out. Such dogs are seldom false tree barkers.

In either case, night hunter or field trial dog, the training to bark up can be accomplished by and with several other signals than *Speak*: Bells, footsteps, car noises, horns, odors, etc. A Galton whistle is the best signal I have found. One of the top field trial dogs to compete in New England won many a trial by responding to his owner's Galton whistle; the dog heard it and the crowd did not. This hound never barked unless he heard it.

If your dog will bark under some special condition, get him thirty-six hours hungry and reinforce as he barks and blow a calibrated or set Galton whistle as you feed. By the end of twenty barks and reinforcements, he will respond to the whistle alone. At the next session work him thirty times but give the reinforcement every third or fourth time.

To have a dog respond to a bell, use the same technique. Have him hungry, make him lonesome, as for example, by putting him in the closet, tied so he can't run out when you open the door. When he barks from lonesomeness or frustration, hurry and feed him a tiny bit. Close the door. Condition him to know that when he barks he loses a little of his hunger. When he barks quickly when you close the door, couple the reinforcement with the ringing of the bell —the door bell, the phone bell, whichever you want him to respond to. After 20 repetitions quit until another training period. Now you can try him first in the kitchen, leaving him alone and ringing the bell. If he responds, reinforce his action and repeat 30 times. After that he will bark whenever the bell rings. For a few days give him something he likes every other time he barks and then every fifth time. Kind words thereafter should be sufficient reinforcement.

To Stop Barking. A barking dog can constitute so great a nuisance that dog and owner must part company, or the dog must be taught not to bark. Having helped many grateful clients, I know that the following negative conditioning processes are successful.

If the dog is a small house dog, the instant he barks, say *Quiet* and pop him into a dark closet. Do it with dispatch. Pick him up by the scruff of the neck and swing him in, closing the door quickly. If he is large, keep a leash on him and pull him into the closet.

If he is an outside dog, and it is summer, try the water cure. Arrange it so he cannot run into his kennel or under a bush. Sit a bucket half filled with water close to him. Go inside and be ready to run. The moment he barks, run toward him so he gets the impression that his barking is calling you. In the past you may have fed him to quiet him and spare the neighbors the annoyance, so you conditioned him to bark. Now reverse it. Grab the bucket and slosh him, saying *Quiet* as you do it. Fill the bucket at once and go back inside. Keep repeating the action until he stops "asking for more."

And then of course, there is the electric method described in Chapter XVIII. A wire leading from one's home out to the dog house, threaded through the chain and attached to the dog's shocking collar, is simple to arrange. The battery and coil are kept in the house.

The Effect of Debarking on Dogs. At this point we must consider the effect of a greatly misunderstood surgical operation which is becoming increasingly popular, especially with persons who won't train their barking dogs not to bark. I refer to debarking. Many, if not most, scientific institutions debark their dogs instead of training them to be silent.

The reaction of many persons when they hear about the operation is, What cruelty! Deprive a dog of his God-given voice! Horrors! Actually, the voice is not entirely eliminated, rather, it is toned down. Dogs like to bark, they enjoy it much more than they enjoy keeping quiet. It is natural for any dog to react to surprises by barking. So the kennel of dogs which is kept mute by discipline is a kennel of less happy dogs than one in which all of the dogs are permitted to bark all they want, muted.

Having debarked over 100 of my own dogs used for nutritional research and from having observed the results, and from talking with clients who have had their dogs debarked, there is but one honest conclusion: Whether the dog makes noise or not, makes not the least difference to him. Going through the motions is what he enjoys. This is simply a reflex reaction to a stimulus. He has just as good a time making only a slight sound as he does making a great deal of noise.

Hundreds of dogs' lives have been spared by the simple debarking operation, dogs whose owners could not or would not train them. Some dogs were just too much for them. In one of my kennels there are thirty-six Beagles, all debarked and I don't know of a happier lot of dogs anywhere. They can bark to their hearts' content yet the neighbors never hear them.

Those who worry about the humane aspects of the procedure usually ask. "How would you like to be deprived of your voice?" I wouldn't. But I'm not a dog. I know enough to control my voice. However, if I could only speak in a whisper and never needed to yell, I would not be unhappy. That's how it is with debarked dogs - they bark in whispers and are happy doing it.

To Respond to Whistles. Whistles are used differently for retriever, upland bird dog or shepherding work. It takes some patience to condition a dog to the desired response to a variety of whistle toots, One toot should be equivalent to the response expected at the sound of the dog's name - "look at me." "Give attention." Two toots are generally used in training to signify *Come.* So in training retrievers or shepherds or any breed where response to whistles is expected, it is well to use a whistle for an attention getter. Thus, when you want your dog to *stay* or *sit* instead of saying, *Jim Sit,* toot once and say *Sit.* Later on, when your retriever is working in water or your shepherd is concentrating on a flock of sheep, and you want him to look at you for signals, one toot will get his attention, but will not call him in.

Come. The word *Come,* or a whistle, a bell, are essentially the same in this case; we want our dog to come to us when we want him. It is truly amazing how few dogs pay any attention to their owner's call to them. "I can't make him come," is the owner's usual lament. From what you know now, surely you can see how to train him.

If you are starting to train, get into an enclosed area and, having decided on the method you will always use, begin to train. This dog is told to *Come,* and he, being very hungry, soon becomes conditioned to the signal, because he comes to get a tidbit each time you call *Come.* In two minutes he makes the association. Let him wander off to the far corner of the enclosure and call *Come* each time as you slowly condition him to head in your direction at the sound of that word.

After two sessions of ten or twenty minutes each, you have his preliminary training all complete. Take two weeks to further condition him by calling *Come* only when there is no strong attraction calling him away from you. If he chases after another dog, don't call *Come*, or your conditioning will lose its effect; you will be shouting *Come* when he is headed in the wrong direction, which will confuse him.

Only when you feel sure he is conditioned, should you quit giving him tidbits when he responds. By then, you can call him when he is headed in the wrong direction, and he will turn and come to you despite any other attraction. If he proves exceptionally stubborn, obtain a strong light cord. Attach it to his collar. Take him where he can see other dogs and let him start after one and call *Come*. If he fails to respond, let him run out the length of the cord and pull hard on your end, upsetting him. Call *Come* and feed him when he comes. The upsetting conditions him not to disobey. Several of these experiences, and you have him trained.

Conditioning to *Come* can also be quickly achieved by two persons, a twenty foot long training cord and an anchor. An anchor-crowbar, post or what-have-you—is driven into the ground, perhaps your lawn, and the hungry dog tied to it. One person armed with twenty tidbits stands twenty feet away from the anchor. The other person, also supplied, twenty feet in the other direction.

One calls *Come* or if one is training a retriever toots two blasts on a whistle. When the dog comes it gets its tidbit, meanders away and hears the signal from the cooperating trainer. When it goes to him or her, it again receives the reinforcement. You will be surprised how quickly it learns to alternate. This behavior you must extinguish by stopping the alternation yourselves. Let the dog get away from you, not knowing which signal to expect next and call several times in succession.

Use up the forty tibits and your dog is quite well conditioned. Of course you will not permit the conditioning to become extinguished by lack of use. What was said about distractions above can be applied to a single person with the dog on a long training cord.

To Retrieve. Almost any puppy will chase a ball and pick it up. The only part of the whole procedure that requires conditioning, is to have the dog bring the ball to you and let go of it. Do you want him to drop it at your feet or in your hand? The latter? Very well.

Start with your pupil thirty-six hours hungry. Take a tennis ball and your tidbits and go to the park or your backyard, the country, wherever there are few distractions. A friend of mine uses the word *Thanks* when he wants his Setter to let go of the retrieved object - usually a grouse or pheasant. Let us use *Thanks*. Throw the ball. The dog will probably pick it up and come near you and drop it. Wait until he brings it right to you - near enough that he can smell the tidbit in one of your hands. Exchange the tidbit for the ball which he will have to drop to satisfy his hunger. Catch it as it comes from his mouth and instantly say *Thanks* and give him the tidbit. Throw the ball again as soon as he has licked his lips, but don't give him any tidbit until he brings the ball to you. At first you may have to kneel down and make the exchange only a few inches from the ground, but at each retrieve, hold his reward higher until - if he is a large enough dog - he will exchange the ball for his reinforcement without your bending over. If he is a small dog, you can train him this way to stand on his hind legs to deliver the ball.

Hunters who train the retrieving breeds use various objects other than balls. Most use a stuffed soft leather "bird" which is about the size of a grouse and called a dummy. After the dog has learned to retrieve, if the dog shows evidence of having a hard mouth, they place cut-off steel darning needles crossways of the "bird" so that if the dog clamps down hard, the needles prick his mouth and in this way, he learns to carry his bird gingerly.

A further extension of retrieving is teaching your dog to *Fetch* which is easily done after he learns to retrieve. Up to now, he has associated your tossing the ball with retrieving it and if you notice carefully, he has watched you and learned where to run for the ball by observing the swing of your arm. I am often amazed at how quickly this fact is learned. Sometimes it seems it is instinctive, but probably it is not. After only a few tosses, your dog runs in the direction he saw you throw it. Retriever trainers also know how quickly a dog learns which way to go by watching their handlers point.

Usually the dog need only glance over his shoulder at the motion of the handler's arm and away he goes in the correct direction. In golf ball retrieving, once the dog knows that he is to retrieve the balls, the handler can then dispense with throwing a ball, but, simply move his arm and away goes his dog in that direction. Because retrievers respond from the first "empty" throw correctly, they obviously have not seen the ball flying through the air most of the times it is tossed. They have heard it strike and possibly tied the motion direction with the sound and have been conditioned that way. However, I have taken dogs who have only seen a ball roll in one direction and retrieved it until they learned the smell of rubber. The next session has been with empty tosses along the edge of golf courses and again the dog retrieved from the rough.

This instant recognition of arm motion is the basis of guiding dogs in retrieving and in sheep herding. We shall see how it is used.

If you live near a golf course and if you own a Cocker or Springer Spaniel, or any of the retrieving breeds (or any kind of dog for that matter) you can exercise him and be well paid for your efforts, by training your dog to retrieve golf balls. When he is trained, go around the edges of the golf course or anywhere in the rough and just pretend to throw a ball. Your dog will note the direction you seem to throw it and dash off in that direction. He can smell an old golf ball and just as the bird retriever smells the bird, your dog will find the golf ball you seemed to throw. I have known one man to come home with forty-two golf balls his Cocker retrieved in a few hours.

A Beagle, which I could not make retrieve by throwing any object, was finally taught by the use of a little ingenuity. I had tried everything, even a rubber ball with a bell in it. Sticks, rolled newspapers, a tennis ball and balls of other sizes wouldn't interest her. She would run to the point they had dropped but would not pick them up.

Since I was using small cubes of boiled beef liver for her reinforcement, and knew how avidly she worked for it, I cut a square stick 1½" thick and a foot long. This was sawed lengthwise, hollowed out, and several slots sawed lengthwise. I filled the hollow with liver. She ran to it when I threw it and instantly picked it up. As she started in my direction I said *Fetch*. She happened to come all the way. I took hold of the stick with my left hand, and in the right hand a piece of the reinforcement which she wanted. As she let go of the stick to take the liver I said *Thank You*.

In ten minutes she was conditioned. When she responded to the signal, *Fetch,* 100 per cent, I wrapped it in two layers of newspaper and she retrieved it many times. Next session, I had her retrieving any object I threw.

Few dogs are as stubborn about retrieving. Among other hunting dogs, jealousy can be used to teach retrieving. One of my best coonhounds, if hunted double, would pick up a coon and carry it away so the other dog couldn't touch it. If he caught one on the ground he would carry it, not to us hunters though, but back to the car. He was a silent trailer and many times at the end of the hunt when we went back to the car we found coons had been placed there.

I learned from a man who had successfully trained Lurchers in England, that he was, without knowing anything about modern psychology, using precisely the method I have been describing.

After the dog had learned to *Fetch* he was then taught sounds for various articles he would be used to steal. Most of the Lurchers were used in catching rabbits on the English estates, but many were used even to steal clothes off clotheslines and were amazingly proficient. My English acquaintance said, "All the boys train them that way."

To Learn Names of Articles. Since it is assumed that the reader owns a house pet and wants to train the dog to fetch legitimate objects and also assumed the dog knows what to do at the word *Fetch!* let us teach your pupil to fetch the newspaper which the newsboy has scaled onto the front porch.

We fold an old newspaper and say to your hungry dog: *Fetch Paper* as we throw it. He retrieves and gets his tidbit. After a few such exercises, we lay the paper down instead of throwing it and walking to him tell him *Fetch Paper*. He usually will. Repeat and reward until he dashes for it quickly every time and then put the paper on the porch, open the front door and have him retrieve it. Be ready when the paper boy comes, and as soon as it plops on the porch, tell the dog *Fetch Paper*. He usually will. Practice him every other day and usually by the third session, he will learn that the paper plopping on the porch is his signal to retrieve it and will in the future get it without command. If you do not permit your dog to come into your home by the front door, he can easily be trained to go to the front porch and carry the paper to the rear door and deliver it to you. But for several weeks, give him a tidbit and pet him and say *Thanks* when he hands it to you.

To teach names of objects, there is no better way of which I know than to teach them in combination with retrieving. Therefore, before we teach the names of objects he can carry, we should teach retrieving. It is then a matter of coupling the name with the word *Fetch!* Suppose he has learned *Paper*. Now we teach *Ball*. There is considerable difference in the two objects. So when he knows both, we place the two on the floor across the room and tell him *Fetch Ball*. You will be somewhat surprised how difficult it is to teach some dogs to make correct choices, but with patience and rewarding only to make correct choices, they all can be taught.

A dog's repertoire of objects learned by name can be quite large, as can a dog's recognition of words. One dog I knew, was said by his owner to know and remember 400. How many persons would have the patience to teach so many?

In obedience trials dumb-bells are used for the fetched object. If your dog has learned to fetch it will be easy to condition him to any object you throw, dumb-bell, newspaper, or whatever.

Likewise he will carry it until you take it or use the word *Hold*. Dogs are easily taught to carry baskets and other objects.

Housebreaking. Most dogs housebreak themselves even though the owners believe they are responsible for the training. The dog prefers to relieve himself out of doors where he can investigate the scents left by other dogs and leave some of his own scent on gate posts and other landmarks. Dog-owners have caught their pets in the act of defecating indoors on a few occasions and made it unpleasant for the dogs. The same dogs found no objection on the part of anyone when they defecated out of doors, and so a habit developed and also a trained aversion to relieving themselves indoors.

Conditioning a grown dog and conditioning a puppy to use the out-of-doors are quite different matters. The puppy needs to relieve himself six or eight times a day. He often has a heavy worm infestation, which makes his feces almost liquid and at some time during his puppyhood, he goes through the three week long siege of coccidiosis with the consequent bowel looseness. He may have several sieges if he contracts more than one form of this parasitic disease.

Let us first housebreak a puppy. If you *don't* do it, it is because you just refuse to give the time and attention to it. If you say you *can't,* I don't believe it; you just *won't.* Any puppy can be house-broken. It takes some time and attention and a knowledge that you already have obtained from having read this book. But let's review some of the essentials to remember:

A puppy starts life retaining his urine and feces until he *feels* his mother's tongue lapping his external organs of elimination. When he is a few weeks old, he trundles outside his den and *feels* the grass under his feet, so urinates and defecates. It is a fact that the pup-pies raised in a wire bottom pen will seek out the grating in the floor over one-pipe furnaces and eliminate on the heating system. In just that fashion, the puppy raised where he went out on grass and eliminated, when brought into a home and given his liberty, will almost always seek the rug or carpet with the tallest nap. A puppy kept on newspaper in a pet shop will seek out newspaper to use, or whatever feels most like it to him. If he has been using packed dirt in his kennel run, he won't object to using hardwood floors.

The puppy actually has a *need to eliminate.* You can permit him to gratify that need - to obtain satisfaction - by putting him where he can obtain it. If you have permitted him from the first to obtain satisfaction on your kitchen linoleum, you have conditioned him, and the longer he does it, the more strongly conditioned he is.

Obviously, you can't very well starve your pup ever other day so he will be 36 hours hungry, nor do you need to, because a growing puppy gets more hungry in twenty-four hours than a mature dog does in thirty-six. So, if during the training period you will feed the pup once a day, he will be hungry at feeding time and he will not have so great a desire to relieve himself during the night and can wait until morning.

A puppy seldom soils his own bed if it is just large enough for him to curl up in.

When in company with his litter mates, a puppy seldom defecates until he has played for several minutes. You will be a substitute for his mother and litter mates.

So with only the above principles in mind, here is all there is to housebreaking a new puppy, in a suburban or city home with a back yard:

Make a box for him from which he cannot escape, with its dimensions the same on each side as your pup is long from front of shoulder to the end of his body (without the head and tail.) Make larger boxes as he grows. You will need a door for the first or housebreaking box.

The second box need have no door, but merely be a bed with a ring at the back to which you can attach a light chain with a swivel in it. At night, or whenever you have to leave him, the pup is chained up and his chain is just long enough to keep him from getting out of his bed.

Keep in mind that your dog, by morning, needs to relieve himself and that putting him out can become a conditioned stimulus and his reinforcement, being able to fulfill his need. If he is permitted to fulfill the need in the house, he quickly becomes conditioned to using that place, so every effort should be spent to see that he never does.

If he is a puppy you acquired, you should ask the breeder what kind of material the puppy was accustomed to, when he urinated. Was it newspaper? Did he run out on packed dirt? Did he use a plot of grass? Whichever the pup was used to going to, is the kind of footing you should try to supply. If he was used to going on grass, put him down on grass; if on newspaper, take newspaper with you and spread it out for him, every day supplying him with a smaller and smaller piece until he learns that it is the outdoors, not the newspaper which gives him this chance to relieve himself. As he gets older, as I mentioned previously, he will like to go out to investigate as well as to satisfy his need.

This is the first step in the morning. The next will be to feed him the first meal about the middle of the morning. He will look as if he has swallowed a croquet ball, and naturally all this pressure of his dilated stomach will put pressure on his bladder and colon. But don't rush him outside as soon as he is through eating; rather, play with him a short time, and as you do, watch him for any tendency to squat. If he makes even a little squeal and turns toward the back door, let him toddle out if he is large enough. If not, carry him out. When he is through let him do what he wants for a while, and then take him inside again. Keep him in one room; no freedom of the house until he is surely housebroken.

What to do on rainy days? The same thing. Dogs don't mind a warm rain. And in the winter? The same again, but if you live in the snow areas, the pup will have to learn to use snow, which makes housebreaking more difficult.

There are those who live in apartments where there is no place but the curb where the dog can be taken to defecate and urinate. It may be, and often is, necessary to train dogs raised in such circumstances to use newspaper. This is accomplished as follows:

A puppy pen is made or purchased. An ordinary folding, bottomless baby pen is adequate if the puppy is of a large breed. If he is too small, a pen can be made, or the top and sides of a refrigerator box can be had from an appliance store. Placed on its side, it is adequate. A box for a bed is placed at one side of the pen. Layers of newspaper are kept on the floor and gathered up each time the puppy soils or wets. When he has become used to the newspaper so that he comes out of his bed and uses it, then, when you are around, you can remove the pen and leave only the newspaper. Some folks cover the whole kitchen floor with paper during the training process, but this is unneccessary and probably poor teaching, because the object of the paper is to let the puppy learn *to go to a place* once he has learned to couple the feel of the paper with satisfaction of relieving his need.

When he goes to the paper, its size can be reduced, while at the same time it is left nearer and nearer to the door to the outside. When the pet has shown you he makes no mistakes, and of course he is growing older daily, the next step is to place the newspaper outside the door with one corner sticking through where he can see it. The dog may make an attempt to use it. He may scratch at the door, which is the behavior you hope for, or whine, whereupon you quickly open the door and show him how pleased you are.

After he invariably behaves in this manner, move the paper outside to wherever it is you want him to use. After he goes to the paper outside, begin to reduce it in size. Set out smaller and smaller pieces each day. I've known dogs to try to use a scrap of paper. I have also known many dogs which were paper broken and whose owners did not use paper outside, to be taken for long walks and hold everything until they were back in the house, and the accustomed newspaper.

Housebreaking a mature dog usually is a simple matter compared with accomplishing it with a puppy. Any kennel dog which has slept in a house which permitted access to the kennel run at all times, is partly housebroken when you acquire him or her. Kennel dogs which are shut in rooms in which there are beds, often learn to relieve themselves in the room, and such dogs are difficult to housebreak.

In the case of a mature dog, a bed the dog's size is almost a must, and a chain and swivel to tie him so he cannot leave the bed, are part of the equipment. He should be kept on the bed all the time he is in the house when you are not present to watch him. A week spent in close supervision is almost always sufficient to condition your adult dog to go outdoors for relief.

Whereas it is most inadvisable to punish a little puppy for misbehavior, the mature dog can and should be punished once he has learned to go outside. We saw that negative reinforcing can be ever so much more effective for rapid conditioning than positive. The question is, what can one do to negatively condition for bad behavior after the job has been done? Put the dog's nose in it? Of course not, because the dog cannot associate your effort with the misbehavior; it comes too long afterward. The negative reinforcing to be effective must be almost part of the misbehavior.

This can take any form but a verbal explosion from you often suffices. If you catch him in the act. Quickly plopping him into a dark closet or tingling him with a switch or electric shocker are excellent.

To stop a dog wetting on evergreen shrubs you may have seen a neighbor rig up some chicken wire which he connects to the electric current. Along comes a dog, lifts his leg and urinates. The stream of urine forms electric connections from the wire to the dog.

To Stop. A useful signal for any dog is the word *Hup.* It is used by many hunters and there is no reason not to use it for house dogs, guard or shepherd dogs even though it is not always part of the language used in all of these categories of dogdom. It is the signal to stop and sit. Some trainers insist that it be the first signal to which a dog learns to respond. *Hup* first, then *sit*. The force system uses the method of a choke collar to stop the dog and then pressure on the hips to make him sit. We have seen a better way to have a dog respond to *Sit*. Now how do we make him respond to *Hup* which will be a combination of stop and sit but not at one's side. First it is necessary to provide some lure which will trigger his action. It can be a strange dog he feels the need to approach. Or it can be a dish of food if he is hungry. A training cord is necessary equipment. The conditioning may be carried out in the home, on the lawn or any place without distractions.

With the dog thirty-six hours hungry, place his food dish the length of your training cord away. Holding the dog by his collar drop a tidbit of food into the pan and walk to your starting place. He will be eager to get to the food. Play out a foot of leash and as he tightens it, say *Hup, Sit*. As he does so, give him a reinforcement tidbit, say *Go On*, letting him go to the pan and eat the other tidbit. Take him by the collar, drop another tidbit, take back to the starting point and repeat. Do it over and over stopping him at various distances and each time he stops and sits walk up to him holding the leash tightly and give him his reinforcement, immediately letting him go to the pan to get another at your signal *Go On*. Some trainers say *Hie On*.

After he is proficient you can exercise him at feeding times. If he is a house dog, put him in another room, fill his dish with food, open the door and as he runs toward the pan, say *Hup* and after he has responded, say *Go On*.

This is especially useful in stopping dogs in the open. Of course you can call *Come* to keep him out of trouble but that should be used only when you want him to come. If you are walking and approach a busy street crossing, having your dog respond to *Hup* and sit before you on the curb is as good as having him respond to *Heel* and often better because you check his forward progress wherever you wish. And as you will see, in spaniel training especially, it is an important signal.

To Escape. We have some examples of modern training methods. Now here is an example of what not to do. Let's say my dog is entirely unfamiliar with word sounds. By *unfamiliar,* I mean that he has not once learned to couple a certain sound with an action.

In the morning, I want to walk into his run and feed him without his escaping. After having fed him I want to remove feces from the run, again without his rushing past me as I open the door. But suppose that he has learned that to make a dash for it, slipping by my legs, gains him his freedom, and each time as he dashed away, I call after him, "Come back here you........." This occurs every time he escapes. What have I done to him?

First, my presence and the opening of the gate are his signals to try to escape and he has succeeded often enough to become conditioned. He doesn't make good his attempt every time but, he, to become conditioned, doesn't need to. When I call *Come* after him, instead of the word having the effect I want, I am reinforcing, in a measure, the whole act of escaping. But this is what the majority of dog-owners do. Each of us, unless we ourselves are conditioned to silence, after such behavior of a dog, will explode with words. We should not.

Chapter XVIII

NEGATIVE CONDITIONING WITH ELECTRICITY

Back in 1950, in *That Useless Hound,* a book for juveniles about a boy and his Bloodhound, I told how the hero of the story used an electric shocking device for practical dog training, and described how he made it. In physiological and psychological laboratories, various arrangements for shocking test animals have been used for many years but it may be that this description for juveniles started the application of shocking to practical dog training. In 1935 I carried out the method of indoor conditioning described later in this chapter.

Recently, the electric method for negative conditioning—training, as the hunters call it—has been developed to include wireless shocking. My simple method involved, depending on the length of my lead wire, one or two 6 volt dry cells, a small induction coil, a switch, a limber strong lead cord containing two wires, which served as a leash, a harness and a collar with prongs which extended through the hair under the collar and touched the skin. One pair of prongs was insulated, the other not, so the shock ran through the neck. A very weak shock was sufficient negative reinforcement.

There was also another modification of it in which I had a wire running down my leg from the battery box on my chest to a spike on my shoe; a spike that pushed into the ground when I walked. Only a single wire was necessary running from me to the dog. On days when the ground was damp this use of the ground to return the current was excellent.

An outfit with wire running to the dog was marketed but the manufacturer felt that the wireless one was superior and discontinued the former product.

One device is a collar holding all the equipment necessary for a 20 second shock and it all weighs only 10 ounces. This device works in principle like the apomorphine injection but costs much more. A dog is taken to where the off-game is known to be and is started running the trash with the device set to "go off" in a given number of seconds. It does, and shocks for 20 seconds. Because it occurs while the dog is in the act of misbehaving, he associates the shock with that misbehavior and stops. A dummy collar is an essential or he could build up an association, and would run off-game in a light collar but not in the 10 ounce device.

The expensive wireless shockers are more elaborate and can operate up to a mile distant. They have many advantages over those with wire cords running from trainer to dog. Chief of these is the fact that a dog can learn that when the wire is detached the trainer has no power over him. For instance, once a track entices the dog to follow and despite the trainer's signal to quit, the dog feels no shock and frequently does learn that he is safe from punishment as long as the wire is detached.

It is necessary with wireless shockers to use dummy collars of the same weight as the shocking device and for the same reason as above. If a dog in an ordinary collar learns he is safe from negative conditioning for misdeeds then he will not react properly unless he feels the added weight. But after he has learned that misdeeds bring pain, he may be run in the dummy collar.

The electric devices most often advertised use hound dogs in the illustrations but do not let this imply to you that this negative conditioning method is not useful in all fields of dog work. With it the mongrel who kills chickens can be cured, the Airedale, Boxer or German Shepherd which chases sheep, the Doberman Pinscher which panics horses can all be taught.

The manufacturers of all of these devices stress the fact that the dog does not associate the trainer with the punishment but that the dog learns he is being punished by the animal he is running. From the literature accompanying the electronic shockers it is obvious that the use of such devices has not reached its full development, perhaps partly because of a lack of knowledge of basic psychology. For example, there are times when the dog should associate a command signal with misbehavior, or, in the case of sheep herding dogs, with a whistle. If he learns that you have control over him even at a distance, this is precisely what you want to achieve. What harm if he "thinks" you can shock him for misbehavior?

For ordinary training a small wire cord conditioner with a light collar is all that can be desired. Only for a very small percentage of outdoor hunting and sheep herding dogs, is the wireless device necessary. In the case of sheep and cattle dogs, all the early training is done with a cord. The cord may just as well contain wires or a single wire and if a shock is coupled with a voice command, the trainer is using a typical conditioned reflex procedure: The dog reacts to a stimulus, hears a voice sound, feels a shock. Soon he will react properly at the voice sound without the shock. Then too, his good behavior is reinforced by your tidbits.

The wire method I described of letting a dog, as his first lesson, run right up to the trashy animal—a rabbit in a wire cage—and when he gets close administering a severe shock, has been more effective than simply shocking or punishing for running on the trail of an animal he has never seen.

One should not expect results from a wireless collar if hunting near power transmission lines. It must never be applied when thunder storms are imminent. Keep the dog wearing one away from running electric motors such as one finds in shops, filling stations. Better to wait to apply it after you reach your hunting grounds. These devices work best on high ground and the range on hot days is considerably shorter than on cold.

Many hounds start their misbehavior by first coming close to a trashy animal and running it by sight until it has outdistanced the dog and he had to run by scent. One of my best young hounds never touched a deer track until one night, he almost ran into a deer under a hemlock tree. The deer tore away and the young hound couldn't resist the temptation to follow. Beagle men have found that one of the best ways to start a pup as I said previously, is to jump on a brush pile and frighten out a rabbit which the puppy sees and tries to catch. True, many will follow rabbit tracks without seeing a bunny, but they will follow not with the zest they would use if they had a memory of the rabbit running. In the same way hunters—even those who never shoot rabbits for sport— shoot a rabbit now and then and let the Beagle nuzzle it.

So it pays to teach a dog what the animal that leaves the track is like, whether you are training positively or negatively. If the rabbit dog takes up running foxes, let him run right up to one in a wire cage or chained to a tree and as often as necessary until he will have nothing to do with a fox track, which he learns leads to a shock. And by adding your command *No!* you can reinforce the effect all the more.

The Cattle Starter. A club shaped device with contact points at the tip is used on cattle to move them about in stockyards, load them into trucks or make a "downer" get up. But I hope no one reading about the use of electricity in dog conditioning will ever say this book recommended the use of one in dog training. There are few instances where one is adaptable. Some boarding kennel owners have run at barkers, jabbed them and quieted the dogs. House dog owners too, have used them. The result is often to cause a dog to cringe at the mere sight of a stick or cane in a man's hand.

In training barkers to be quiet, the dog needs only feel a slight shock accompanied by the word *Quiet.* After a dozen repetitions the word *Quiet* is all that is necessary. A collar with a wire running to it, or, if a dog is in a cage, a grid made by running parallel wires about on a sheet of one-half inch plywood. The dog's feet are first dampened. To produce the shock, a switch is thrown.

By either method the dog feels the bark brings a shock together with the word *Quiet.* But coming at him with a club-like device, jabbing him, and nothing else, while it will cure the barking, makes the dog afraid of the wielder of this instrument.

In 1930, work was begun on training dogs for hunting without taking them into the woods or fields. The effort proved successful. A small house 5' x 10' was built; a door at each end, and a partition in the middle. A one-way glass door was installed in the partition. The experimenter was on one side, the dog was chained in place on the other.

The dog stood on electric grids made by running parallel bare copper wires back and forth to cover the false floor on which the dog stood. A light chain on each side of his collar was fastened to a hook, so that the dog had to stand and could not turn around.

In front of the dog, chest high, was a metal pan with a pipe connected to it, so arranged that the experimenter could drop a reinforcement into the opening on his side of the partition and it would roll down into the pan.

A switch enabled the man to shock the dog gently. The wires were connected to a battery and small induction coil.

Outside of the house, directly behind the pan, a small slow speed fan was attached which blew a light breeze over the pan.

A number of twenty foot, three inch pipes were used. Each was attached to a box containing an animal. One held a raccoon, one a rabbit, one a fox, one a porcupine, another a wad of bedding on which a tame deer had slept.

The object of the study was to condition a dog to bark when he smelled the scent of a raccoon and further, to distinguish this scent from all other animals' scents he might run across while hunting.

To carry out the procedure, the dog was first conditioned to bark when the valve opened and he smelled raccoon odor. Three dogs were so conditioned—dogs which had never been in the woods. All were mature animals.

The sound of the fan starting and the valve opening acted as the signal. The odor was a second or two coming through the pipe. Each dog was first taught to bark at the word *Speak*. He heard the word a few moments after the valve opened. He barked, and instantly the reinforcement rolled into the pan. Only a few minutes elapsed before the dogs would respond to the odor and the word *Speak* could be dispensed with.

During a fifteen minute session, the dog was reacting as desired. Two sessions were sufficient, with their many separate trials, to have the dogs fairly well conditioned to raccoon odor.

The third session was devoted to ten minutes of raccoon trials, after which the pipe was changed for the pipe coming from the procupine box. Barking resulted, and the dog whose feet were dampened, was mildly shocked. Three trials taught the first dog that porcupine odor brought a shock if he barked at it. Then the odors were alternated; raccoon and porcupine. At first, the dog was afraid to bark at the raccoon odor, but did so when he heard the word *Speak*. By the end of this session, he was fairly accurate. It took another session before he responded correctly—was properly conditioned.

Fourteen trials were conducted before the first dog would clearly refuse to bark at all odors presented to him except that of raccoon.

The outdoor testing consisted of planting the animal boxes behind a stone wall, fifty yards apart where the wind blew the odors across a field. The dog, on a long leash, was taken across the field where he had to cross the odors borne by the breeze. He showed anxiety at smelling all odors except that of the raccoon, which was the last. At this, he turned and barked once, head in the air and ran upwind toward the source of the odor, being praised by me as he ran.

This dog was then taken hunting only three times where there were coons. He treed one which we shot, and hunted well. He was sold and made an outstanding record as a silent trailing coon dog.

Another big blue tick hound, whose only fault was running deer, was solidly conditioned off deer in this training house. After three sessions, he cringed when the deer odor came to him.

Chapter XIX

CONDITIONING FOR OBEDIENCE COMPETITION

Cᴏɴᴅɪᴛɪᴏɴɪɴɢ ꜰᴏʀ Oʙᴇᴅɪᴇɴᴄᴇ Competion is one of the most salutary developments in the realm of dogdom. Obedience classes bring together persons interested in dogs where the class members *do something* with their companions. What the field trial and hunting is to the suburban and country dog owner, the obedience class is to the urbanite and many suburbanites as well. Obedience classes draw owners of pet dogs principally. They should be encouraged. Many lasting friendships are made through the meeting of persons with this mutual interest.

Persons who do things with their dogs are those who learn the real joys of dog ownership. Obedience classes meet under the tutelage of an experienced trainer.

In 1964 the methods used are mostly the force training system developed by the German army dog trainers before and during World Wars I and II. That the method accomplishes results cannot be denied, but the findings of the science of psychology were seemingly unknown to these men. Most of the books which instruct the dog owner are written by Germans. They are excellent considering the knowledge of the day. Force is still in vogue, but the natural method excells it in every particular. It is enjoyed more by the dog, is quicker, easier on the owner, and instructive in the principles of psychology. But unless leaders adopt it, progress will be slow and dogs will be forced, as at present, into obeying rather than becoming conditioned joyfully.

Obedience training can be cut to a fraction of the time usually consumed in such conditioning if that is desirable. Obedience class teachers must learn something of modern conditioning in order to teach their pupils.

I want to make their work more pleasant and have the dogs enjoy the training a great deal more. Efficient methods of conditioning for several of the usual commands taught in obedience classes were described in Chapter III. Here follows some methods of conditioning for others.

Heel. The command (signal) *Heel* used to mean to walk behind the trainer or owner just as the heel-driving cattle dog naturally follows the animals he herds or as the Dalmatian followed closely behind the heels of the horse drawing the brougham. When I was a boy, we said *Side* to have our dogs stay at our sides. So many persons insist on teaching their dogs words they personally understand that it is curious how the word *Heel* doesn't mean to the dog what it means to us: Since it has become a part of the obedience schedule ritual, *Heel* will mean, in this case, for the dog to walk at the trainer's left side.

The usual method of training a dog to heel is to place a choke collar on it and after training the dog to sit at the signal *Sit,* the trainer walks and walks holding the dog back to the proper position or jerking on his neck and saying *Heel* each time. This is the usual force method.

The natural method, on the other hand, is as follows: With the dog thirty-six hours hungry, take him into a room free from all distractions. A back yard or a park and a long, light leash will also do. He has already been taught *Sit* and *No.* So condition him to come beside you and sit.

Your pupil is hungry, he knows you have a tidbit (the reinforcement) in your hand. He naturally goes to the side where the food is. As he does so and turns around into the proper position, say *Heel* and give the tidbit. He will wander away. Coax him back again, wait until he is where he should be, and again say *Heel,* then reinforce. It may be five to fifteen minutes before he reacts properly and has associated the signal and his action with the slow satisfying of his appetite. If he sits when he arrives at your left side, so much the better. Repeat 20 or 30 times. At the next session have him heel and sit. Repeat this 30 times.

Next session walk with him on a leash. If he pulls ahead say *Heel,* stop and say *Sit.* You will be amazed how quickly you can condition your dog positively. He will sit at signal, get up and walk when you walk, sit when you stop.

At first he will look up at you expectantly but when he is conditioned, the reinforcements can come less and less frequently until he forgets them and will not look up, but pay attention to the environment.

But you can't stop there. You must next let him see distractions. If you own an electric conditioner, it can be used to advantage. If he disobeys and jumps ahead when you say *Heel,* say *No,* buzz him and he will quickly learn he must not disobey. He won't know that you shocked him, rather he will feel he shocked himself and perhaps like you even better. He can't get beyond the leash.

When he is thoroughly conditioned at home, he is ready for further conditioning in the hall where other dogs distract but he won't be long responding because you have conditioned him. In competition, no talking is permitted, the dog must react to the handler's motions instantly and from habit.

The standard obedience trials, where the dog competes for a certificate, involves walking and turns. Many hours of walking and making turns are necessary before most dogs are ready for competition. When the time comes, the dog and handler almost appear to be parts of the same organism.

Stay. This obedience item is one of the most showy of the tricks in the repertoire of a well-conditioned dog. It can be done with words, whistles, or motions as signals. Shepherds train their dogs at distances as far as their dogs can clearly distinguish the handler. In the sheep dog field trials, there is often a quarter of a mile between shepherd and dog. The short distance, possible in a hall, is nothing compared with the outdoor trials.

As performed in the obedience trial, the dog is told to lie down and the handler then backs and walks away to the predetermined distance. The dog must lie, keeping its eyes on the handler who, at the judge's indication, motions the dog to run to its handler.

Stay can be taught quickly and easily by two persons. One is the handler, the other anyone whom the dog need not know but who will cooperate carefully. I have watched trainers using the force system and seen them spend hours trying to persuade the dog to stay lying down, as if they thought the dog understood

English. Had one of them asked a friend to stay behind the pupil, even behind a fence with a hole in it and through which a cord passes, how much quicker the dog could have been conditioned.

To train *Stay* by yourself, and with no electrical equipment, using a spike or choke collar, chain your hungry dog to some object and have him lie down. Say *Stay* and back away. He does not know that signal so he lunges forward to get to you. His neck hurts and he lies down quickly. Repeat until he does not lunge and then reinforce with a tidbit. One of the most interesting facts, I have learned about the natural method of training is that it requires so little time for a dog to associate his receiving a tidbit with the realization that he has done right. It is like saying *Good Boy!* Everything you teach him to do increases his recognition of this fact. Now that you have come to teaching him that he should not move when you say *Stay* and that he gets his tidbit when he remains motionless, he seems to learn it quickly, much quicker than as though it were his first lesson, shaking hands for example.

Now give him more chain and do not reinforce if he moves toward you, only when he stays put. When he finally "comprehends" your signal, repeat it twenty times, but do not back away over twelve feet. Next period go through it all again and when he behaves as you want, repeat thirty times.

Now he is ready to be tried where other dogs and distractions exist and when he responds properly you can begin using hand signals and condition him to respond to them. This you do by calling *Come* as you move your hand, reinforcing when he reaches you. Soon you can use only your hand motion and he will respond.

The quickest method is the electric. You can hold the switch at the end of the wire. The dog is chained. If he lunges or tries to run to you, administer a slight shock. This takes the place of a choke collar.

A friend's cooperation is a great help. The friend stays far enough behind the dog so the pupil doesn't know that the friend is pulling the strings. He can act as the bird hunter does and talk to the dog, steadying him until he is conditioned. He can pull on a leash to give pain through a choke or spike collar, or press the switch to shock the dog if you are using electricity. But he must use the same word signal as you. He can unsnap the leash when you beckon the dog to come. And he will soon be unnecessary.

To Jump A Hurdle. Here again height depends on the size of the dog. This time we shall say that the dog is a Doberman Pinscher. In his case, a cricket can be used since such a stunt is strictly for exhibition purposes.

A thirty-six hours hungry dog, a cricket, a hurdle, and a training cord are what you will need to start. If the hurdle is to be solid, in the nature of a board wall, we use a lot of boards and side pieces with grooves into which boards can be slid. If the barrier is a pole, two heavy dowels with a sheet of transparent cellophane rolled on them is an excellent barrier. A pair of side supports with holes in them into which pins can be pushed on which the crossbar (pole) is rested. A pair of athletic high jumping standards make ideal supports.

The pupil is held to one side of the first board, his pan on the other. Reinforcement is dropped in the pan, the cricket snapped as the dog steps over the board. When he has learned that the cricket and food go together, the cricket is his stimulus and the way to get the food is to hop over the board. As the height is increased to two boards, the pan is moved farther from the hurdle because he can't see it and must not land on it and be distracted. Be sure his take-off and landing areas are not slippery. Before giving exhibitions, it is well to train your pupil out of doors.

At first, snap the cricket as your dog jumps and gradually snap as he is getting ready to jump, then just when you want him to jump. Stop when he shows any inclination not to respond.

With each lesson, start with the hurdle considerably lower than where you left off last time. Watch that the cord does not become tangled. If you are working in a fenced enclosure, you can soon stand beside the hurdle without having put food in his pan and as he comes down, quickly move to the pan and drop in his reinforcement.

You may ask, why not have him come to you to collect his tidbit? Obviously, he will be disinclined to make the effort to jump.

The bar barrier with plastic is unrolled as it goes up with one bar lying on the ground. Otherwise the procedure is the same. And you must play out plenty of cord to prevent its distracting your pupil. After he is conditioned, a bar alone is used.

How high do you want him to jump? Well, that depends on the breed of dog you have. If he's a Greyhound, he can be taught to jump even a ten foot fence.

Now let me tell you how I used a different incentive to teach another dog to jump. I bought him from a man who found him too large to get through any fences in his area of Ohio. I trained him to tree squirrels first and he was a most adept pupil. In the area of Michigan where we were hunting, there were fences of many heights; hog, sheep and stock fences. So a friend held the dog on one side of a hog fence only thirty inches high while I took Mack's constant companion and walked away from him in the direction of a patch of trees. Mack began to bark and carry on, but my friend held him until I was fifty yards away. The big hound ran back and forth and finally half climbed and half jumped the fence rather clumsily. My friend said *Jump*. When Mack caught up with me, I petted him and took both dogs back again and repeated the conditioning. The third time he jumped the moment he was liberated.

So, he was tried in the same way with a sheep fence, about forty inches high. The very first time he cleared it as gracefully as a deer, so we all went squirrel hunting. That night, by moonlight, we repeated the procedure with a fifty inch stock fence between us. There was considerable hesitation on the dog's part but my friend told me afterward that the dog looked up and did not run back and forth. All that was necessary for my friend to do, was take him back from the fence a few yards and say *Jump* and over he bounded. Never again were we troubled by fences. My pupil actually jumped a seven foot kennel fence without touching it. He had thenceforth to be kennelled in a covered run.

To Broad Jump. This is a matter of negotiating a series of low hurdles. In principle, conditioning for broad jump is the same as for high jumping. For indoor conditioning the need for floors covered with runners or mats where there is no chance for slipping is obvious.

Use a lead at first until the dog becomes conditioned to your signal which can be a word, a sound such as clapping ones hands or only a motion. After the dog is conditioned to one hurdle, the number can be gradually increased and he usually responds as if he were playing a game. His tidbit awaits him at the conclusion of each jump until he invariably responds. After that, a tidbit now and then is sufficient reinforcement.

The famous Keeshond Obedience star, Ch. Rovic's Chimney Blaze, U.D.

Chapter XX

CONDITIONING FOR GUARD AND ATTACK

Now for another aspect of dog work: Germany used 30,000 trained dogs in World War II, France 20,000. The United States used some and the soldiers, sailors and marines who trained them were first trained themselves. Each man was assigned to one dog. The dogs were conditioned for special purposes. The guard dogs who accompanied sentries proved to be morale builders.

After the war some dogs were said to be "detrained," but few were found to be reliable house dogs. Von Stephanitz, who developed the German Police Dog (in the United States, the German Shepherd) said that the breed was developed for guard and attack. Weber, an authority on training guard dogs says, "In private life, then, where the dog goes about freely most of the time and is independent of owner control, protection training and police training are decided menaces."

Everyone who trains a dog for guard and attack work should know that such a dog must be under constant surveillance and had best be handled by only one man.

The army issues instructions on how the "Brass" wants their dogs trained. There is little explanation of the basic psychology back of such training. In what follows here, it is assumed that you now understand that basis. It will help you be efficient and you will see why repetition is necessary.

I had the opportunity of watching a German Army trainer instructing a class of American Army Dog Corp men and watching them drill the dogs. Every action was forced. The signals (commands) were barked in staccato shouts at the dogs, who obeyed like the soldiers. All the dogs were German Shepherds and Doberman Pinschers—breeds ideally adapted for this work; bred for it, in fact.

You know now that this would be accomplished quicker, better, by the natural method in quiet tones. It would seem that sentry work especially should be accompanied by whispered signals. Even in attack work no sharp loud words are necessary. Few today remember the goose stepping walk, the barked commands of the German Army but those who do, associate German dog training and German dog temperament with that type of human temperament and conditioning. German trainers were brought here to show Americans how to do it. Some of the remnants of this are still found in our obedience work today. This does not make it right. Indeed such training, applied to breeds which are bred for other work, such as shepherding, trailing, bird hunting, coursing, can be more harmful than helpful.

To condition dogs, bred for the purpose, to attack is one of the very simplest forms of dog conditioning. What we need to do is to control the pupil. Those with most experience with police and army dogs emphasize that here is the one man-one dog combination par excellence. Thus one man stays with one dog. The dog is always handled by that man and no one else. Army dogs trained in some uses may have more than one handler but those dogs trained for protection should be one man-one dog combinations.

The dog must attack on command, he must guard an object or person, must refuse food, not so much because of the danger of poisoning, but so he cannot be lured away by proffered food. In fact, many dogs are conditioned to attack anyone offering food.

Police or protection training is more than a one-man job. The handler is always one of the two, but the assistant can and should be an assortment of men. If the handler tries to act as an assistant should, in attack training, the results may be tragic; his dog may attack him.

All the dogs in police, army or protection work are first conditioned to respond to the usual obedience signals and the handlers often have them responding to various other signals such as *sit up, say your prayers, roll over.* After this preliminary conditioning, the attack work starts.

Male dogs without noise- or gun-shyness are used, the bolder the better. Several service organizations buy their dogs which are frequently dogs which have become more dangerous than a family can handle; instead of having them killed, they sell or donate the dogs to the services. Such dogs are already on first base. Temperamentally, they are excellent for attack training.

In the early days the German method was to control by strenuous use of the whip by the handler. Electricity is much more effective. The assistant, clothed in padded bite-proof clothing simply enrages the dog by all means possible so that the dog tries to get loose to attack his tormentor. As he is liberated by the handler, he hears the words *Get Him* and after sufficient repetitions, at the words *Get Him,* the dog will attack even a non-tormentor.

The problem is to control the dog with a word. He is so savage and enraged that his blood adrenalin is high and he feels pain less than at normal times. The German method was to whip the dog hard enough to make him forget attacking and listen to his handler. A shock will do a better job and require fewer trials to condition the dog.

We are permitting the dog to do what he wants: Attack and chew on the padded garment of the assistant, the fulfillment of his desire. He loves it because basically he is that kind of dog.

In this work, to have a dog refuse food it is necessary for the handler to be ready to unleash the dog and say *Get Him* just as the padded assistant proffers the food. After sufficient repetitions the mere stretching of a man's hand toward the dog will be the signal for attack. If he is guarding an object, he will attack. Of course in the general scheme of things, no handler will be near a dog on a chain when food is offered but the dog will growl and bark fiercely, his attention on the man and not the food, and the handler will respond to the barking by unleashing the dog, and the dog will lead the handler to the one who attempted to poison the dog.

It is too bad that television has done so much harm to the public's knowledge of dogs in this respect. Thousands of persons, seeing the remarkable exploits of Rin Tin Tin bought German Shepherds expecting they could do with their dogs what "Rinny" did. I asked his remarkable trainer, Lee Duncan, how he had trained his dog to be so kindly and yet at times, so ferocious. My friend laughed, "I use two dogs, of course." One was the attack dog, the other the kindly one—the real Rin Tin Tin. That he was well conditioned when not on the lot, I can attest, because at a banquet at which Rinny was to appear as a surprise, Mr. Duncan hid him under the table between my feet for a full ninety minutes. He was told to stay and he remained with no one aware of his presence but Lee and myself.

Dogs which are used to accompany watchmen on their rounds can easily be taught, following the obedience lessons, to uncover anything unusual on the rounds, by teaching them attack behavior first. If a department store is being patrolled, the padded assistant is planted behind a counter or display case. After dogs have walked through any area a few dozen times, they observe by ear and nose anything unusual and want to investigate. No other stimulus is needed, no other reinforcement than being permitted to do so.

When a dog hears the slight movement, or smells an unusual odor which was not there at other trips, he, encouraged by the handler, investigates. If the man freezes, he will not be so easily discovered as when he moves. Movement is fatal because the dog loves to pursue as well as attack and the assistant is "apprehended."

When conditioning, it is well to have the padded "robber" run and attempt to escape. The process can become almost a game. The "robber" hides at different places beside the path taken through the store and the dog becomes more alert looking for him. The "robber" is changed after a dozen trials and changed several times after that if it is possible to employ willing assistants.

In department store patrolling, there are so many attempts at robbery that strangers occasionally substitute for the friendly accomplice. Thus, it is important to be able to control the dog before he inflicts disfiguring or fatal wounds on the thief.

Chapter XXI

CONDITIONING TRAIL HOUNDS

FEW WORDS ARE NECESSARY to the hunter or hound man on the subject of starting a foxhound, rabbit hound or Bloodhound trailing. Every rabbit hunter knows that if he jumps on a brush pile and his dog sees a rabbit run out, the little hound will be after it. He may not run it long at first, but each successive run will be longer and he will tire less each time.

Taking him with one or more trained Beagles will help, too. The main object in training is to condition him not to run off-game.

So with the foxhound. He is a "natural" at following a fox trail even if he never sees a fox in his life; your job is to see that he runs only fox.

Conditioning to Discriminate Odors. As I said previously, it is the odor left by an animal which triggers or signals the dog to satisfy his drive to pursue. This odor is also called a spoor, or scent, or trail. I said that the dog must be conditioned to discriminate. We saw that the wolf will pursue the odor of a single caribou right through where the caribou herd has been and not quit to follow a fresher trail. So will most hounds stick with the first trail each starts. But many hounds will follow the trail of any species of animal. The owner, of course, wants his hound to trail only one species.

How then, can a dog be conditioned to hunt one species only? This involves both positive and negative conditioning. The system which I have found excellent in the open, involves first making sure that the hound has plenty of opportunity to follow the tracks of the species I want him to follow. This may be accomplished in several ways.

You may take your pupil with a sure hound, and not until the sure hound has a trail going, liberate the trainee. He will run with the sure dog and fall in on the basis of contagious behavior.

They may run together, or one may lag behind the other. Let your trainee run the trail as long as he will. All the time he is doing it, he is becoming conditioned. If he leaves it for the trail of an animal of another species, you must catch him off as quickly as possible. Simply taking him off the wrong species acts to condition him. No punishment at first. I can well imagine a foxhound man asking, "How do I catch him, if he is running free?" In this day of automobiles, it is generally easy. In the first place, a trainer will not take his hound where there are mountains, or inaccessible places. If he does, he can't catch him. He takes him into areas where he can drive to cut him off when he needs to.

Another way of starting the new dog, is to obtain an animal which you want him to follow, and let it go where the dog can see it run away. If you can liberate the animal in an open field where the dog can give chase by sight until it is lost from view in a woods, the hound will have his nose affectors to follow. I saw a wonderful demonstration of this in one of my big Bloodhounds. The late Captain V. G. Millikin, America's greatest Bloodhound detective, saw my untrained dog and admired him greatly. The hound had just recovered from what we then called distemper, and was putting on weight. "There's a hound won't need training," he said, and offered to demonstrate. "Here, Sonny," he said to my fourteen-year-old son, "Go through that hole in the fence over yonder, and take a walk out through that pasture and sit down." My son did. We improvised a harness of rope, and while big Red strained to follow the boy, keeping his eyes on the hole in the fence, we attached a leash to the harness, and the Captain took the leash and went after my son. Red pulled the Captain to the fence, jumped through the hole, the Captain stepped through, and at once Red put his nose to the ground and trailed through cow and sheep tracks to the lad. Captain Millikin eventually owned this dog.

In principle, trail hounds do this naturally and should be encouraged to do it frequently until they show great zest and proficiency. Only then should they be punished for following what the hunter calls *trash*. Trash to a coon hunter may be fox, deer, rabbit, porcupine. Trash to a fox hunter can be coon, and trash to a beagler will be fox and coon as well as other game, but no insult is meant by a hunter who uses the word to other hunters whose hounds follow what would be trash to the first.

To punish—negative condition—properly and efficiently, one must be able to control his hound, and the hound must know what *Don't Touch!* means. The methods found most useful are: The one already mentioned, namely, take the dog home every time he runs trash; catch him and thrash him and take him home; use a training cord and scent of the "wrong" species. In the first two methods the hound is not controlled. The second method is quicker than the first.

In one fall, I broke six confirmed deer dogs which were also coon dogs from following deer by this method: We drove around at night to areas where we knew deer yarded. By turning a flashlight into such a field, we could pick up eye reflections. Attaching the training cord to a dog's collar, I took him into the field and said nothing. Long before we reached the precise spot where the deer was seen, the odor was generally strong enough for me to smell it. The hound took off on the trail, whereupon I called, *Don't Touch!*, hauled him to me and thrashed him properly with a limber switch. This is where most trainers stop. But in each case we had a fine trail ahead of us, a trail made to order. And when there was snow on the ground, it was all the better.

Taking the hound in a half circle of about 200 yards, so we could cross the deer's trail again, we walked until the hound grew excited and started pulling and baying, whereupon I called, *Don't Touch!*, hauled him in and thrashed him again. This was repeated going on the opposite side of the trail, thus having made an S, and punishing the hound each time he misbehaved. It requires only a few such treatments and the hound is "broke off" deer. If one session doesn't do it, there are other opportunities later.

Since rabbits run in circles, it is a simple matter to catch a hound on a rabbit track. Coonhounds which run foxes can be hunted in the daytime and if they run anything except squirrels or tree housecats, they can be negatively conditioned.

There have been a few dogs which learned to break other dogs of running trash. If you know of one and the owner will permit you to hunt with him, you will find no quicker way of conditioning in proper behavior. Spike, a cross of Farm Shepherd and Redbone, was one such dog. He would have no part of hunting anything but coons and bobcats. Nor would he permit another hound which we took hunting with us to run anything else. Before he stopped the other dog he apparently had to feel frustrated at not being able to hunt. If we were on a woods road listening, and Spike had covered the area in which the other dog was running a trail, Spike would become increasingly restless. He would run forward and back along the road and then, when his frustration reached a certain point, would plunge into the woods. Soon we would hear the misbehaving dog yelp and then all would be quiet. Out of the woods Spike would come with the other dog, tail hanging, close behind. Spike expected to be petted and he was.

Electricity can be applied effectively in many ways for negative conditioning (see Chapter XVIII). It is particularly effective in long distance training of hounds or dogs which are running off game. But in that use, is not safe except in the hands of an expert.

As soon as the dog has become accustomed to the weighted collar, it is changed for the collar with the receiver attached. In the North, the hound can be taken on the snow where the tracks are plainly visible. He is a cougar hound and starts off on a deer's trail. Not a word need be spoken but after he has run the trail a hundred yards or so, the trainer throws the switch and the shock knocks the dog down. He usually quits. But he may try again and feel the shock. An intelligent, not too stubborn dog associates the shock with the deer odor and quits after a few lessons. In most cases, after a time he responds again to deer scent and needs another lesson.

As you may realize, a dog can be quickly negatively conditioned against running the proper game if another trainer happens to be working in your area. The waves his device transmits to condition his fox hound against fox, can also condition yours against coons when your dog is wearing his receiver but doing the desired thing.

The Chemical Method. This is one which I think I originated. If others used it before I used it, I have not heard about it. My method is to take a hound at night where I can locate deers' eyes with a flashlight or my car lights. I say nothing to the hound, simply let him out of the car on a leash, fill a syringe with a small amount of apomorphine, inject it under his skin and let him go. Away he goes after the deer, but soon he begins to feel neauseated and vomits, feeling so sick he can't hunt and returns to the car. He associates deer scent with his sick feeling. It usually takes three doses before the dog no longer is enticed to follow a deer's scent.

If I am conditioning him against fox running. I have a companion lead a fox to make a trail, I inject the apomorphine and liberate the dog. Apomorphine is a prescription drug which must be obtained from a veterinarian or physician who will give you the proper dose for your dog depending on his weight.

BEAGLES

Beagles usually show trailing behavior as early as three months. Some show it first at five months.

The ideal method of conditioning a pack or litter of Beagles is to permit them to run "to their hearts' content," in an area well stocked with rabbits. Some of the top beaglers own farms remote from roads and give their pups free range. One can hear the merry voices of some puppies at almost any hour of the day or night. Others fence and stock areas.

Given the opportunity almost any Beagle will run a rabbit, but only a small percentage run it stylishly to conform to field trial requirements. Beaglers say they do not like to train their hounds, but because the dogs are small, easily reared and inexpensive, they prefer to let them "train themselves," and these men cull heavily, choosing only those dogs whose natural behavior on a track most closely approximates the rigid field trial specifications.

For these dogs, four signals are used: *Come, Down, Tallyho* and *Hark*. If you attend a field trial, you will hear these terms used.

Come. Already explained (Page 225) .

Down. The dog must drop on his belly and wait for the handler to pick him up. (See Page 214) .

Tallyho. When the rabbit is spotted the competitors take their dogs quickly to the hot line. Dogs learn this in the field because they are eager to find a line and after hearing their handler call the signal, they very soon associate it with their innate drive.

Hark. This is used as a whistle is used in other kinds of hunt-ing. It too is quickly learned because the handler uses it to call a dog to a line another dog has found.

For the individual dog, jumping out a rabbit and a signal *sic 'em* or *find 'em* with a lot of hiss in the use of the words will usually send the dog away after the bunny. The signal can be used when the dog makes a loss and at such points he feels you are with him, helping. If he is not gun shy he soon learns that the crack of your gun and the dying warm rabbit which he nuzzles are all part of the game.

More and more, beaglers who live in suburbs are using the spotlight method of conditioning, because by this means it is so easy to find the rabbits. Late at night, the men drive about subur-ban areas or country where they know rabbits are plentiful. A spotlight picks up a rabbit which will usually sit in its glare until the beagler carries his dog quite close. The dog sees the rabbit and chases, soon loses sight of it and thereafter must run by scent.

Since this is not a book on breeding, the findings and opinions of beaglers as to what faults constitute reasons for eliminating dogs are not appropriate here. Suffice it to say that one of the best methods that can be used to uncover undesirable characteristics is to run the dog in a pack. This conditions while at the same time it enables the handler to compare the dog's behavior with that of other dogs. If some of the pack misbehave and the dog being tested sturdily refuses to follow, he is a dog worth owning.

TREE HOUNDS

A fact not realized by city folks, who know about dogs chiefly from having attended dog shows, is that in America a type of hound called tree hound, coonhound, varmint dogs and other names constitutes one of the largest of all dog groups. Sport with them is enjoyed by thousands. Coonhound field trials rank first among the field trials of all kinds, over 1000 being held annually.

The dogs used are mainly of six breeds: Redbone, Bluetick, Black-and-tan, Plott, English and Treeing Walker. Each of these is a breed more numerically abundant than many registered in the American Kennel Club; these breeds being registeded by the United Kennel Club. The Black-and-tan of the U.K.C. has ears of medium length and is a fast hound quite different from the long-eared A.K.C. type and less inclined to run fox than the long-eared type.

With a little encouragement these hounds will be treeing the family cat or squirrels at the age of four months, but if let alone, the treeing aptitude shows itself at between seven and eight months of age. This was determined by turning different litters of Redbones into an acre lot in the center of which was a raccoon den. It was a tall cage with a tree trunk in its center and a hole in the trunk, into which the coons crawled, then downward to the nest. The dogs were turned out in the run in the morning. They did not see the coons, but could smell them. The coons were wild coon and kept themselves hidden when they knew dogs were near.

Possibly the behavior was allelomemitic. Often the first dog stood against the cage and barked up. It was probably the natural exhibition of the inherited behavior pattern. Some pups did not bark up for two weeks after the first littermate.

Bloodhounds, English Setters, a cross of Bloodhounds with Bull Terriers, never barked up naturally even though they were tested until a year or more of age. After so many generations of selection for the tree-barking aptitude, it would seem reasonable that the characteristic should be well established.

We are discussing the natural pattern; almost any dog can be taught to bark up. A dog of any breed seeing a cat run away from him, climb a tree and sit on a low limb will bark at the cat. Thousands of mongrels learn that way and are trained as coon *dogs,* not coon hounds. Mongrels even trail quite well by scent, but seldom do as well on cold trails as pure hounds, and many trail mutely.

A tree hound is practically useless if he will not bark tree. It is essential, therefore, in a tree hound's training that he be conditioned to bark tree. He will run a trail without conditioning but he may run trash: deer, fox, rabbit, skunk, armadillo, sheep, cattle, horses, and other animals. So the hound must be educated to ignore all but tree animals. The discrimination in time can be confined to treeing only one species of tree animals. A hound owned by my son trailed only male coons, a feat quite unusual. I could follow with my hounds in the same territory and my hounds would tree the females my son's hound had left.

Conditioning a dog to tree should be the first step in tree dog or tree hound education.

To Train a Dog to Bark Tree. In chapter XVII you found some hints on getting a dog to bark. As we have seen, a well conditioned tree dog should follow the trail of his game until the animal has climbed a tree, and should then stand at the foot of the tree and bark tree. Nor is it difficult to condition a dog to do this, while at the same time helping to make a first class tree dog of him. Having trained many very proficient night and tree dogs, I can assure you the following method based on modern knowledge is efficient. It can be useful for any breed of dog, but only one who needs to know more about dogs would begin to train any but a dog of a breed bred for the purpose.

If your dog does not respond to *Speak* by barking, see that he does. In this task, starving is entirely unnecessary, because he will respond to his drives to trail, or to chase, even when his appetite has been satisfied. In this case, we are conditioning a drive. We suppose your dog is to be trained for squirrels.

The equipment you need is a gun, a cage made of light wire, a light rope long enough to reach over a limb high up on a tree, and touch the ground while you hold the other end. Put a live squirrel in the cage and have a recently shot dead squirrel, with a small cord attached to its neck. Attach the cage with the squirrel in it to the rope and pull it up to about seven feet from the ground.

Have an assistant hold your dog far enough away from the tree with the cage so he cannot see it. While your friend is holding the dog, you show him the dead squirrel, but shake it to make it appear lifelike, and back away from the dog, pulling the squirrel by the string. When you have reached the tree, call, and your assistant will liberate the dog which will follow the trail to the tree, and looking up, see the squirrel in the cage. To excite him to bark tree, pull the cage up and down. When he jumps for it, pull it up and let it down again to excite him more, and encourage him to *Speak!* After a minute or two of this, pull the cage up into the tree and shoot. Wait a moment, then throw the dead squirrel which you have concealed in your coat, up high in the tree. When it drops out, let your dog shake it. Some hunters skin the squirrel and let their hounds eat it, doing this once a day while hunting. But feeding a squirrel is not at all necessary. Once your dog learns that you will generally shoot out the game, seeing and hearing you do so is all the reinforcement he needs; his behavior will soon become habitual.

If your dog is to trail and tree coons and possums, you need a wild small coon with a collar attached, a lead stick so the coon cannot reach your legs to claw or bite you. You need four or five feet square of two inch hexagonal mesh chicken wire. Also, about 40 feet of one-eighth inch steel cable. Find four trees about 15 feet apart on a square. Cut the cable in half, and thread each piece through the rough edge of the chicken wire, leaving 7 feet at each end to wrap around the trees. Attach the cables to the four trees, eight feet from the ground, so you have a small trampoline above your head, right in the center of the square of trees.

Now, go to work while an assistant holds the dog. Let him see the coon, which you lead away from him, while he makes frantic efforts to follow.

When you get to your objective, let the coon crawl up a tree, and then assist him out onto the wire mesh and let go of him. The coon will not try to escape. Call to liberate the dog. The trail will lead to the tree, and the dog will look up. He can't escape seeing the coon. As he jumps and barks at the coon, that animal will walk about on the wire, with an up and down springy effect, which will tantalize the hound. Let the dog bark and jump, until he appears to be tiring, and then shoot the coon between the eyes. If he doesn't fall off his trampoline, push him off with a stick. There is less to be gained by permitting a dog to attack and kill a live coon than to shake a dead one.

Two such training periods will be all any keen hound needs. I trained two Redbone puppies who were nine months old in this way. Neither ever ran any off game (trash), and together they treed eighty coons, which we took, before the pups were two years old.

Your next job is to let a coon climb a real tree, but one in which you can see him. The dog will probably do a good job on this coon, too. Now you climb the tree, and shake out the coon while your assistant holds the dog. When the coon has a good start, liberate the dog. The coon, hearing him coming, will climb another tree, and this time, shoot the coon out.

The pupil is now ready for night hunting. You can take him with another sure coonhound, or by himself to where you are sure there are coons. He will do the rest, up to where the coon climbed a tree, or is lost in a hole or rock ledge. If you start your dog this way, he will be better grounded than he will in any other way that I have learned.

He must be trained, of course, to discriminate among the odors of all other animals and tree only raccoons, bobcats or whatever game you hunt.

A raccoon may have meandered over several miles before a keen coonhound runs across his trail. Working it out, slowly at first, is a joy to watch. As the trail becomes fresher to the hound, he can run faster. At this point, some neophyte hunters conclude that the hound has jumped the coon and that the animal is running. Observing the course the hound has covered, leads one to that conclusion but it is seldom warranted. The hound is simply following a fresh trail, following it where the coon went when he was not being pursued. The curious raccoon ambles along on a most extraordinary track and every hunter should take this into consideration.

Occasionally a three-footed coon, unable to climb a tree, will lead a hound for hours. Indeed, one of my hounds tracked one for four hours, a coon we saw in our flashlight beams several times. Yes, it is possible for one to elude a hound, but such chases are rare. Any good, trained hound will follow such a trail at a fast gait. The point is this: When you have a newly conditioned hound he may need much encouragement on stale tracks. Encourage him and don't conclude that, because the trail goes through culverts or over fallen logs that the coon is playing tricks; no lower animal makes plans ahead to such an extent.

But how encourage? You have already conditioned your hound to associate the words "get him" or "find," with following a trail. As you catch up to him on his difficult trail tell him, *get him* and put feeling into your voice. He will soon feel you are part of his pack and work harder because of it.

When a dog sees you, or one of your party climb a tree, this cooperation on your part also makes you one of his pack. The rifle shot or the sound of a pistol shot high in the tree and the dying coon falling out all become associated and make him a surer dog.

For those interested in coonhound field trials, I suggest a perusal of the section on training your dog *To Bark*.

MAN TRAILERS

I am not ashamed to say that training man trailers and tree hounds has occupied more of my time than any other kind of training, unless we count the training for the usual kennel manners which all dogs should have. But training the above two classes of dogs embodies so many kinds of training that the experience has equipped me to handle the simpler kinds of canine education more easily.

Any dog of any breed can be taught to man trail, but only a few breeds of dogs have demonstrated superiority at the work. These are Bloodhounds, Long Eared American Foxhounds (registered as Coonhounds by the American Kennel Club), Basset hounds, Redbone Coonhounds (which have Bloodhounds in their ancestry), and cross breeds among the above. I'm sure I could train a Toy Manchester Terrier, or a German Shepherd, but when I was finished with all I could do, I'd still not have a proficient man trailer.

In principle, Bloodhound conditioning differs only from that of other trail hounds in the initial discrimination. Lest you happen to be one who still feels the breed name means trailer-of-blood, be assured that this is not the case. Centuries ago the word *blood* was synonomous with *heredity*. They spoke of the blooded horse, blue blooded human beings; the Bloodhound name signified the pure hound, the acme of hound breeding. No blood is needed on a trail. Blood is ignored as I have observed in several murder cases on which I have used my hounds.

The success of a man trail depends principally on the start. A Bloodhound is not often used in man trailing until all other

Redbone Coonhound, one of the superior trailing breeds.

Cross of Airedale with Bloodhound, an excellent trailer, alert, courageous. This cross would be excellent for police work.

Capt. Volney G. Mullikin of Kentucky, the greatest man hunter that ever lived. Captain Mullikin's work with his Bloodhounds accounted for more than 2,500 convictions.

means of locating a human being are exhausted. Usually hundreds of human beings have tramped an area hunting a lost person and the Bloodhound must follow one trail—the oldest—among them all.

He must be permitted to smell the odor of the person whose trail he is to follow and conditioned to ignore all other human trails which are in the same path or which cross the trail he is following. That dogs can do this is no more amazing than the fact a wolf can pursue a single Caribou trail through the tracks left by a herd. We lack anything like the capacity to differentiate odors to such a degree but the hound possesses it and the hundreds of successful human trails followed by Bloodhounds attest to this almost incredible capacity.

In my book *Bloodhounds and How to Train Them,* I detailed three methods to condition a man trailer. To reiterate: The ordinary method of following many trails with a "reward" (as I said then) at the end; the missing member method; the quick method.

The usual method consisted of using the hound's drive to trail as his incentive. The garment of the person to be trailed was dropped by the runner. The dog was taken with head held high to a point close to the garment, the leash transferred from the collar to the harness and the dog was told *Find Him.* He started off first on a short trail and the runner fed him when he was located. Three or four trails were run consecutively, always with the same runner. The method worked; I should know because I trained many highly successful Bloodhounds that way.

The missing member method involved taking the dog and runner in a car to the place where the trail was to start. The dog knew the runner had his food and he was eager to get it—being thirty-six hours hungry. The dog saw the runner leave and disappear into the woods or around the bend in a woods road. Fifteen minutes later the dog followed the man's trail and got his meal, or part of it if several trails were run. After six or eight such experiences, the runner was sent ahead but some of his clothing was carried beside the dog on the way to where the trail began. While the handler kept the dog in the car, he took the clothing and placed it where he wanted to start the dog. It need not be at the very beginning of the trail; ten or a dozen feet away would suffice. The clothing substituted for the runner and the dog whose head is dropped over the clothing as he hears the words *Find Him,* finds the trail and follows it.

Naturally each trail is made older. After a dozen such trails, another person rides in the car, as well as the clothing of the man to be trailed and the hound gets his first lesson in discrimination. The man is let off to walk along the same path as the runner, who has left a trail half an hour earlier. By the time he is out of sight the car is driven back to the starting point, the clothes placed on the ground and the hound started. The man who was let off takes a short walk turning off the trail after 100 feet and waits only a short distance from the trail. The hound should ignore him. If he does not, much more trailing is needed.

A proper Bloodhound leash is an old fashioned horse rein with about twelve or fifteen inches of chain at the end. For negative conditioning along a trail, a slap with the leash causes the chain to strike the hound's back. If he becomes more interested in trees where dogs have left their identification, a light slap and a *Don't Touch* soon eradicates that reaction when trailing. The kind of Bloodhound which is most successful is so intense on getting to the end of the trail that nothing else matters.

After he shows he knows that the clothing scent, and not a rider, is the trail to follow, the runner should run trails where people walk, and the hound, an hour later be able to follow the right trail—to unscramble the odors in his nose and brain, and respond accordingly—the one of many odors is his stimulus.

The third method which is quicker and requires much less physical exertion from the handler but does require most patience, involves conditioning in an empty building such as a garage. Since my original book was written, I have learned that a building or large bare room with two entrances is preferable to one with only one entrance.

By this method, discrimination is taught first with the knowledge that the dog does not need to be taught to trail; that is part of his built-in mental equipment—one of his drives.

Two persons are used. One enters by one door and walks to a position at the back of the room. The other enters by the other door and leaves a shoe in the doorway. He stands beside the other person. The dog is brought to the door with the shoe, he hears the signal, *Find Him* and his head is dropped so his nose goes down over the shoe. Now so far as odor goes, the shoe is superfluous but it is part of a chain reaction that you will use later. The odor is so strong the dog doesn't need the shoe.

You lead him across the room to the person who matches the shoe and the dog gets a tidbit which both persons have previously handled, the reason for which is obvious.

The hound is led out and in a few minutes the action is repeated. After four or five trials, the "lost person" changes places with the other. At least twenty repetitions should be conducted the first day by which time the hound will have perhaps half of his appetite satisfied.

I have trained Bloodhounds which "caught on" during the first session while others—possibly because of some ineptitude of my own—took five. Gradually the errors become fewer, however, and we find a typical curve of learning emerging, with the improvement becoming markedly rapid at the end. This is when the dog seemingly "catches on."

When he makes no errors, four persons are employed. I found that it was especially useful to have them at first stationed well apart. When the dog makes no errors, group them together. The dog will then stand before the right one and wait for his reinforcement. This is useful in actual trailing because if a dog is trailing a man who is found standing among a group of persons, the dog will go straight to him and wait for his tidbit; thus providing positive identification.

Having learned to connect the initial odor on which his head dropped with the person who gives him tidbits, every dog I have conditioned followed his first trail unerringly. This consisted of my four "fugitives" walking single file along a path in the woods. The one whose shoe or other garment is left behind, turns off the path and walks fifty yards, more or less, and waits while the others go on for 100 yards along the path.

The Bloodhound's head is held high. The leash is transferred to his harness, he is led to the garment which had preferably not been dropped directly in the path, his head is dropped as you say

Find Him, and he is away with you, the handler, jogging behind. He may over-run the turnoff of the fugitive, but do not speak to him. Within twenty-five feet, he may whirl and unless you are alert, spin you off balance, as he goes back to find the missing odor. When he does find it and follows to the end, the fugitive should not only give him his generous tidbit but both fugitive and handler express their happiness at the achievement.

This should be repeated a dozen times in different places at each session. But do not change fugitives that day. Each day thereafter, use a different fugitive and increase the length and time of the run. When you are up to a half a mile and your assistants have left an hour before you and the hound start out, he is as good as trained.

Because several golf courses are available in our area, I found there was no better place to test a dog. Early in the morning, my fugitive took a walk around at least half of a course and sometimes, using a map, through the entire eighteen holes, ending up near the clubhouse. All day, golfers played over his foot tracks. In the evening when the course was deserted, I would start my hound. It would take me half an hour or more, depending on the length of the course. With a strong hound tugging a man along he can jog at eight to ten miles an hour. After I had left, my fugitive drove to the clubhouse, left his car and waited at the end of the trail he had made.

The hound had to follow through the maze of invisible tracks for three to five miles until he found his man. Every trained dog I sold had performed this feat. All made good except one. He was sold to a Negro penitentiary superintendent in Arkansas. The buyer wrote me he would not trail, but he liked the dog. I had to be in Arkansas, so I stopped to learn the difficulty. The hound, even in my hands, would not trail a Negro. So we had the Superintendent lay a trail and the hound trailed meticulously. I sold him then to Captain V. G. Millikin who followed twelve trails, seventy-two hours old and dozens of easier ones with the dog making finds and convictions on all. These hunts were scattered over the period of his life.

Bloodhounds are useful in locating drowned persons. In my experience I found several. The odor apparently rises to the top of the water. My dogs have jumped into streams and ponds where the water was still, but where persons have been drowned in moving water they have only led to river edges. The trail ends at the bank, or perhaps a spring board from which the person or persons either jumped or fell.

In a narrow river, however, the dog can often easily trail along the shore, for enough of the body odor clings to the edges to make it appear to be a trail. So it pays for a professional to condition his man trailers to water. Sometimes when a fugitive wades or swims a narrow river, the trail may appear to run along the bank when actually it is the chemical emanations from his body clinging to the stream's bank, in which case the trail fades and the handler realizes why the hounds have been mistaken.

The starting being so important, every well conditioned hound should be acquainted with as wide a diversity of starting paraphernalia as possible. You may often be called to start from the driver's seat of an automobile, from a wrench or gun handled by the fugitive, from underclothing or bed sheets of a lost person.

What the hound trails is not the shoe scent as has been amply demonstrated by my own hounds. I trailed one murderer who broke into a home and left his shoes, changing to a pair of knee length rubber boots. This did not deter the hounds in the least, for we followed him over a mile after that.

It is also well to understand that a hound's memory for scents is excellent but that since he is so used to being taken home when a trail ends at a road or a lake's edge, he becomes conditioned to regard that as the end of his job. Every professional Bloodhound should be conditioned to expect to follow the trail again when he recognizes it. If the fugitive rows a boat across a lake, the hound should be taken in another boat, rowed across, or taken in a car to the nearest point on the other shore and be told *Find Him* as he walks along the shore. If the boat is there, he can be started again from it.

This is not a book on Bloodhounds, but on principles and further refinements of man trailing will occur to every handler as he works with his hounds.

All Bloodhound work, like all of the work with trailing hounds, is simply conditioning a drive. The force system almost always fails when applied to trying to force dogs to prevert their natural propensities. At least two dozen Bloodhounds I sold as puppies in the past were given to training kennels to train and every one was ruined. At first they were forced into "obedience training" and then expected to trail. Actually, the long chases behind a Bloodhound while he is becoming efficient are a lot of work, which also accounts for the scarcity of expert man trailers. Many people buy Bloodhounds, but do most of the training sitting comfortably in a chair, thinking about it. I sold 60 puppies one year, and after a year wrote to the buyers. Not one had made a man trailer of a dog, although a few had started. Actually, it is wonderful fun and a trained Bloodhound has many uses. When our children were off in the woods behind our home, we often tied a note to a hound's collar and gave him a scent. The dog would trail to the youngster who read the note, and came home.

To Condition for Car Hunting. Where game may be scarce, or hunters tired, or where they consider car hunting more efficient, hundreds of dogs are conditioned to hunt ahead of a car. The method of locating game tracks is used by coon-, fox-, bobcat-, deer hunters but mostly by the first. On lonesome back roads, relatively free from traffic, one man drives, the owner of the hound walks with the dog with the car close behind. The dog soon goes well ahead. At this point the owner waits for the car to catch up and then rides on the mudguard. If the dog hesitates, the owner gets off and walks. When the dog is confident the owner is coming, the owner then rides inside and watches, calling out, encouragement if the dog seems to lose confidence. When the dog crosses a trail, his actions are visible to the hunters who park the car and follow the dog on foot after they ascertain where the trail leads. One evening's experience is sufficient for this conditioning.

Chapter XXII

CONDITIONING BIRD DOGS

RETRIEVERS

THE SAME PRINCIPLES apply to training for bird retrieving as applied to retrieving a golf ball or newspaper from the front porch (see Page 228). In this case, more firmness is required and a greater response to signals.

Certain standard equipment is necessary as well as standard behavior, because if a retriever is to compete in a field trial, his handler must follow established rules. Moreover, it is much easier to train a dog of a breed selected for generations for bird interest and retrieving ability than to train a Fox Terrier or a German Shepherd. Also we have water to contend with and natural water dogs are usually easier to train in water than dogs of non-water-going breeds.

The equipment consists of a choke collar—one which tightens about the dog's neck when he strains at the leash—at least two whistles, preferably emitting the same sound (one is a spare), a cord to go around your neck to hold a whistle, a leash about 18 inches long, a long cord and/or "belt cord" as it is usually called. A six foot long piece of belt lacing is excellent. Make a 3 inch loop in one end through which to pass your belt. The other end of the cord is slipped through the D in the dog's collar and the end is held by you, the trainer. In conditioning your dog to retrieve you need only drop the end and your dog is free. Lastly, you will need dummies to be retrieved. These are canvas or leather bags about three or four inches in diameter and a foot long. They can be had from any ship chandler where they are sold for attaching around the sides of boats for protection against the sides in mooring. Or you can make them of tough canvas and stuff them with fine shavings. Some trainers fasten a foot long cord to one end. If a dog carries with his head low, he steps on the cord, so it tends to cause him to retrieve with head held high. Actual training consists of steps. He must *Come* on command. *Sit, Stay, Heel, Retrieve, Hold, Drop, Go On or Back,* some word to start the dog, and *Over.*

We have discussed means of conditioning to *Come, Sit, Stay, Retrieve,* but here we have a specialized form of retrieving. Also, the judges in a retriever trial like to see a retriever when told to Heel, walk to the rear of the handler, but to one side, as far back as one's heels in walking. Then too, retrievers are taught to respond to a whistle rather than to words. Two blasts in retriever trials means *Come* (see Page 225).

The well-conditioned retriever does not come in with his bird and drop it at the handler's feet; he holds it sitting before the handler. In his case the retriever is trained by not exchanging the tidbit for the dummy or bird for increasingly longer periods, while the handler says *Hold.*

Where you want your pupil to give his retrieve to you, well knowing that he then will receive his reinforcement, you can say *Thanks,* or as most retriever men say, *Drop It.* This does not mean literally to spit it out, rather to release his hold so the handler can easily take it from the dog's mouth.

Retrievers' trainers expect their dogs to have retrieved a dummy hundreds or thousands of times during the course of the dog's education. One of my clients made a specialty of training his Golden Retrievers to retrieve under as many different conditions as possible. One day he threw a dummy 60 times in our parking lot.

The signal used in field trails for the dog to start may be any the handler wishes, but more and more only the dog's name is used. He has been held back with the belt cord and is eager to run. It amounts to a release. Teaching this signal is practically unnecessary because you will use it so many times, as you wave your hand forward, that the pupil becomes conditioned automatically.

If all of the separate items of behavior have been mastered, the whole complicated performance seems like a single act. When the dog retrieves well on dry land, he is ready to have his lessons in retrieving birds. In our section the retriever men use pigeons for the first live birds.

A pistol with blank cartridges is employed at this point and some trainers use it along with the dummy. As the dummy is in the air, the pistol is discharged. The dog sees the dummy drop and associates the sound with the fall.

Pigeons, which may be obtained from a poultry market, are used effectively. The belt cord should be used at the start. A bird's neck is broken, the bird thrown, the pistol discharged and the dog told to go. He can scarcely help retrieving the bird just as he did the dummy because of his conditioning. The same bird can be used several times. This is sight retrieving. When you know your dog has a soft mouth, use a pigeon with clipped wings; the fluttering excites the dog.

Now come lessons in finding the bird by scent. Naturally you need a field with low growing bushes such as an old blueberry pasture or one with hardhack bushes. Throw the bird and your dog will see it until it drops in the bushes. At your signal to go, he will have to find it with his nose.

To increase the distance it will require an assistant who will throw the bird or dummy. Some trainers have the assistant do the shooting and they probably have good reasons, such as thus preventing dogs from becoming gun-shy, but this is not necessary because the dog can be accustomed to the sound in his early conditioning.

For field trial work, the dog must be trained to the sound of the gun being discharged by a person other than the handler and at a distance; for personal hunting the dog is usually in a blind with the owner, and the gunblast is close. A dog trained first for personal hunting can be conditioned later to a field trial etiquette.

The pupil may at first retrieve to the assistant but will hear you blow twice and if the assistant pays him no attention the dog will retrieve to you. The distance of retrieves should exceed 150 yards before you finish this stage of his education.

You are now ready for double retrieving. Again, go back to the area of clear visibility. Toss out a dummy or a bird fifteen or twenty yards away, another five or ten yards in a direction about ninety degrees from the first toss, all the while holding the dog on your belt cord. Let him see you swing your arm as you toss the short bird and that, being the latter, is the one he will retrieve first. That over, wave your arm in the direction of the long bird and say *Back* and he will dash out to that one and retrieve it.

Many a puppy, first learning double retrieving, will try to bring both dummies to his handler. If a dog in competition tries it or brings both birds in, he is automatically disqualified. This is called *crossing over*. The way to stop it quickly, in a neophyte, is to toss the first dummies in opposite directions, at 180 degrees from each other, instead of 90.

When he is proficient at the job, work him in brush on doubles until he follows the same routine by scent and at the next training period employ two assistants, one short, say thirty yards away, the other at fifty yards, first in the open and then in the cover where he must search. Your arm gesture and *Back* will send him forward. It may require several weeks to accomplish his thorough training to this point.

Now comes the lesson in water retrieving. If you have not accustomed your dog to water, do so. He must love it. He will splash about the edge, swim with you, retrieve sticks. But if he does not by nature do these things, don't give up. Rather, get him to love it by showing him there is nothing to fear and fun to be had.

Coming out of the water, your dog may drop his retrieve and shake. Every retriever trainer has had this problem and knows that prevention consists of being right at the water's edge to take the retrieve and give the reinforcement before the dog can drop his retrieve. Each time the dog comes in, the handler is a little farther back. He expects his pupil will shake as soon as he has delivered the retrieve, so is prepared for the shaking.

The stylish retriever does not hesitate to jump in the water. One of my friends, who was especially successful, trained his dogs along a river bank. At one point the shore was a beach, upstream the shore was increasingly higher above the water. The dogs were first trained on the beach, then to jump off a point two feet above the water and next they made a four foot jump. The last was at least eight feet high and the dogs would land with a great splash, but loved it. A pond with a steep bank also makes an excellent training area. The retriever should make a run for it and without hesitation jump into the water.

Since your retriever, when retrieving live game, will be working among decoys, you should accustom him to be at home among them. If he becomes confused upon finding himself swimming among a lot of them and tries to retrieve one, you can call *Don't Touch* or *No,* whistle him in and toss your retrieve beyond them. In this way you can encourage him to *Back,* which to him, means keep going. After he has swum past decoys he will no longer be confused by them.

As the retrieves become longer, have an assistant in a boat toss the dummy and when the pupil is fully proficient, use two assistants and again double retrieves as you did on land. Make the retrieves in water without obstructions, one close, the other more distant and at an angle to the first.

The next stage is, of course, retrieving in water with obstructions where he uses his nose.

When pigeons are used they often land with wings outstretched and any retriever is likely to pick it up by the wing. Therefore, experienced trainers tie the wings to the birds' sides. A piece of Scotch Tape will do the job and then the dog picks up the body, not a wing.

When you next come to the live bird stage, do not shoot a shot gun over the dog; it is better to accustom him to the blast from a distance. Your assistant can do this from a position perhaps fifty feet away. Again the retriever sees the bird go up, hears the shot, sees the bird drop. He will probably try to break for it but your belt cord will restrain him.

Pheasants come next, provided you can obtain a few. In double training you can use them many times but at first with wings tied down. In double training use a dead one as the distant bird, a live one, shot, as the close bird.

Ducks are last. Tie the wings, legs and neck. The retriever may again hold the bird by the wings but much more likely by the body because he learns quickly that the wings are an awkward handle. You can use a duck many times provided the dog doesn't crush it.

Blind retrieving is next in your dog's conditioning. Assuming that he responds to one whistle toot by looking at you, you can now use signals.

Later in your training, you will have to condition your dog to respond to a hand signal and come to you. This can be taught while accepting the retrieve. Bend slightly and extend your arm toward him and draw it backward at your side. After he has brought the dummy fifty or 100 times, seeing your arm movement will cause him to come whether he is retrieving or not.

Field trials have their own language. Three words are used to accompany hand signals. Actually the words do more to please the trainer, they are not necessary to the dog. If the handler wants his dog to go farther on than where he is the word *Back,* is accompanied with hand motion. It is assumed that the dog is looking at the handler. The other word used is *Over* together with a hand signal to have him move right or left.

To train the dog to associate the hand signal with the word, you need scarcely be told of the need for repetition. Condition your dog to the signals, *Over* and *Back* in any order you desire. Start him sitting before you and back away so that twenty or thirty feet separate you. Toss the dummy off to his left and, while he is looking at you, move your hand with a throwing motion and say *Over.* Repeat this forty times. At the next session, work him twenty times left and switch to thirty times the right. Next session work him twenty times right and thirty times back when you toss the dummy over his head. Next time work him twenty times back and then try all three signals in any order using only the words without motions.

He should be ready to retrieve any one of three dummies you throw in approximately the same positions he has been used to. This makes a showy performance and is much easier to accomplish than one might think. Pigeons can now be planted in cover, your dog taken into the area and by hand and voice signal told which direction to retrieve. No retriever needs to be shown how to locate game with his nose; all you need do is guide him reasonably close to where it lies.

Confusion results where the same area, especially in water, is repeatedly used because game odor may persist over the whole section. This is especially true where the birds are plentiful and you are hunting from a blind or competing in a field trial. Thus conditioning to hand signals is especially valuable. He already knows that your arm extended toward him and then drawn backward as you bend slightly means to come to you. If he does not, practice him in it using reinforcements and the words *Come In*.

With all of this conditioning accomplished, your task now is to be sure you can control your pupil under any and all ordinary circumstances. He must stop when you blow one toot on your whistle no matter how eager he is to get to the fallen game. You must be able to have him go on when you give him the *Back* signal. Should he pass it by in his excitement or exuberance, he must stop at the whistle toot, look at you and come toward you at two toots.

But for all of the seeming complexity the whole picture, composed of its separate conditioned parts, is actually the simplest kind of training especially because we work with a dog whose behavior patterns are so ideally adapted to the actions expected of him.

The foregoing are the basic responses. There are refinements to be sure. Watch a retriever trial, read the many retriever books and especially read the elaborate American Kennel Club's Rules Governing Retriever Field Trials which may be had by writing that organization at 51 Madison Ave., New York, N. Y. From these you can get ideas and really *work your dog;* don't train him by only thinking about it.

In an actual field trial competition, the dogs may have to have demonstrated their technique in as many as a dozen different situations on land and in water. These range from easy to difficult. The judges arrange beforehand what these situations will be, in order to eliminate as many as possible in the early stages of the contest and run the diminishing number of contestants through the difficult later events.

In the 1960 National Trials, fifty-five contestants had dwindled to thirteen for the last event. The first situation—a simple one—involved retrieving three ducks. Two were shot over water; one of these was dropped among decoys. A third was planted on the opposite shore of a pond. A second test was the finding of a hidden bird 125 yards away while bypassing a marked pheasant lying close by.

The best dog does not always win. Luck plays an important role; a sudden slight gust of wind can mean all the difference, as it can in bird dog competitions of all sorts.

The point is that the dog should be conditioned for as many varieties of situations as he is likely to encounter. It pays to work the dogs diligently because the top dogs here have sold for between $5,000 and $10,000.

UPLAND BIRD DOGS

The desired actions of any of the several breeds of dogs developed by selection to possess certain distinctive, inherited behavior patterns in hunting upland birds, are quite standard. The exceptions are the spaniels whose modes of action differ somewhat and are used differently. They too were bred for their work.

A well-trained pointing bird dog should hunt for birds with his nose, stop and point in the direction of the game bird while showing as much style as possible. He should point until the bird is flushed, shot and drops, at which point, at the owner's command, he should retrieve the dead or injured bird to the handler.

This, of course, applies to the personal hunter. Retrieving is no longer a part of the expected behavior in the big horseback field trials. The trainers find it difficult to hold a good retriever steady to shot and wing. Occasionally, one finds a dog steady, particularly if the bird is not killed, but if one falls the dog breaks. Training to be steady to shot and wing is much easier when retrieving is not part of his act.

Many books have been written on the subject of training dogs of these breeds but I have seen none which consciously applies any psychological short cuts.

What needs can we use to condition bird dogs? Hunger is one but, as useful as that is, the need of the dog to fulfill the innate urge to hunt can be even more useful to us. Watch a pen of Pointer or English Setter puppies when a butterfly flutters over them; every puppy is dancing in rapt attention and soon is trying to catch it. Giving these pups the opportunity to pursue their desire is an excellent incentive. Couple this drive with hunger, which one can also slowly satisfy, and we have enough basis for conditioning for all of the things we want our bird dogs to do.

Retrieving can be established using food. So can the refinements leading up to field work, such as *Sit, Heel,* and such responses to signals as will cause the pupil to jump into his crate in the car.

Equipment for training is a whistle, a training cord and some pigeons. For preliminary training: A long fish pole with six feet of line on the end of which is a bird's wing.

Older dogs which have run wild on farms until they were several years old have been successfully trained but the easiest pupil is a four months old puppy. At this age the bird interest has become pronounced.

We have already discussed ordinary obedience training. Here we condition a bird dog. And it depends on our use for the dog, how we condition him. For horseback field trials, where dogs make great reputations? Or to be a personal hunting dog? The former rushes off at liberation along with his brace mate and finds his birds while traveling at top speed. The personal hunter works closely, quartering back and forth and paying attention to his handler. Because the big field trial winners become in demand as sires, bird dog men with bitches to breed have been sending them to these winners; with the result that the general bird dog population is tending more and more to be wide goers, and today it is becoming increasingly difficult to buy puppies which tend to be close workers.

For the "walking" field trials of many parts of the country the bird field where the birds are planted is usually small so the fast close worker is at no disadvantage in competition with the racer who may over run birds. The close worker is a joy to the walking man carrying his gun who wants to bring home the birds.

Before you start, you should decide which kind of dog you want and buy or breed that type of pup. Start him learning your signals, verbal, whistle or motion at about four months of age. Start by leash-breaking.

Dangle the bird wing above him in his pen and try to let him catch it. He'll love it. Keep it up until he seems to be tiring. Do this for several sessions once a day.

The next lesson is to respond to the word *Whoa.* Using the fish pole and bird wing, attach a four or five foot cord to the pup's collar and, holding him with your left hand, the pole handle in your right, dangle the wing out in front of him letting it touch the ground and move it to make it appear alive. The pup will try to lunge at it, when you quickly flick it away.

With your training cord holding him, you can teach the signal *Whoa* at an early age and control him nicely.

Take him where there are birds and let him dash about hunting them. Birds will flush out but he can't catch them. Simply giving him the opportunity to hunt is reinforcement enough. Do not restrain him until he has learned to hunt. A good bird dog is interested in body scent of the birds and hunts with head high. Should you have obtained one which is more interested in following trails than body scenting, he is a poor prospect for conditioning unless you are interested only in pheasants. Grouse especially will crouch quietly when they know a bold energetic dog is moving rapidly about, but a slow trailing dog will cause them to move.

The field trial dog is expected to *go Away* at two sharp whistle toots, therefore in the early loose field work, toot twice every time you give the dog his freedom. Later on two toots will cause him to work wider and sometimes faster.

If you have taught your hunter to respond to the word *Come,* you should condition him to also respond to a long drawn out whistle blast. It calls off the hunt in that area and in field trials gets your dog out of the field to make room for the next contestants.

If you plan to use a whistle at below freezing temperatures, buy one made of plastic because a metal one will stick to your lips.

Part—an essential part—of every well bred bird dog's natural behavior is the pause he makes before attempting to catch a bird. (Bird dog men call this "Flash" pointing.) Many fine pointers learn by themselves; they have raced and tried to catch so many birds and found they could not that they have given up and simply point.

After some training of the extension of the "flash" point into a long steady point there is evidence that the dog actually becomes hypnotized. There are records of both Pointers and Setters having pointed so long, that they have become stiff. A gun's blast quickly frees them from this state.

Many, if not most trainers, give their dogs freedom and hope and wait for the time when their pup will point at a place close enough so they can snap a leash on the collar and stroke the pupil who is fulfilling his drive to hunt birds. Strangely enough, a pointing dog does not like to be pushed from behind toward his bird. If you place your hand quickly on his rear and push him toward the bird he is pointing, it tends to make him staunch on point. The method is used by experts. It is only a part of the training. If you are there close to him and also interested in the bird with him, you become part of his pack and he is happy to work with you. After a minute or two, you flush the bird and liberate the dog who dashes after it and, if the wind is right, is more than likely to point it again.

Now he must become conditioned to long points and what a gun's blast means and to "steady to shot and wing." If you have conditioned your pupil with the fish pole and wing, to respond to *Whoa,* you now proceed to use it in steadying. When he is pointing a planted pigeon, snap a ten foot long checkcord on his collar. Shoot a twenty-two gauge blank pistol. Or, better still, have a companion flush it. Say *Whoa.* If he does not respond but, instead, bolts for the bird, upset him when he comes to the end of the cord. Repeat the act as often as he bolts. At the next session use a larger bore gun, but don't shoot close to him. After he associates a bird dropping with the gun's report, you can graduate to a twelve gauge shot gun.

If you want him to retrieve it, then you must condition him as explained previously (Page 271). If he does retrieve you will get many wounded birds you might otherwise miss.

In order to reinforce those dogs which show a lack of interest in birds, some trainers shoot one, pluck it and hide it for another point, throw it like a flush and let the dog eat it. This is not recommended for dogs to be trained to retrieve where soft mouths are essential.

SPANIELS

This section applies to Springer and Cocker Spaniels, not to Brittany, which are classed along with Setters and Pointers. The Spaniel field trials have become quite standardized and one wishes their numbers would increase greatly because they are a kind of field trial which many Spaniel owners can compete in and thoroughly enjoy. Fortunately, the Springer owners have not made the mistake the Cocker show enthusiasts made and demanded a dense long wooly coat which makes them completely impractical as hunters. There still are, though few in numbers, enough of the old flat coated dogs remaining so that Cocker field trial enthusiasts can have their wonderful sport.

The field trial spaniel is not necessarily a pointing dog. He is a hustler who gets about in the brush and flushes birds which his handler shoots and the dog retrieves. Whereas a Pointer or Setter which drops his head and trails is no longer wanted, a spaniel does hunt in this way, almost as a hound hunts.

Spaniel training starts with retrieving (see Page 227) and responding to whistles or words. They are active dogs and when turned out in bird country, busy themselves scooting about. Rabbits run ahead of them and Springers especially follow them as a Beagle does. All Spaniels, surprising a deer, which jumps out of its hiding, will pursue it for awhile. But their chief love is birds, for which they have been bred by generations of selection. Even the show spaniels which for generations have been only pets, when taken into the field, show that the breed has not lost its propensity.

So in Spaniel training, the retrieving is generally taught first and you know how to do it. The next conditioning is quartering. A spaniel working properly stays within twenty-five to forty yards from his handler and moves back and forth ahead of him, covering all the area. It is better to hold him close enough so that if he flushes a bird, it will be close enough to you to drop it with a shot. A dog too far out will also have his bird too far, often for you to shoot effectively.

The same applies to the quartering distance to the side. It should not exceed twenty-five yards but that depends somewhat on the wind's direction. You are going to condition to quartering first with a dummy which your pupil is going to have to smell.

Assuming you have conditioned him to follow arm signals in retrieving and that he responds to your whistle—one toot to get attention, two to come to you, you can now either throw a dummy off at 9 o'clock and while he is retrieving it, throw another to 3 o'clock, or you can use pigeons tied so they cannot fly and plant them at these positions. Six pigeons planted before the session starts can give a spaniel a lot of conditioning. But you must remember the spots they are planted or you can push long sticks into the ground to mark the spots where cover is thick.

With you standing at 6 o'clock, let your dog go out ahead. If he runs straight, whistle and as he looks give him a hand motion to indicate where the bird is planted. He will find it and retrieve it. Put it in your hunting coat pocket where he can't see it and send him out with a *Go On* or *Hie On.* If he quarters toward 3 o'clock let him. If the wind is coming from that direction, he will probably smell the bird and find it. If not whistle and give him the direction.

In hunting with spaniels the attention-getting blast is usually followed by two short toots when the dog gets either too far to right, left or ahead. The hand signal coupled with the toots turns him and after many responses, the toots alone turn him. Some dogs naturally work close, with an eye on the handler while others high tail it for parts unknown. The latter may require many hours of working and much tooting to keep them quartering close. A long blast on the whistle should cause the dog to sit; this is a field trial essential but not for a personal hunting dog.

To teach it, spend time conditioning him to the whistle immediately followed by the word *Hup.* The responses can be conditioned in one's back yard. After thirty or forty trials the word can be dispensed with and the dog is conditioned to sit at the long whistle blast.

Now you must see that he differentiates the normal toot for attention from the long blast for *Hup.* When you work your dog in water, your control becomes essential. He can be running toward the water and you can have him stop and sit on the bank. Or in upland hunting you may know where a live bird is and you want to get closer for a shot. *Hup* him with the whistle, walk up and then let him flush.

As a live bird flushes the spaniel should hup and remain, just as a Pointer remains steady pointing. The whistle establishes this behavior. When the bird is shot the handler tells his dog to *Hie On* and retrieve it.

The dog's conditioning is now nearly complete. Many handlers use pigeons (see Page 273) and plant homers alternating with market pigeons. The homers are flushed and fly home, the hunter purposely missing them, but the market pigeons are shot and retrieved. Next lesson is with pheasants—much more expensive but necessary for the finishing off process, their greater size and weight present an obstacle to a Cocker Spaniel for retrieving but not to a

Springer Spaniel. Both breeds must become accustomed to them if they are to be used for pheasant hunting. The same applies to ducks retrieved from water.

What's wrong with this picture? One not acquainted with dogs might conclude that the Setter was a rabbit dog. However, the rabbit is of a tame domestic breed, and the dog is only curious about it.

Chapter XXIII

TO CONDITION DOGS AGAINST
ATTACKING ANIMALS

Few persons on vacations realize the importance of teaching their dogs to avoid certain wild creatures notably skunks, and in the suburbs, porcupines. Every year thousands of dogs are killed or blinded by the latter and more dog owners inconvenienced by their dogs who have attacked skunks. Owners complain, "My dog can't seem to learn." Many dogs, despite severe quillings or repeated heavy spraying, attack over and over. They will not, if properly conditioned.

Northern coon and cat hunters often find themselves without hunting dogs. I have had my dog quilled within ten minutes after I entered the woods on a two week hunting vacation and then have had to spend days trying to buy another hound, mine being completely incapacitated by quills in his feet and leg muscles. Hunters are not so much troubled by skunks; in fact many get to enjoy the scent being immune to its foulness because of the association of it with so many wonderful nights hunting.

The following suggestions are for those who do the educating. Buy a small wire mesh rubbish burner or build a wire cage. Get a porcupine and put him it it. His quills will stick through the wire. Sit the burner in a yard with the dog, or if no yard is available, put the dog on a chain. He will snoop close to the porcupine and get quills in his nose. As he does so, say *Don't Touch,* assuming that your dog already responds to *Don't Touch.* This conditioning will reinforce that education. Catch the dog and pull the quills. Let him go again. The burner is so small the animal can't flip his tail although he may try. Every time the dog is quilled say *Don't Touch* and pull the quills.

You should know that the porcupine's large quills can be extracted more easily than can those from his tail. The porcupine's tail is his defensive weapon. It is heavy and strong and he flails it against an enemy, driving the quills with their barbed ends deeply into the flesh of any antagonist. They work in out of sight quickly. If the quilling of a dog takes place in the woods and you have no pliers, by the time you reach home, many tail quills will be out of sight. So will many of the long white body quills. You will need pliers with tight jaws to pull quills.

To pull quills, chain the dog to a tree and pull any quills on his body. With a hand under his jaw, push him over so that the top of his head rests on the ground. This stretches the vagus nerve and in this position (he is partly in shock) he feels less pain. Pull as fast as you can. If quills' tips are through his lips, pull them on through; it hurts less than extracting them. Pull out his tongue and be sure no quills are left in his mouth or throat and next work on his legs and body.

If he breaks away, he can't go far because of the chain which is of the utmost importance.

Dogs attack porcupines and often feel no pain at first. It may take several attacks before they suddenly realize the animal has defenses. It is interesting how dogs differ in their propensity to attack many times despite severe quillings while in the case of others, a few quills in a dog's nose may be a lesson for life. Bull Terriers, Airedales, some hounds, may need three quillings to end their stubbornness.

Dogs used to savagely attacking raccoons get the worst of all quillings because they are conditioned to kill and have done it many times.

After your dog has been taught, through the method described above that the porcupine is dangerous, put a slipnoose around the porcupine's neck so you can handle him on a pole. With the dog chained to a post or tree, lead the porcupine close to the dog and if he makes an attempt to attack it, step on the porcupine's tail (I assume you are wearing heavy hunting boots) so he cannot flail it, and have a companion ease the dog up to the animal. If he attacks it, say *Don't Touch* emphatically. Finally, if he persists, push his nose against the porcupine as you say *Don't Touch* and pull the quills. These you can usually pull with your fingers.

If a hunting dog trees a porcupine after this training, shoot it out, and have a companion let the dog go only after the animal can't flail its tail. Say *Don't Touch* and walk away. If you can see any other porcupines he trees, don't shoot them but tell him Don't Touch and walk away from the tree. A disgusted tone of voice will help.

If you have an electric shocker, you can have him discriminating coons, cats and porcupines with a few shocks. When he gets close to his first porcupine, shock him. Next time he trees one, attach the shocker and when you have shot it, shock him as he is almost to it. To him, porcupines give off radiations. He will leave them alone.

Skunks are easily conditioned against by using a descented animal and an electric shocker. Lead it on a dewy evening across a field and put the skunk in a little cage in a clump of bushes. Let the dog trail it on a leash. When he arrives at the box, shock him, saying *Don't Touch* as you do.

Next put the skunk in a cage covered with as inconspicuous wire as possible, into the dog's run, and each time he goes near the cage, say *Don't Touch* and shock him. If after this the dog attacks a skunk in the fields or woods, and gets a spraying, he will be cured for good.

To cure a dog of killing poultry, some persons tie a hen to the dog's neck and leave it there until it almost decomposes. A home pet, or a dog of bird dog breed can be cured before he starts; put the pup or young dog in a run with a hen and chickens. She will usually fly like a fury, straight at the dog's head and peck and scratch so the dog will try to keep away from her. At this point, remove the dog from the pen. A second experience will be enough to condition a dog for life. One dog has been known to kill over 100 chickens and end up exhausted.

Conditioning all hunting bird dogs against chickens is a common practice of professionals. Their dogs learn early that farm poultry is not their game. These men usually use a whip at first attempt of a dog to chase a chicken. An electric shocker is even better.

Chasing sheep, not to mention killing them, is one unforgivable offense. Many state laws prescribe that the sheep-killing dog be destroyed. If the dog's owner is known, he must reimburse the sheep's owner to the full value of the killed or chased animals. A sheep which has been terrified by a dog, even if it is not killed, may be valueless for breeding or anything but the wool it wears at the time. Such sheep are usually paid for at full value by the dog's owner. If no dog is incriminated, the sheep's owner is reimbursed by the state.

Any dog showing the least tendency to chase any sheep should be reprimanded strenuously. If he still is interested, the electric shocker is the best method to condition against this serious behavior. Let the dog get close to a ewe and shock him so he gets the impression that the sheep does it. This is the same procedure to be used with deer which are confined in a park but tame enough to come close to a fence.

When your dog shows no more interest in running after a sheep, leash him and take him quietly among a flock of tame sheep. If he wants to chase horses, cattle or what-have-you accustom him to them in this way.

Some hunters find that tying a dog with a 10 foot long cord to a tough billy goat and leaving them together in a field will eradicate his sheep and deer interest.

Where swine are permitted open range as in some of our southern states, dogs sometimes enjoy chasing young pigs. This can be most annoying with wide running bird dogs. The electric shocker can quickly cure the propensity. Don't try the hen and chicken method by putting your dog in a pen with an old sow and her pigs because unless the dog can jump out, the sow will most likely kill him.

Some of the most tragic examples of stock killing are found in areas where the expanding suburbs are crowding out the farming areas. Families buy guard dogs as property protectors and, living on the edge of farm land, these big dogs roam. Their wandering takes them into sheep and cow pastures where like any untrained red blooded dogs, they enjoy chasing creatures strange to them. It is a lark. The poor farmer suffers. Thousands of farm animals are killed or damaged every year in this way. Having been a farmer myself I know the anguish which livestock owners feel at finding a flock of sheep ruined, or cows with their tails cut short or udders gashed.

And having had to suture damaged animals in my veterinary

work and helped appraise damages for which the state partially compensates the owner, I realize how just is the farmer's grievance.

But having helped clients choose their dogs, I have also known well the disastrous results to the dog owner when he chooses a dog of the wrong breed for his home location. I have advised many clients who disregarded the warnings and who bought potential livestock killers which grew up and killed, and cost their owners thousands of dollars in the aggregate.

All this I say because I know so many will wonder, now that they already own large guard dogs, how these dogs can be trained not to chase and harm livestock. Frankly, I do not know and I know of no one who does know because the dogs stealthily disappear and usually do their maurading at night. The killer sheep dog has never been conditioned against going many farms away and getting in his deadly work. Once discovered he is destroyed by his owner who wants to be a good neighbor.

My advice to those who own dogs of the kinds which might damage livestock is to keep them well penned. They have to damage farm animals only once to cost the owner so much that the dog won't be worth it. And, as I said, in many states, the dog must be destroyed.

Chapter XXIV

THE PROBLEM DOG

As I THINK BACK OVER the years when, as a veterinarian, I was consulted by clients about their dogs' behavior, what looms largest among the questions asked and the help needed was not so much positive conditioning, but rather, how to cure dogs of undesirable behavior.

First of all, came questions about how to stop dogs from biting. This characteristic was much more prevalent in large breeds. Inquiry usually revealed the fact that the dogs were too large for their owners. Many had been brought into the home at the half grown stage after they had developed dominance over kennel mates. When taken into homes and fed, and a person in the home approached the food pan, the dog continued in its acquired habit and snapped at the person. Some form of negative conditioning should have been administered to the dog instantly but it was not, and from then on the dog dominated the household. When it was grown, the dog was not safe and was too large to discipline. These dogs had to "have their way."

A second kind of biter was the fear-biter. These were timid dogs, usually conditioned to be timid by the manner in which they were handled. In time they behaved rationally, but in the presence of strangers. cringed and bit if approached too closely, or if placed in a boarding kennel or hospital, bit when being moved from a kennel cage.

"Piddling," as it was called, "weakness of the bladder sphincter muscle" as it is also called, ranked high as a problem. When, as previously stated, Cocker Spaniels accounted for one in every four dogs I saw, and when a high percentage of Cockers then would squat and urinate when approached by even their owners, it is no wonder that so many owners wanted to learn how to end this obnoxious behavior. Some male dogs would jump up in their happiness to see the owner, and then urinate against the owner's dress or legs. Was this seeming urinary incontinence bred into the dog by lack of proper selection, or was it acquired by conditioning, or both?

Another problem is what I would call being over-protective. This characteristic was not necessarily evinced by guard dog breeds, but was seen in all breeds to some degree. It is exhibited by the dog which "chases cars." He is guarding the premises. Shepherd dog breeds - Collies, farm shepherds, Pulis - for example, are the worst offenders but one finds even Bull Terriers, Poodles, Airedales and others doing it. The dog almost never runs at cars unless in front of his owner's property.

The dog which refuses to permit strangers to approach its owner is over -protective. So is the dog which barks at and threatens or bites the postman, a meter man, laundry man.

The dog which just barks at every strange sound may have started by being protective but soon becomes conditioned to bark needlessly.

Probably because I have been known for my interest in hunting, I've been asked many times to explain why old hunting dogs seem to revert to their early behavior. Foxhounds ran rabbits or deer when they have been conditioned against them and have not been known to run one for perhaps seven years. Beagles ran deer, coonhounds ran foxes, Setters chased rabbits. This behavior is much more common than the average dog owner knows. Sometimes we see it demonstrated when old dogs soil in the house - dogs without kidney disease or intestinal ailments; they behave puppyishly.

Irrational fear is commonly demonstrated by dogs toward certain objects. Some may fear a man with a stick or with even a flashlight and dash into a corner and cringe or perhaps run to the owner. Many women's dogs fear all men and there are dogs which fear women. Almost everyone has known dogs which panicked at the sight of a child. Thousands of dogs fear loud noises, and especially thunderstorms.

In our veterinary hospital many forms of odd behavior were noted. Boarding kennel owners have become worried and have asked how to get dogs to eat so the owners would not think the dog had been underfed while being boarded. I have seen dogs vomit soon after the owner has left, seen others lie almost comatose for hours on end, not sleeping but fearful if one could judge by the expression; others have developed diarrhea.

Male puppies which make sexual motions on pillows, the legs of children or company, present another problem.

Vomiting after eating gives owners of Boston Terriers, Boxers and Bulldogs much concern.

Hypnotic spells are not unusual.

Seeming inability by males to copulate or non-receptivity by bitches is very common.

Fear of places, such as certain rooms, the rear seat or the trunk of an automobile, small patches of woods, veterinary hospitals, boarding kennels, a dog house, a kennel run, are observed in some dogs.

The ruining of the contents of homes on a large or small scale is a common form of misbehavior. Small: chewing on a mahogany table leg; large: tearing all the furniture, rugs, beds and bedding asunder.

Dogs which eat their own stools or those of other dogs constitute common problems. Those which defecate or urinate away from their own premises may be such problem dogs that the owners have to chain or pen them.

These then, are some of the more common problems. Besides them, definite neuroses are occasionally found in pets. Some observers would list all problem dogs as neurotic. We have seen in Chapter VI how it is easily possible to condition almost any dog to be neurotic and we know by incorrect conditioning methods, dog owners have unconsciously produced truly asocial pets. Also by constant repetition of acts which produce anxiety as evidenced by frustration a dog may do things normal dogs do not do.

Most of the problems could have been avoided by having obtained a young puppy and never permitting it to become dominant over the owner and, as it grew, conditioning it properly. You now know how to condition properly from having read this book, but the following suggestions may help specific instances.

How would a psychologist "straighten out" a problem dog? Pavlov and others cured dogs they had made more neurotic than any pet owner is likely to make his, by reconditioning. Some would call it brain washing. We can't suggest one single method to treat all problems; we must use one appropriate to the particular case.

Conditioning man-shy and noise-shy dogs has been discussed, as has the problem of the barking dog.

Frustration can be prevented by the owner becoming dominant over his dog and creating situations in which the dog cannot "have his way." Instead of always taking a dog with you in the car, take him on fewer and fewer occasions, but leave him chained where he can do no damage. It is much better, however, to have refused to let him have his way from puppyhood onward.

The biting problem is often solved by destruction of the dog. Everyone has heard the expression, "Any dog is entitled to one bite, but no more." The biting dog in many sections of the world is an expensive dog. He is usually suspected of being rabid and that calls for quarantining, unless he has bitten a member of the family. He can be very expensive if he inflicts a wound which results in a disfiguring scar on a person not a family member. Most suspicious dogs are insured and more than one bite has cost someone $5,000. or over.

We can scarcely condemn as a biter a dog which chases a boy on a bicycle, sticks its paw out, has it caught in the chain and sprocket, causing bicycle, boy and dog to end in a heap and in the resulting panic the dog bites the boy; he may be biting at the bicycle. However, such accidents have cost the dogs' owners a great deal of money. They illustrate the need for proper conditioning; no dog should chase a boy on a bicycle, a man on a motorcycle, or an automobile.

Properly conditioned dogs of the non-guarding breeds will not bite unless under blinding pain and many not even then. Yet occasions arise when even the most trustworthy dogs bite when in a pack pursuing a fleeing person. A pack of Bull Terriers which had been kept in isolation on a barge killed a boy who ran from them and attempted to climb a fence. These dogs and their relatives had been never known to bite a person before that disastrous occasion.

Boxers and German Shepherds left to guard children have apparently been jealous of them. Newspaper accounts tell of at least a dozen which killed the children. Every one of the dogs was a male.

Some partially ate the babies. Two Great Danes jumped a fence and killed a boy. Two Greyhounds chased a boy on a bicycle and killed him.

Dogs that kill are not a problem because they seal their own death warrants by the act, but dogs that nip or bite occasionally definitely are, provided the owners insist on keeping them. Why do they bite?

They bite because of having learned the biting kept other puppies away from food pan and later, as I said, they dominated the owner. They bite to protect what they feel is their own. The Cure?

Let them learn that their action brings on negative conditioning, until their protection activity is extinguished. Or, if it is desirable that the dog protect, then he must learn what persons are his friends. The mailman will cooperate usually. When it is time for him to come along the street, the dog's owner walks a few houses away, leaves some tidbits which the mailman picks up. When he gets to the home with the protective dog, he gives that dog the tidbits. He becomes a friend, not to be frightened off, but looked for.

Women's dogs who show dislike of men can be fasted thirty-six hours when a man is coming to visit. He can be given the tidbits, sit down, use a signal - word, clucking sound, finger snap - and give the dog a tidbit. And another and another until he has given about thirty. One man is his friend. After the conditioning has been conducted by several men, his dislike of them will be ended.

The same treatment of dogs who dislike women or children is effective in their case, too. If I were a meter man, I should always carry tidbits for dogs which I knew might "be ugly."

I estimate that 10 per cent of all pet dogs squat and urinate under certain conditions. This is due to a relaxation of the circular muscle (sphincter) which holds the bladder closed. A puppy, improperly handled may remain a piddler all of his life. It is not the reaction of panic, and once it has become established by conditioning it is difficult to extinguish.

If it were reaction to panic, then the anal glands would also discharge and they do not as may be witnessed by "confirmed piddlers" "playing sleigh ride" on the living room rug. When they do this they are putting pressure on the anal glands to squeeze out their contents.

Try to imagine yourself a tiny puppy. An enormous human being bends down over you; you'd be frightened too! The fright causes relaxation of the sphincter muscle and some urine escapes.

But there are dogs which only discharge urine when in an ecstasy of happiness. This too, is the result of a strong emotion, producing a relaxation of the bladder sphincter. Dogs which discharge anal glands as the result of panic may not leak urine. You may have seen a dog fight and have smelled anal gland discharge on the whipped dog, but you probably have not noticed urine.

The way to extinguish the early conditioning of the piddler is never to bend over the dog to pet him or her. Each time you do so reinforces the habit you wish to break. Ask all visitors to refrain from bending over the dog.

Car chasing is an easy response to extinguish. Response? Yes, to the excitement of turning wheels, the moving car and a bark. The dog barked; the car moved. Naturally the association occurred. A passing car also moved at the second barking. The dog was responding to his instinct to protect (ideal in the shepherd dog bred for that behavior). Here we have an excellent illustration of conditioning. If you want to see a bewildered dog, next time a car chaser charges out and runs beside your car, simply apply the brakes and scold the dog; you'll be the first who ever did it.

To cure car chasers or chasers of any vehicles, make chasing unpleasant and this undesirable behavior will be quickly extinguished. How? Obtain the cooperation of neighbors. Carry half a bucket of water on the floor of the back seat and squat down so your dog can't see you. When he comes alongside, slosh him with the water. Repeat from different cars until he finds car chasing is unpleasant.

Another way is to have the friend stop suddenly and you jump out with a switch and tingle him. Soon he will learn that not all cars are afraid of him. Another excellent way is to procure some Fourth of July torpedoes. These are a small packet of pebbles together with an explosive cap. When the dog rushes out slam a few on the road in front of him. Some persons make a weak solution of ammonia and water and squirt it from a water pistol into the dog's face. This can be dangerous if the solution is too strong.

When old dogs seemingly exhibit puppy characteristics or

seem to have lost much of their conditioning, i.e., the old fox hound running deer, it may be a typical illustration of senility. In elderly human beings senility shows itself by the person being able to recall events of the past but quickly forgetting recent ones. For this condition, sex hormones are sometimes used but most of canine senility is hopeless.

Irrational fear in dogs can often be overcome by hand feeding, much petting, taking the dog for a walk. Tranquilizers are used a great deal in veterinary hospitals but had best be used under veterinary prescription when given at home. It is not unusual to hear that the owner of a Pomeranian has given the dog a tranquilizer pill strong enough for the 150 lb. human being—twenty times the proper size dose for the little dog.

As for thunder storms, the dog which fears them will, by his actions, tell the owner far in advance of the storm. Many dogs become so frightened they are sick, and in the name of kindness should be given some drug to tranquilize or partially anesthetize the pathetic animals. These, your veterinarian can supply in the proper size dose.

In my researches with Malucidin I found that dogs which seem to freeze stiffly in strange environments are dogs whose adrenal glands discharge adrenalin into their blood. When in this condition the dogs seem to feel pain much less than others who are more tranquil. Tranquilizing drugs counteract the adrenalin and the effect lasts twenty to twenty-four hours.

If a dog has a phobia or unwarranted fear of some object, take him near the object despite the dog's objections and hold him there long enough for him to learn not to fear.

I mentioned how coonhounds which feared a gun shot sound were caused to like it. In many such ways the feared object can be turned into a potent signal.

Some neurotic dogs have been successfully treated by keeping them away from whatever agency caused the neurosis and after their actions were normal gradually introducing them to the agency again when they learn it will not harm them.

Dogs which hypnotize themselves must be kept from the situation where it occurs.

Stopping male puppies of their propensity to make sexual motions, a form of behavior which can be most embarrassing, is simple. A rolled newspaper slapped beside the pup's head on every occasion will quickly stop it. Unfortunately a group of small children may not understand the significance and thinking it is cute, encourage the pup. The behavior, unless extinguished, may persist.

This is not confined to puppies alone. Sonetimes older dogs will perform this way but only on certain persons, both men and women. It is a matter of smelling the person first. I have seen this in several pet dogs. This is not a matter of the person owning a dog because the offending pets do it regardless of dog ownership. And they behave that way toward the same persons in different suits or dresses. The behavior is occasionally seen in spayed bitches.

Inability by male dogs or indisposition to copulate, or unwillingness on the part of bitches to permit copulation is common. Among my many dogs there have been males which because they seemed unable to connect and had been helped by me, would pay no attention to a bitch unless I was present in the run with the pair. I knew a Boston Terrier which was conditioned to copulate on a table and would be uninterested in a bitch when on the floor. In the proper conditions these dogs were normal in their behavior. There are males which, even when the bitch makes all the advances, plays, licks them, even mount, the dogs will refuse to show interest. Over the years I have encountered this problem in many of my clients' dogs.

If the dog is friendly, he can usually be made to be interested by having an assistant hold the bitch from in front, placing the dog on her and pinching the sensitive area behind the bulb of the penis. This initiates a thrust reflex and the dog usually begins to make sexual motions. I have even helped vicious males by first tying their faces and placing the dogs on the bitches, and pressing the thrust reflex area.

If a bitch refuses to copulate despite teasing by the stud, and if puppies from her are wanted, she can be held by an assistant and her vulva held upward by the stud's owner. If she is bred at about the fourteenth day of her period, she will become pregnant if she is otherwise normal. And after one copulation, she may stand normally the next day.

Frequently, simply turning dog and bitch out in a large enclosure will be enough for the bitch to overcome her reticence. If she is one who is overly attached to her owner, then the owner's presence in the enclosure helps greatly.

One must keep in mind that bitches often show monogamous tendencies. If a bitch has been kept with a male dog until propinquity has had its effects, she may refuse to copulate with another dog without a great deal of coaxing.

Cophrophagy—the eating of dung—is one of the foremost problems and one of the most obnoxious practices which dogs exhibit. Is it a psychological problem? To a large extent it is one of nutrition but in some cases it is psychological. It often starts from the need to play and the lack of anything to play with. Retrieving breeds like to carry things. Among my Cocker Spaniels there were many which would carry a stone if nothing else was available. Lacking a stone they carried pieces of stool. From this practice, coprophagy developed. It was stopped simply by leaving old tennis balls in the runs.

In the case of dogs which show no repugnance to stool eating, faulty nutrition is frequently the cause. Sometimes insufficiency of only one essential vitamin will be responsible and even after the diet is complete, the habit will persist. If an abundance of food is supplied, and left where the dog can nibble at any time—dog food in a self feeder is good—the dog usually stops consuming feces. Electric shocks can be tried but dogs learn quickly which stools have been prepared and then avoid them.

While we are discussing eliminations, how does one stop male dogs from urinating on evergreen shrubbery? There are sprays available which must be reapplied after each rain. Electricity proves a powerful deterrent, too. A piece of poultry netting is draped over the shrubs. It must not touch the ground. One pole of an electric current is attached to the netting, the other attached to a rod which is pushed into the ground. Dogs' urine is not passed in a steady stream except when the bladder is full. Hence the urine becomes a conductor and the dog feels a sharp shock which is almost instantly interrupted. Even one shock will keep a dog away for a long while. When the ground is very dry this treatment does not always work. In that event, the dry lawn or soil can be wet with the hose before the dog is due to visit.

Besides these common problems many others are prevalent among dogs. The way to extinguish undesirable asocial behavior will occur to you. Some ingenuity may be required. You can now manage most of the exceptions to normal behavior.

Last but not least is the problem of dying. In this case the dog's behavior is normal but owners often cannot understand their old pet leaving home. From my experience with the thousands of dogs of my own and my clients, I feel certain that dogs know when their natural death is imminent. How does one act? He leaves home and walks as far as his tired old body will go, then he crawls under a protecting bush, under a verandah, anywhere he can hide, and dies peacefully, usually curled up as if asleep. He is not a problem dog.

RECOMMENDED READING

Wolves Don't Bite, Curran, Sault St. Marie Press, Canada.
Lives of Game Animals, E. T. Seton, Doubleday.
The Wolves of Mt. McKinley, A. Murie, U. S. Government Printing Office.
Experimental Psychology, I. P. Pavlov, Philosophical Library.
Animal Behavior, J. P. Scott, University of Chicago Press.
Principles of Animal Psychology, M. R. F. Maier, & T. C. Schneirla, McGraw Hill.
Animal Courtship, M. Burton, Fredk A. Praeger.
Animal Psychology, N. L. Munn, Houghton Mifflin.
How Animals Behave, H. E. Wells, J. Huxley, G. P. Wells, Cassell, London.
What is Hypnosis? A Salter, Richard R. Smith.
Hormones and Behavior, F. A. Beach, Hoeber.
The Behavior of Organisms, B. F. Skinner, Appleton-Century-Crofts.

BIBLIOGRAPHY

Anderson, O. D.: The Role of the Glands of Internal Secretion in the Production of Behavioral Types in the Dog. *Amer. Anat. Mem.*, No. 19, Wist. Inst. of Anat. and Biol., 1941.

Humphrey, E. S.: Mental Tests for Shepherd Dogs. *Jour. Hered., 25:* 129, 1934.

Iljin, N. A.: (*Genetics and Breeding of the Dog.*) 162 pp., illus. Moscow and Leningrad, (In Russian) 1932.

Iljin, N. A.: (Segregation in Crosses Between A Wolf and A Dog and Material on the Genetics of The Dog.) Trudy Din. (Moskva) *Razvitia* (Trans. Dynamics of Devlpmt.) *8:*105–166, illus. (In Russian, English summary, pp. 165–166.), 1934.

James, W. T.: Morphological Form and Its Relation to Behavior. *Amer. Anat. Mem.*, No. 19, Wist. Inst. of Anat. and Biol., 1941.

Keeler, C. and Trimble, H. C.: Inheritance of Position Preference in Coach Dogs. *Jour. Hered., 31:*51, 1940.

Kelly, G. L. and Whitney, L. F.: Prevention of Conception in Bitches by Injections of Estrone. *J. Ga. Med. Assoc., 29:*7, 1940.

Kreps, E. M.: Conditioned Reflexes of A Dog in Heat. Report *Fiziol. Bes.,* 1923.

Krushinsky, L. V.: Hereditary "Fixation" of an Individually Acquired Behavior of Animals and the Origin of Instincts. *Jour. Gen. Biol.,* T. V. 5, 1944.

Krushinsky, L. V.: Interrelation Between the Active and Passive Defence Reactions in Dogs. *Bull. Russian Acad. Sci.,* No. 1, 1945.

Krushinsky, L. V.: A Study of the Phenogenetics of Behavior Characters in Dogs. *Biol. Jour. T.,* VII 1938 No. 4, Inst. Zool. Moscow State University.

Marchlewski, T.: Genetic Studies on the Domestic Dog. *Akad. Umiejetnosci Krakow (Acad. Sci. Cracovie). Bull. Internatl.,* (B) *2:* (117) –145, illus., 1930.

Pavlov, I. P.: *Lectures on Conditioned Reflexes; Twenty-five Years of Objective Study of the Higher Nervous Activities (Behaviour)* of *Animals.* Transl. by W. H. Gantt, and G. Volbroth. 414 pp. illus., New York, 1928.

Rosenthal, I. S.: The Effect of Pregnancy and Lactation on Conditioned Reflexes. *Rus. J. of Physiol., V,* 1922.

Stockard, Charles R.: *The Physical Basis of Personality.* W. W. Norton and Co., New York, 1931.

Whitney, L. F.: The Mating Cycle of the Dog. *Chase Mag.,* 1927.

Whitney, L. F.: Heredity of the Trail Barking Propensity in Dogs. *Jour. Hered., 20:*561–562, illus., 1929.

Whitney, L. F.: Inheritance of Mental Aptitudes in Dogs. 6th Internatl. Cong. Genetics, Ithaca, 1932, *Proc.,* 2:211–212, 1932.

INDEX

conditioning for game animals, 260

highly sensitive in dogs, 193

how formed in dog, 47

learned more quickly with greater incentive, 193f

too fine, dogs become neurotic, 193

unlearning generalizations, 193

Disgorging, Wolf, for puppies, 23

Distractions, bad for learning process, 196

Doberman Pinschers as war dogs, 250

Dog, ambidexterous, 43

and laboratories, ix

awareness of noise, in sleep, 39

back to wolf environment could not survive, 32f

basically wolf in anatomy, physiology & behavior, 31

behavior, exemplifies forebears, 29

behavior never uncaused, 37

classification of, for purpose, 171ff

combination of conditioned and unconditioned reflexes, 122

conform in behavior, 33

discrimination between tones, 52

eating skunk, 56

emotions of, 73

escape artist, 33

examples of intelligence in, 33

exterior or interior most interesting?, 37

faculties of, that need educating, 38

feces eaten by, 56f

flesh, eaten by, 55

giant, trouble in copulation, 156f

head shape, 39

hearing ability tested, 52

hearing greater than man's 50

how he eats, 55

how he learns, important, 37

in war, 250

intelligence of, 82ff

is not human, 7, 45

knowingness, reflection of teaching, 46

known by his acts, 46

language of, 83

learned reaction to what he hears, 48

like wolves, keeps nest clean, 22

nervous system of, should be understood to train, 37

no imagination, 45

no language, 45

not killer from taste of blood, 56

personality of, 46

preferences in foods, 55f

reaction to movement, sound or odor, 44

remembering while owner's away, 45

specific, fitted to do special job, 169

superior in odor detection, 46

superiority to wolf, 33

susceptibility to pain, 66

three uppermost drives in, 37

why easily poisoned, 55

Domestication, pups of wild dogs similar to wolf, 110f

raccoon, story of, 111

wild pups, example of, 110f

wolf, must be done early, 30, 110

Dominance, in puppies, effect on later life, 292

when bully develops, 107

Dominant, behavior patterns, examples of, 180

behavior patterns, which are, 178

gene, 177f

Don't Touch!, 211

as used in man trailing, 266

useful in stopping dogs from attacking animals, 285f

useful signal, 256

Double retrieving, conditioning for, 274

Down!, used as Beagle signal, 258

Drink, for fluid in mouth not just to replace water lost, 144

what causes dog to, 144

Drinking, by overheated dogs, 145

Drive, sex: bitches' escape behavior, examples of, 157

strengthened by occasional consummation, 146

to be part of pack, powerful, 145

Drives, combination of, best for conditioning, 149

necessity for understanding, 6

uppermost in dogs, 37

Drop It!, signal used for retrievers 272

Drowned persons located by Bloodhounds, 268f

value of concurrence in, 197f
value of frequency and recency, 197
wolf through hunting with parents, 26
wolf through play, 26
Lee Duncan, trainer of Rin Tin Tin, 252f
Left, being, produces potent drive, 145
Leg lifting, in male, effected by testosterone, 128, 149
Lemmings, food for wolf, 20
Lie down!, training to, 214f
Lightning, fear of, 219
Lights, as signals, 203
Litter, protection of, 163
    when copulation produces maximum size, 155
Little Red Riding Hood, book, 9
Liver, use as reinforcement, 228f
Livestock, killed by dogs, examples 228f
"Loafer wolf," method used in killing, 19
Lone wolf, 25
Luck in field trials, 277
Lurchers, English, bred for intelligence, 33f
used as thieves, 229

M

McDonald, Dan, description of wolf's capacity for food, 20
Mahangun, Indian name for wolf, 11
Male, castrated, activity in, 151
    vigorous, force bitch to copulate a-head of time, 154
Mailman and dogs, 294
Malleus, 49
Malucidin and dogs which freeze, 296
Man-shyness, conditioning to over-come, 219
Man trailing, 264ff
    along shores, 269
    by any breed, 264
    discrimination taught in garage, 266
    methods of training dogs for, 265ff
    starting dog on, 267f
Maneuvering, of wolf in attacking, 18
Manhandling, example of value of, 138
    puppies, important in behavior of dog, 138
Marchelewski, Dr. T., study on inherit-

ed behavior, 179f
Martin, Abe, of Algoma, 9
Master absent, effect on dog, 87
Mate, call of wolf, 16
    selection of by wolf, 21
Mating cycle, errors in working out, 154
    physical manifestation of approach, 152
    termination of cycle, 155
    time and procedure, 154
Maturation, definition of, 133
    develops instinct, 133
Mature dog, housebreaking a, 234
Medulla oblongata, 42
Memory, ability to alternate, examples of, 88
    and association, in cerebral hemispheres, 41
    better for smells than appearance, 88
    dog's work in mazes, 88
    examples of dog's smell, 58
    how tested, 87
    of dogs for odors, 269
    makes vocabulary, 85
    wolf, 27
Men, dislike of, overcoming, 294
Mendel, Law of Alternate Inheritance 177f
Mental aptitudes, inheritance of, 169
Mental capacity, description of, in dogs, 89
Mental characteristics of human beings and other animals, 7
Metabolism, control of, by hormone 166f
Metallic clicks, as signals, 204
Meterman and dogs, 291
Metronome, Pavlov's use of, 120
Midbrain, hearing, 42
Migration of birds, cause of, 91
Milk, temperature of, important, 111
Mind, of dog, 117
Misfitting, dogs into wrong job, 169
Missing member method of training Bloodhound, 265f
Modern method using volition, 201
Modern Training methods, appeal of, 6
Modification, extent of, in behavior patterns, 181f
Mongrels, sometimes useful as tree dogs, 260

BIBLIOGRAPHY

ALL OWNERS of pure-bred dogs will benefit themselves and their dogs by enriching their knowledge of breeds and of canine care, training, breeding, psychology and other important aspects of dog management. The following list of books covers further reading recommended by judges, veterinarians, breeders, trainers and other authorities. Books may be obtained at the finer book stores and pet shops, or through Howell Book House Inc., publishers, New York, N.Y.

Breed Books

AFGHAN HOUND, Complete — Miller & Gilbert
AIREDALE, Complete — Edwards
ALASKAN MALAMUTE, Complete — Riddle & Seely
BASSET HOUND, Complete — Braun
BEAGLE, Complete — Noted Authorities
BOSTON TERRIER, Complete
  Denlinger and Braunstein
BOXER, Complete — Denlinger
BRITTANY SPANIEL, Complete — Riddle
BULLDOG, New Complete — Hanes
BULL TERRIER, New Complete — Eberhard
CAIRN TERRIER, Complete — Marvin
CHIHUAHUA, Complete — Noted Authorities
COLLIE, Complete — Official Publication of the
  Collie Club of America
DACHSHUND, The New — Meistrell
DOBERMAN PINSCHER, Complete
  Noted Authorities
ENGLISH SETTER, New Complete — Tuck & Howell
ENGLISH SPRINGER SPANIEL, New
  Goodall & Gasow
FOX TERRIER, New Complete — Silvernail
GERMAN SHEPHERD DOG, Complete — Bennett
GERMAN SHORTHAIRED POINTER, New — Maxwell
GOLDEN RETRIEVER, Complete — Fischer
GREAT DANE, New Complete — Noted Authorities
IRISH SETTER, New — Thompson
IRISH WOLFHOUND, Complete — Starbuck
KEESHOND, Complete — Peterson
LABRADOR RETRIEVER, Complete — Warwick
MINIATURE SCHNAUZER, Complete — Eskrigge
NEWFOUNDLAND, New Complete — Chern
NORWEGIAN ELKHOUND, New Complete — Wallo
OLD ENGLISH SHEEPDOG, Complete — Mandeville
PEKINGESE, Quigley Book of — Quigley
POMERANIAN, New Complete — Ricketts
POODLE, New Complete — Hopkins & Irick
POODLES IN PARTICULAR — Rogers
POODLE CLIPPING AND GROOMING BOOK,
  Complete — Kalstone
PUG, Complete — Trullinger
ST. BERNARD, New Complete
  Noted Authorities, rev. Raulston
SAMOYED, Complete — Ward
SCHIPPERKE, Offical Book of — Root, Martin, Kent
SCOTTISH TERRIER, Complete — Marvin
SHETLAND SHEEPDOG, New — Riddle
SHIH TZU, The (English) — Dadds
TERRIERS, The Book of All — Marvin
TOY DOGS, Kalstone Guide to Grooming All
  Kalstone
TOY DOGS, All About — Ricketts
WEST HIGHLAND WHITE TERRIER,
  Complete — Marvin
YORKSHIRE TERRIER, Complete
  Gordon & Bennett

Care and Training

DOG OBEDIENCE, Complete Book of
  Saunders
NOVICE, OPEN AND UTILITY COURSES — Saunders
DOG CARE AND TRAINING, Howell
  Book of — Howell, Denlinger, Merrick
DOG CARE AND TRAINING FOR BOYS
  AND GIRLS — Saunders
DOG TRAINING FOR KIDS — Benjamin
DOG TRAINING, Koehler Method of
  Koehler
GO FIND! Training Your Dog to Track
  Davis
GUARD DOG TRAINING, Koehler Method of
  Koehler
OPEN OBEDIENCE FOR RING, HOME
  AND FIELD, Koehler Method of — Koehler
SPANIELS FOR SPORT (English) — Radcliffe
STORY OF DOG OBEDIENCE — Saunders
SUCCESSFUL DOG TRAINING, The
  Pearsall Guide to — Pearsall
TRAINING THE RETRIEVER — Kersley
TRAINING YOUR DOG TO WIN
  OBEDIENCE TITLES — Morsell

Breeding

ART OF BREEDING BETTER DOGS, New
  Onstott
HOW TO BREED DOGS — Whitney
HOW PUPPIES ARE BORN — Prine
INHERITANCE OF COAT COLOR
  IN DOGS — Little

General

COMPLETE DOG BOOK, The
  Official Pub. of American Kennel Club
DOG IN ACTION, The — Lyon
DOG BEHAVIOR, New Knowledge of
  Pfaffenberger
DOG JUDGING, Nicholas Guide To
  Nicholas
DOG NUTRITION, Collins Guide to
  Collins
DOG OWNER'S HANDBOOK, The New
  Hajas & Sarkany
DOG PSYCHOLOGY — Whitney
DOG STANDARDS ILLUSTRATED
DOGSTEPS, Illustrated Gait at a
  Glance — Elliott
ENCYCLOPEDIA OF DOGS, International
  Dangerfield, Howell & Riddle
JUNIOR SHOWMANSHIP HANDBOOK
  Brown & Mason
SUCCESSFUL DOG SHOWING, Forsyth Guide to
  Forsyth
TRIM, GROOM AND SHOW YOUR DOG,
  How to — Saunders
WHY DOES YOUR DOG DO THAT?
  Bergman
OUR PUPPY'S BABY BOOK (blue or pink)